The Time-Life Gardener's Guide

FLOWERS FOR CUTTING AND DRYING

A

BOOK

TIME® LIFE BOOKS

Other Publications:

AMERICAN COUNTRY
VOYAGE THROUGH THE UNIVERSE
THE THIRD REICH
MYSTERIES OF THE UNKNOWN
TIME FRAME
FIX IT YOURSELF
FITNESS, HEALTH & NUTRITION
SUCCESSFUL PARENTING
HEALTHY HOME COOKING
UNDERSTANDING COMPUTERS
LIBRARY OF NATIONS
THE ENCHANTED WORLD
THE KODAK LIBRARY OF CREATIVE PHOTOGRAPHY
GREAT MEALS IN MINUTES
THE CIVIL WAR
PLANET EARTH
COLLECTOR'S LIBRARY OF THE CIVIL WAR
THE EPIC OF FLIGHT
THE GOOD COOK
WORLD WAR II
HOME REPAIR AND IMPROVEMENT
THE OLD WEST

For information on and a full description of any of
the Time-Life Books series listed above, please call 1-800-621-7026
or write:

Reader Information
Time-Life Customer Service
P.O. Box C-32068
Richmond, Virginia 23261-2068

This book is one of a series of guides to good gardening.

The Time-Life Gardener's Guide

FLOWERS FOR CUTTING AND DRYING

TIME-LIFE BOOKS, ALEXANDRIA, VIRGINIA

CONTENTS

1
DESIGNING A GARDEN

2
PREPARING FOR INDOORS

3
DRYING AND PRESERVING

Cultivation provides only half the pleasure that comes from a cutting garden. While growing healthy, perfect flowers is gratifying, arranging and presenting them brings equal rewards. This volume will guide you through all stages of growing and using cut flowers, from planning your garden plot, to harvesting flowers, to arranging both fresh and dried materials.

The opening chapter shows how to design and maintain a cutting garden. And for when your efforts begin to bear results, there are chapters on conditioning flowers for fresh arrangements, and on a variety of ways to preserve them. A later chapter details both the basics and the finer points of arranging flowers; it shows how to create a variety of arrangements—from a simple, fresh bouquet to a pressed flower picture. Chapter 5 is intended to serve as a reference guide to which you can refer again and again; it contains information on planting and on maintaining a garden through the seasons, as well as solving any problems that may arise in the process. Finally, the Dictionary of Plants contains more than 150 entries, each of which includes plant descriptions and suggestions for growing, harvesting and using individual species.

<table>
<tr><td>

4

MAKING ARRANGEMENTS

</td><td>

5

WORKING IN TANDEM WITH NATURE

</td><td>

6

DICTIONARY OF PLANTS

</td></tr>
</table>

1
DESIGNING A GARDEN

Unlike viewing gardens, cutting gardens are not intended to add to the beauty of the landscape; they are meant to supply flowers to adorn an interior. And since they are planted not to be seen but to be harvested, the rules of design are different. The best location is one away from public view, where the empty spaces left by large-scale cutting won't matter. Accessibility is equally important; if you plant with your own convenience in mind—leaving space between the rows where you can walk—normal maintenance and harvesting chores become much easier. Naturally, you must also consider how a particular site will benefit the plants themselves. Flowering plants require a sunny location, and orientation is important, too. Be careful to plant tall species in such a way that they won't block the sunlight that other plants need in order to develop and thrive.

With careful planning, you can design a cutting garden that will supply you with a variety of flowers for arranging indoors throughout the seasons. This chapter will guide you in that process by focusing on the most important considerations—space, location, convenience and flower selection.

Once the garden is established, the plants themselves will need attention. Plants grown for cutting require the usual care: watering, fertilizing, weeding and mulching. Information on each of these will help you to achieve the best results with the least effort. In addition, you will find it worthwhile to perform a few extra chores for the special needs of cut flowers. For example, a section on disbudding will help you to encourage plants to produce a few large specimen blooms rather than many small ones. Some of the most striking fresh flowers are those that come atop tall, straight stems, but such flowers require staking to keep them from toppling over from wind, rain or their own weight. The pages at the end of the chapter show an efficient and inexpensive way to support plants as they grow.

A WELL-PLANNED CUTTING GARDEN

Divided by straw-mulched pathways for easy access, rows of red and orange plumed celosia await the snip of the shears in this well-designed cutting garden.

A separate garden where the flowers are just for cutting enables you to have an abundance of flowers indoors without marring the beauty of the flower beds outdoors by removing the finest blooms. Since flowering plants need lots of sun, such a bed should be in a location that receives six to eight hours of light a day. It should be near a water source to make watering easy. And since it is not a viewing garden and may start to look somewhat scraggly once you start cutting the flowers, it should not be placed in a prominent part of the landscape.

Determine how much space you have, then draw up a list of plants that are suited to cutting. To ensure a steady supply, plan on growing at least six plants of each type and choose varieties that bloom throughout the season. Since most flower arrangements call for foliage as well as flowers, you'll want to include some plants just for their decorative leaves and branches.

Because the cutting garden is not designed to be looked at, the plants may be grown as close together as is healthy for them. For information on spacing, consult the Dictionary of Plants *(pages 86-152),* the backs of seed packets or the tags that come with bedding plants sold in nurseries. As with any garden, be sure to prepare the soil thoroughly before starting to plant.

The model cutting garden shown at right measures 25 by 12 feet. Plants are grouped in rows for easy access. The rows are planted with an east-west orientation for maximum sunlight; if the rows ran north-south, one row of plants would inevitably shade its neighbors as the sun moved from east to west across the sky.

Always keep plantings of annuals and perennials separate so you won't disturb a row of long-lived perennials when the time comes to replant the annuals.

NORTH

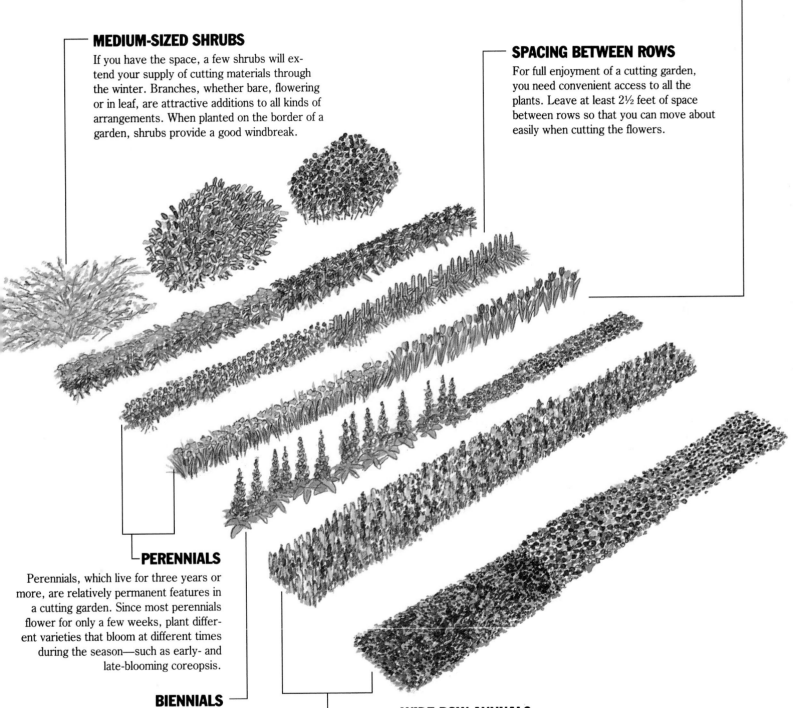

BULBS

The earliest-blooming cutting flowers are typically spring bulbs like daffodils and tulips. They come up reliably year after year with minimal care. To avoid disturbing the bulbs after they are finished flowering, take care not to crowd them with other plants.

MEDIUM-SIZED SHRUBS

If you have the space, a few shrubs will extend your supply of cutting materials through the winter. Branches, whether bare, flowering or in leaf, are attractive additions to all kinds of arrangements. When planted on the border of a garden, shrubs provide a good windbreak.

SPACING BETWEEN ROWS

For full enjoyment of a cutting garden, you need convenient access to all the plants. Leave at least 2½ feet of space between rows so that you can move about easily when cutting the flowers.

PERENNIALS

Perennials, which live for three years or more, are relatively permanent features in a cutting garden. Since most perennials flower for only a few weeks, plant different varieties that bloom at different times during the season—such as early- and late-blooming coreopsis.

BIENNIALS

Biennials live for two years but flower only in their second year; the first year they produce only foliage. For greater efficiency, plant half a row with biennials, half with annuals. After reaping the annuals, replace them with biennials. By the end of the second year, you will have a row of biennial flowers every year.

WIDE-ROW ANNUALS

Since they live for only one season, annuals need less space than more permanent plants, and to get more flowers for cutting, you can crowd your annuals into rows slightly wider than usual. While closer spacing discourages sideways growth, it favors longer stems—a plus for a cutting garden. □

CULTIVATING FLOWERS FOR CUTTING

Neat, colorful rows of celosia (foreground) and salvia (background) bear vivid testimony to the rewards of a well-maintained cutting garden.

ake care of your soil, says an old gardeners' adage, and it will take care of you. For the gardener growing a cutting garden, that means the best flowers come from the healthiest plants. To ensure a steady supply of long-lasting blooms, establish a year-round routine of basic maintenance for your cutting garden.

The end of the active growing season in the fall is a good time to have your garden soil analyzed. If you send a sample to your local agricultural extension service, you will get back a report detailing any nutritional deficiencies. It is best to correct them with the recommended soil amendments before spring planting.

Once the growing season starts, you will need to water, fertilize and weed on a regular basis. For the best results with the least effort, get to know your plants and their individual needs. See the page opposite and the Dictionary of Plants *(pages 86-152)* for specific do's and don'ts.

The best protection against pests and diseases is periodic inspection combined with swift remedial action. Whenever you go out to cut flowers, take time to look for symptoms of disease and insect damage; problems are always easier to control or cure if caught early. For specifics, consult the trouble-shooting section on pages 80-83.

Good grooming makes for a healthier as well as a more attractive garden. Dead plant material, like frost-killed annuals and perennials, can serve as a breeding ground for insect pests and diseases. Dig them up and replace them in early spring to prevent unsightly gaps in your cutting garden come summer.

Once the garden starts blooming, remove faded flowers promptly to encourage continued blooming. The only exceptions are plants you are raising for their seedpods.

WATERING

Most growing plants must absorb about 1 inch of water a week to stay healthy. How much they get from nature depends on local rainfall, soil type (sandy soil drains faster than clay), and evaporation due to sun and wind. If a plant looks dry, water it immediately. Water long and deep; frequent light watering only encourages shallow root growth—which makes plants susceptible to drought.

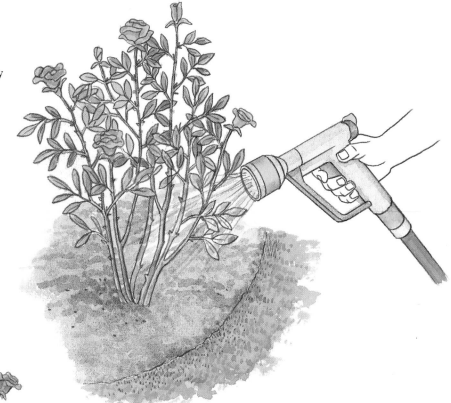

FERTILIZING

The most important plant nutrients are nitrogen (for green growth), phosphorus (for roots and flowers) and potassium (for general vigor). These ingredients are listed on fertilizer packages as ratios of N, P and K; "5-10-5" means the product contains twice as much P (phosphorus) as N or K. For healthy flowers, avoid fertilizers with a high nitrogen content. Keep in mind that it is safer to apply too little fertilizer than too much.

WEEDING

Weeds are interlopers that compete with cutting plants for water and nutrients. Use a weeding tool to remove weeds promptly; deep-rooted weeds like dandelions may require a little extra digging to pull up all the roots. To discourage weeds, apply a 1- to 2-inch layer of organic mulch (such as shredded bark, pine straw or wood chips) over the bare soil between plants. The mulch will also help retain moisture. □

DISBUDDING
TO PRODUCE SPECIMEN BLOOMS

Judicious disbudding early in the growing season allows the showy blossoms of these deep rose-colored peonies to put on a spectacular display.

Disbudding is a special kind of pruning that has one purpose. It is to force a plant that normally produces many small to medium-sized flowers to concentrate all its energy on growing one big, beautiful bloom. Commercial nurseries use the technique to create, among other items, the classic long-stemmed rose. Other flowers that are commonly disbudded are peonies, chrysanthemums, carnations and dahlias. Other plants that respond well to this treatment are delphinium, yarrow, zinnia, China aster and celosia.

To be suitable for disbudding, a plant must have well-defined flowers that grow in clusters. A typical cluster will show three buds of unequal size; the largest will generally be in the middle and be flanked by two smaller buds. The two side buds are removed to allow the middle bud to reach its greatest possible development.

Typically, other side growths on the same stem—smaller branches, additional flower clusters—are also removed. This not only strengthens the main bud by eliminating competition for nutrients, it also encourages the formation of a long straight stem that serves as a suitable pedestal for the king-sized bloom.

In many cases, the single large flower created by disbudding is top-heavy. To prevent the plant from falling over, it is wise to stake the disbudded stem early in its development *(pages 14-15)*.

The best time to disbud is in the early summer, when flower buds are distinct but still small.

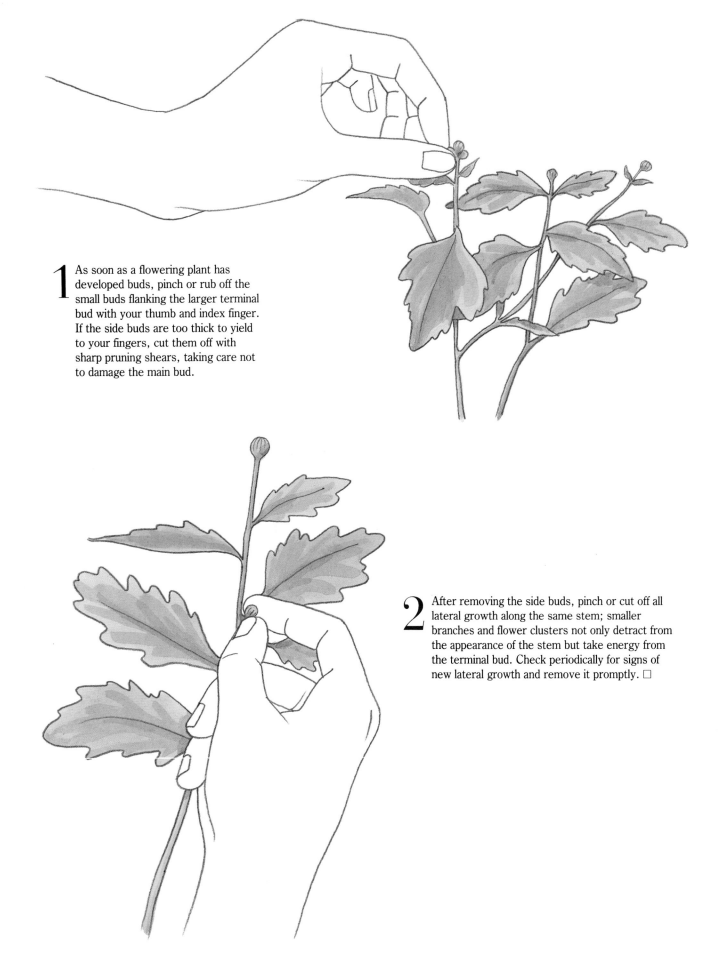

1 As soon as a flowering plant has developed buds, pinch or rub off the small buds flanking the larger terminal bud with your thumb and index finger. If the side buds are too thick to yield to your fingers, cut them off with sharp pruning shears, taking care not to damage the main bud.

2 After removing the side buds, pinch or cut off all lateral growth along the same stem; smaller branches and flower clusters not only detract from the appearance of the stem but take energy from the terminal bud. Check periodically for signs of new lateral growth and remove it promptly. □

STAKE-AND-STRING SUPPORT FOR TOP-HEAVY BLOOMS

Because so many flower arrangements call for big, full blossoms on tall, straight stems, a typical cutting garden has row on row of plants like cosmos, delphinium, stock, celosia, lily and tall marigolds. But the taller the stem and the heavier the bloom, the more likely a plant is to droop under its own weight—or even to break in strong winds and pelting rain.

To keep your annuals and perennials upright until you are ready to harvest their blooms, support them with a system of stakes and string. For optimum results, stake your plants before they get too big so you can guide their growth as they mature.

A staking system should not only be easy to install; it should be inconspicuous in place. The best system for a row of flowers in a cutting garden is a simple line of bamboo canes running down the center of the row, with heavy string woven around the outside edges of the plants *(opposite)*.

Bamboo canes may be either natural-colored or dyed green. They come in a variety of lengths and thicknesses; choose the size you need to support a particular plant. For example: since a lily flower is heavier than a cosmos flower, the lily plant requires a sturdier stake.

When you stake early in the growing season, be sure to get an accurate estimate of how tall your plants will be when fully grown, and buy canes accordingly. Stakes that tower over plants look unattractive; stakes that are too short do not offer proper support.

If you have to guess, it is safer to buy canes that are too long rather than too short. Keep in mind that a good 9 inches of each cane will be buried in the ground.

Unobtrusively supported by lines of wooden stakes and string, these rows of delphiniums can grow tall and full without danger of bending or breaking.

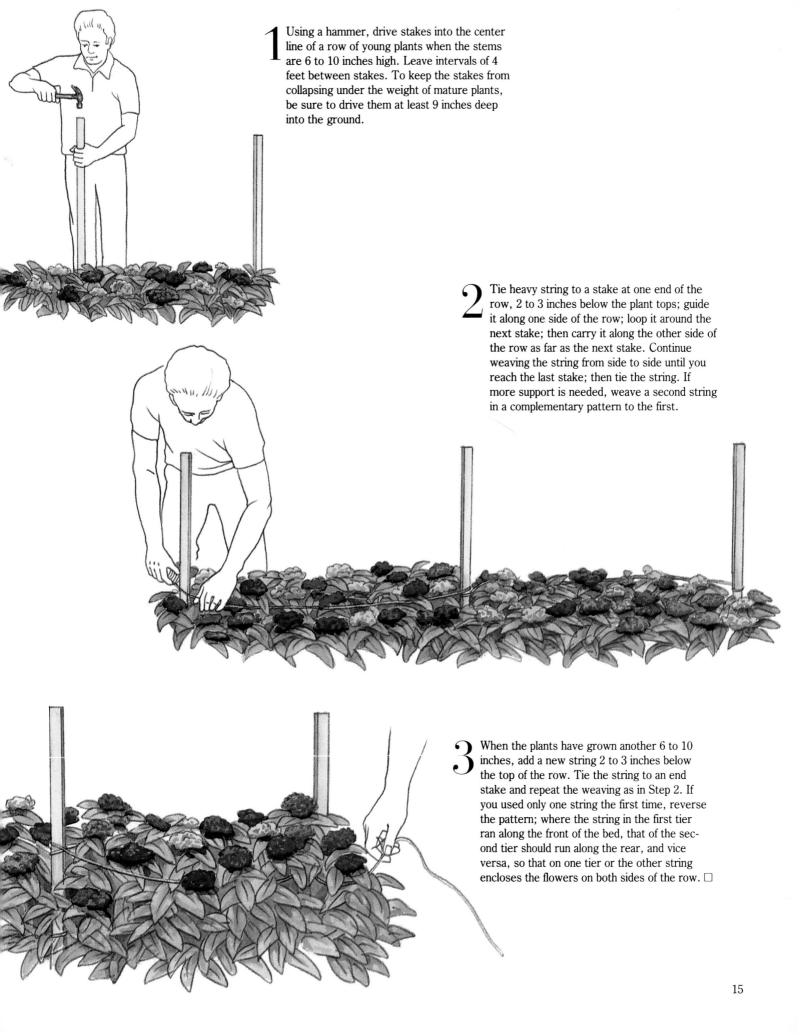

1 Using a hammer, drive stakes into the center line of a row of young plants when the stems are 6 to 10 inches high. Leave intervals of 4 feet between stakes. To keep the stakes from collapsing under the weight of mature plants, be sure to drive them at least 9 inches deep into the ground.

2 Tie heavy string to a stake at one end of the row, 2 to 3 inches below the plant tops; guide it along one side of the row; loop it around the next stake; then carry it along the other side of the row as far as the next stake. Continue weaving the string from side to side until you reach the last stake; then tie the string. If more support is needed, weave a second string in a complementary pattern to the first.

3 When the plants have grown another 6 to 10 inches, add a new string 2 to 3 inches below the top of the row. Tie the string to an end stake and repeat the weaving as in Step 2. If you used only one string the first time, reverse the pattern; where the string in the first tier ran along the front of the bed, that of the second tier should run along the rear, and vice versa, so that on one tier or the other string encloses the flowers on both sides of the row. □

2
PREPARING FOR INDOORS

Freshly cut flowers bring the color, the fragrance and the beauty of the garden indoors. They may be placed loosely in a vase or they may be arranged formally. Either way, they can be appreciated up close. But whether or not fresh flowers hold their beauty depends on how they are treated both during and after cutting. Timing is crucial: harvesting flowers at the right stage in their development—and at the right time of day—can make a difference in how long they last. And the care you take in cutting them—using sharp, clean tools to prevent spreading diseases, and a bucket of water to keep them fresh—can also affect their appearance. Certain species require special attention; poppies' stems, for example, need to be seared, and the stem ends of plants such as lilacs and azaleas should be hammered so that they can take up more water. Tulips should be wrapped in newspaper to keep their long, flexible stems from curving and twisting. The following pages show how to condition a variety of flowers so that they retain their color and beauty for as long as possible.

Also contained in this chapter are ways to improve upon what nature provides. Pages 20-21 show how to make woody branches assume a variety of curves and shapes; the technique is useful whether you intend to create a wreath or to add line and movement to an arrangement of mixed flowers and foliage. In addition, a section on forcing branches into bloom will enable you to make winter branches with buds come alive, bringing on the color of spring months in advance of the season outdoors.

WAYS TO KEEP CUT FLOWERS FRESH

The secret of making arrangements of fresh cut flowers long-lasting comes down to one simple proposition: make sure the blossoms and stems get the maximum amount of water for the maximum length of time. Doing this takes a little effort, more for some varieties of flowers than others *(opposite)*. But if it is done right, your cut blossoms will stay fresh longer than you thought possible.

The first key is in the cutting. Always snip flowers that are fresh and full of moisture, the blossoms just on the point of opening. Avoid very tight buds; they will not develop if cut prematurely. But new blooms will open more after being snipped, and will last longer than older blossoms that have begun to dry out.

A second sort of timing is important. Do your cutting in the early morning or in the evening, when plants are full of moisture. Never cut blooms during the middle of a hot, bright day when the flowers have lost moisture to the sun.

Another key is to carry a bucket of water into the garden, and to plunge the stems into it as soon as you have cut them. When the container is full, carry it indoors, into a cool, dark spot. This conditioning in water is all-important, because it enables the flowers to drink their fill and replace whatever moisture was lost during the cutting process.

When arranging, always use a clean vase, to avoid transmitting any leftover disease. Renew the water often, and recut the bottoms of the stems every couple of days to open up fresh water-absorbing tissues. Last, put a commercial cut-flower preservative in the water right away. It, too, will keep stems from clogging and provide nutrients that even cut plants will welcome.

Soaking in plastic buckets, newly cut chrysanthemums show their deep, rich colors. This sort of conditioning, done right away, keeps cut blooms from fading prematurely.

1 Cut your flowers with a very sharp knife or with florist's shears, to minimize tissue damage, and cut diagonally to expose a maximum of tissue for water intake. Cut just above a node, where a leaf or a blossoming stem grows from the main stem. This will allow the plants to grow new flowers.

2 Strip the foliage from the bottom three-fourths of the stems, which will be submerged; then plunge them into a container of tepid water. Keep the blossoms dry—except for violets, hydrangeas and lilies-of-the-valley, whose blossoms are able to absorb water.

3 Carry the bucket inside and cut the stems once more, doing it underwater this time and, again, at an angle. This prevents air-bubble blockage, which can impede water intake. Put the bucket in a cool, dimly lit place and leave the flowers undisturbed for at least two hours or overnight. The flowers will then be ready for arranging. □

STEMS WITH SPECIAL NEEDS

Flowers with woody or wobbly stems, and ones that ooze sap, need extra preparation before being conditioned, to help them absorb water. The drawings below demonstrate techniques for readying such problem stems for soaking.

SEARING
Poppies, dahlias and some other flowers, when cut, exude a sticky fluid that can clog their stems. To stop the flow, sear the stems with a flame.

HAMMERING
The stems of woody plants (lilacs, azaleas) cannot absorb water well. To expose the inner tissues, hammer the cut ends until they splinter.

WRAPPING
The flexible stems of tulips, stock and snapdragons often flop over. To prevent this, gather several stems together, roll them in a tube of newspaper and plunge the tube into water.

BENDING BRANCHES
FOR CURVILINEAR DESIGNS

Standing alone in a tall glass vase, a bunch of pussy willows forms a striking monochromatic arrangement. The willows on the right and left, shaped into gentle curves, add a soft, graceful accent to those in the middle, which retain their natural upright lines.

Branches taken from flowering shrubs, trees and woody-stemmed plants such as pussy willows make wonderful additions to flower arrangements; they give structure and yet a vigorous look that collections of blossoms by themselves seldom possess. The Japanese have long been masters at employing bare or just-budding branches, sometimes using them alone in arrangements to get a stark, sculptured quality. Or they have placed them in vases of flowers with great subtlety and precision, often bending some of the branches to achieve more delicate, rounded outlines. Flower arrangers in the West, by contrast, have tended to leave branches as they come naturally, using them mainly to add height to arrangements and to provide a relatively simple if pleasing basic structure or outline.

There is no reason, of course, not to make the best of both worlds, East and West, by combining some gently curving Japanese-style branches with straight ones—especially since making even quite stiff branches bend is not a difficult or complicated process. As shown at right, the main requirement is a good soaking in warm water. Long, thin branches will not need much soaking—in fact they may take on curves without it—but stiff, woody ones may need to be soaked overnight. Then it is just a matter of bending the branches manually and tying them with twine until the softened wood takes on the curves you want.

Expert flower arrangers have found that branches from a wide variety of plants and trees work well. Pussy willows and Scotch broom are standbys along with forsythia and the thin outer branches of cherry and apple trees—and there are many more. Branches are most often cut and used in early spring, before they leaf out, because leaves tend to obscure the strong linear outlines that you want the branches to provide.

1 To get branches ready for bending, soak them for several hours or overnight in a large washtub or in a bathtub. Start with warm water; it helps soften the woody tissues so that even stiff branches can be bent without breaking. When the time comes to do the shaping, remove the branches from the water.

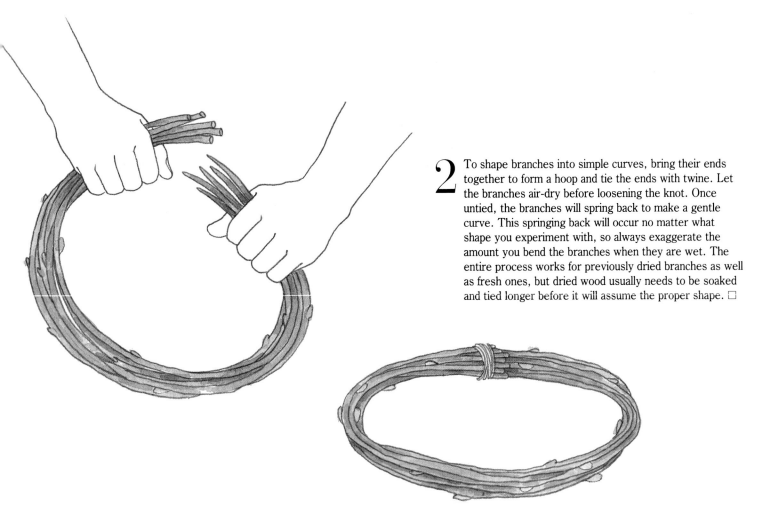

2 To shape branches into simple curves, bring their ends together to form a hoop and tie the ends with twine. Let the branches air-dry before loosening the knot. Once untied, the branches will spring back to make a gentle curve. This springing back will occur no matter what shape you experiment with, so always exaggerate the amount you bend the branches when they are wet. The entire process works for previously dried branches as well as fresh ones, but dried wood usually needs to be soaked and tied longer before it will assume the proper shape. □

BRIGHT OFF-SEASON COLOR
FROM FORCED BRANCHES

Flowering branches are welcome any time of year, but especially during the dark days of winter. And many sorts of branches can be forced to blossom and put out leaves ahead of time, even during the frozen months when nothing else in a garden shows any sign of life. Branches from azaleas, lilacs, forsythias, cherries, apple trees, and other flowering trees and shrubs will produce lovely blossoms if cut, brought into the warmth of the house and given some water, as shown at right. The branches of maples, oaks and beeches can also be forced to sprout attractive young foliage.

The only part of forcing that calls for much care and thought is the cutting itself. The branches should be healthy and laden with buds. Ideally, the branches should also be ones that may need pruning in spring anyway, to improve the shape of the tree or the shrub. Do not do any cutting that will spoil the looks of your plant.

Timing is also important. Most trees and shrubs have formed their next year's buds by the end of summer, but the buds must go through about six weeks of cold to break dormancy. This means you should wait to do any cutting until the middle of January—any earlier and the buds will remain dormant. Also do the cutting in the middle of a mild, sunny day when the plants' sap is running. Do not snip any branches that are frozen; if cut before they are ready to come out of dormancy, they may never bloom at all.

It takes some time for branches to flower or foliate after they have been brought indoors. How long depends on the species and on how early you do the cutting. For example, branches cut as early as mid-January from a shrub that normally blooms in April may take six weeks to blossom. Still, this means you will have fresh spring color in late February, even if winter's grayness seems to be hanging on forever out of doors.

Slender outer branches from a buckeye tree add bright green foliage to a late-winter arrangement that includes flowering sprigs of azalea, also cut early and forced to bloom indoors, as well as some richly colored hothouse-grown tulips.

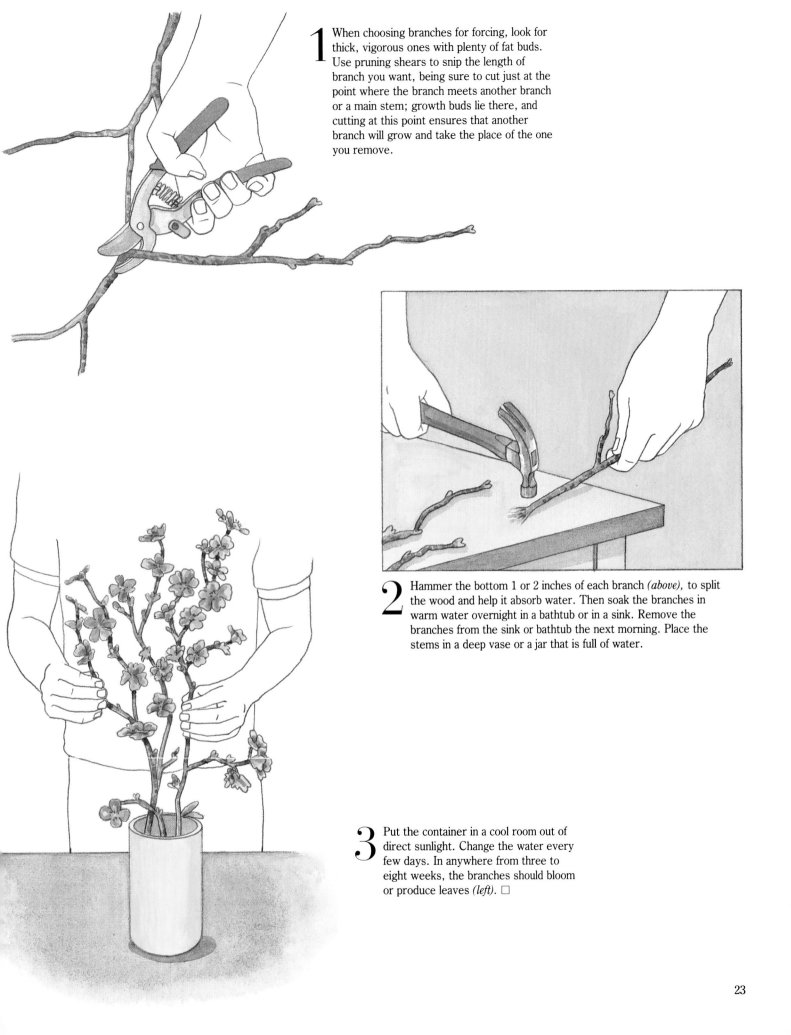

1 When choosing branches for forcing, look for thick, vigorous ones with plenty of fat buds. Use pruning shears to snip the length of branch you want, being sure to cut just at the point where the branch meets another branch or a main stem; growth buds lie there, and cutting at this point ensures that another branch will grow and take the place of the one you remove.

2 Hammer the bottom 1 or 2 inches of each branch *(above)*, to split the wood and help it absorb water. Then soak the branches in warm water overnight in a bathtub or in a sink. Remove the branches from the sink or bathtub the next morning. Place the stems in a deep vase or a jar that is full of water.

3 Put the container in a cool room out of direct sunlight. Change the water every few days. In anywhere from three to eight weeks, the branches should bloom or produce leaves *(left)*. □

3
DRYING AND PRESERVING

Nearly all flowers sacrifice some of their vivid color when dried, but dried flowers make up for that loss by lasting longer than fresh ones. Some preserved flowers last indefinitely. And though their colors are generally muted versions of what they were when fresh, they have a delicate beauty of their own. This chapter provides details on the basic methods of preserving flowers, from traditional techniques such as hanging and pressing, in use for hundreds of years, to more recent ones such as microwaving.

The method of preserving you use will depend largely on the flower and how you intend to use it. Drying flowers in silica gel, for example, preserves more of their original color than air-drying does; standing flowers upright in a vase will often give their stalks a graceful line as they bend while drying; and pressing gives blossoms an unusual, two-dimensional look. By consulting the Dictionary of Plants at the end of the book, you can determine which method works best for a particular species or which will produce a particular effect.

Since dried arrangements often contain materials besides flowers, there are also sections on preserving foliage and seed-pods. Like flowers, branches of leaves can be preserved by air-drying; individual leaves, by pressing. Two other methods—preserving with glycerine and skeletonizing—are reserved for foliage. Seedpods require special attention, since their folds and cavities provide perfect places for insects to hide. Instructions on cleaning and preserving the wide variety of seedpods are also included in the pages that follow.

Finally, since the stalks of many flowers and pods become brittle when dried, a special section on wiring stems will help you to create new stems of virtually any length, so that the flowers can be used in whatever type of arrangement you desire.

AIR-DRYING: A TIME-HONORED METHOD

The oldest and most natural method of preserving flowers and some sorts of foliage for use in winter arrangements is by air-drying—that is, letting air circulate around the leaves and blooms. About the only complication is that different sorts of flowers and foliage dry best in various ways *(opposite)*. Most upright-growing plants with clusters of smallish blooms, for example, need to be hung upside down. Flat, open flowers should be dried right side up, with the petals supported by mesh to keep them from drooping. Stiff ornamental grasses are easiest; they need only be put standing up in a vase and left alone.

But none of the drying methods are complex or difficult. What does take some care is collecting the plant material for drying. First of all, the flowers and leaves should be unblemished; imperfections are magnified once the material is dry. Second, the blooms should be just nearing the peak of their development. Flowers at or past their peak tend to crumble when dried. Then, too, do your cutting and collecting during the middle of a sunny day, after the morning dew has evaporated and before evening moisture has begun to fall. There is no use starting with wet materials. Also, remove at least the lower leaves from flower stems; they generally do not dry well and may lose their shape. (For more on preserving decorative foliage, see pages 32-33 and pages 38-41.)

While it dries, the cut material may be kept in any spot that is dry and dark and well ventilated. After flowers have dried so they feel crisp, spray them with a sealant or fixative, which will help hold the fragile flower parts together and keep out moisture from the air. If you are not going to arrange the dried blooms right away, store them in a box. A few moth flakes will repel insects, and a small amount of a desiccant such as silica gel—laid in the bottom of the box and underneath a layer of paper towels so it does not touch the flowers—will absorb any humidity. Seal the box with plastic tape.

Looking decorative even while drying, bunches of roses of various colors and some white baby's breath hang from a rafter. Like other flowers, roses should be cut for drying before the blossoms are fully open. Unlike most other foliage, rose leaves dry well on the stem.

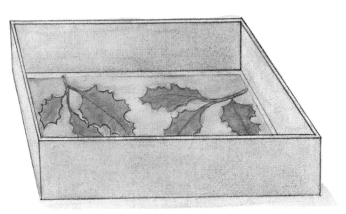

LYING FLAT

The leaves of some trees and shrubs like these oak cuttings should be laid flat in a shallow box lined with sheets of absorbent newsprint or blotting paper. Do not let the leaves overlap one another, and turn them every couple of days so they will dry evenly. The leaves will crinkle some but retain good color. Large individual leaves can also be dried this way.

HANGING UPSIDE DOWN

A majority of upright-growing flowered stems, from goldenrod *(right)* to roses to baby's breath, dry best if hung upside down in bunches. Make small bunches of a few stems each for good air circulation, and stagger the blooms so they do not hit each other. Secure the stems in bunches with rubber bands, then use string to hang them from nails or hooks.

SUSPENDED IN MESH

Soft, flat-topped flower heads such as those of the Queen Anne's lace shown here dry best if their stems are stuck through the holes in a sheet of chicken wire. The wire can be supported between two chairs.

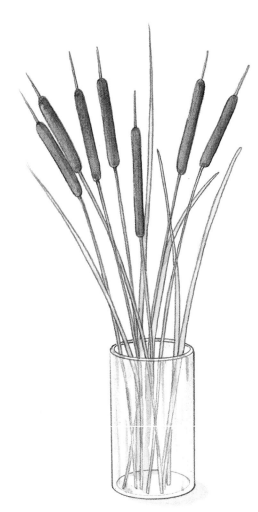

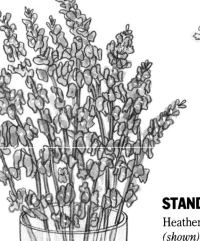

STANDING IN WATER

Heather, bells-of-Ireland *(shown)*, delphinium and some other stiff-stemmed plants can best retain their shape if placed standing in about 2 inches of water. The water keeps them from wilting before they start to dry; then they dry slowly as the water evaporates.

STANDING IN A DRY CONTAINER

Ornamental grasses, cattails *(above)* and bare branches do best simply standing upright in a dry vase, which invites them to bend slowly in graceful curves. Thinner-stemmed grasses should be dried in bunches so the stems in the center stay straight while the outside ones curve downward. □

A DESICCANT
TO RETAIN SHAPE AND COLOR

Looking like a fine old hand-colored floral print, a winter arrangement combines several different kinds of dried flowers—a large peony surrounded by roses and celosias. Drying blossoms like these in silica gel helps preserve their fresh natural hues.

One alternative to air-drying flowers *(pages 26-27)* is to cover them with a desiccant or drying agent. This method is useful for delicate flowers that have thin petals that will fall apart if air-dried. It is also an excellent—though somewhat tricky—way to dry large blooms such as the roses and huge peony in the photograph at left, because it usually preserves their shape and color better than other drying techniques.

One drying agent is common sand; another is a mixture of cornmeal and borax. But both act slowly, simply supporting the flowers while their moisture evaporates. Better is a powdery substance called silica gel, which actually draws moisture from blooms, and cuts the drying time from weeks to as little as only a couple of days. The gel can be bought at craft shops and, while not cheap, can be reused indefinitely.

The flowers you choose should be near their peak. They should also—and this is vital—be absolutely free of any moisture from dew or rain. The silica will cling to even the smallest drop, discolor the blossom and probably cause it to rot.

Then the flowers need some special preparation *(opposite)*. Because stems rarely dry well in a desiccant, they need to be removed; short substitute stems of florist's wire have to be made to take their place. The blooms should be set very gently in the silica, in a tin or plastic container that has a tight lid.

The difficult part is leaving the flowers in the gel the right length of time. They need to be thoroughly dry, but if dried too long they become brittle and will shatter. The proper drying time varies from one sort of flower to another, depending on the bloom's thickness and the fleshiness of the petals. Check your flowers after they have been in the gel a couple of days and each day after that; touch the petals to see if they feel crisp. When they do, they are ready for new, longer wire stems—and for use in arrangements.

1 Pick blooms for drying in silica gel in the middle of a dry, sunny day so that they are not spotted with any extra moisture. Select blooms that are free of natural blemishes and free of damage by insects. Once you have the flowers indoors, snip off all but an inch or less of each stem with garden shears.

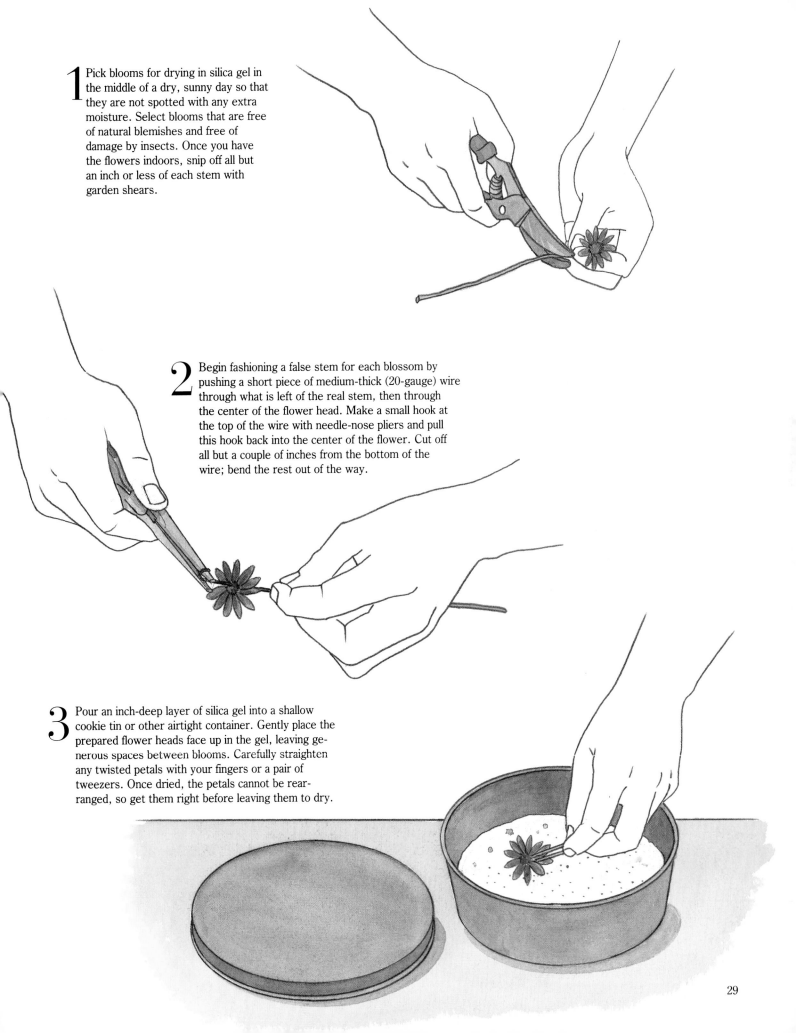

2 Begin fashioning a false stem for each blossom by pushing a short piece of medium-thick (20-gauge) wire through what is left of the real stem, then through the center of the flower head. Make a small hook at the top of the wire with needle-nose pliers and pull this hook back into the center of the flower. Cut off all but a couple of inches from the bottom of the wire; bend the rest out of the way.

3 Pour an inch-deep layer of silica gel into a shallow cookie tin or other airtight container. Gently place the prepared flower heads face up in the gel, leaving generous spaces between blooms. Carefully straighten any twisted petals with your fingers or a pair of tweezers. Once dried, the petals cannot be rearranged, so get them right before leaving them to dry.

4 Using a small paintbrush, push particles of the silica gel under the petals and around and on top of the flower heads. Get the gel into crevices as best you can, and between the petals of intricate blooms such as roses, marigolds and zinnias. This will help the gel draw moisture from the interior of the flowers.

5 Gently sift more silica gel on top of your flowers, covering all the petals and crowns. Put a tight lid on the container and store it in a dry, cool spot. Because different flowers dry at different speeds, it is best to dry only one kind at a time in a container. Try not to inhale the powdery silica; it is not poisonous but can cause sinus irritation.

6 Check your blooms after two days or so by opening the container, tilting it slightly and brushing aside some of the gel. Feel a couple of petals. If they seem crisp and papery, start lifting the blossoms from the silica by grasping their wire stems. Brush off any remaining traces of gel. If the petals seem soft and pliable or the flowers' thick calyxes are not yet dry, cover the blooms once more, recap the container and wait another day.

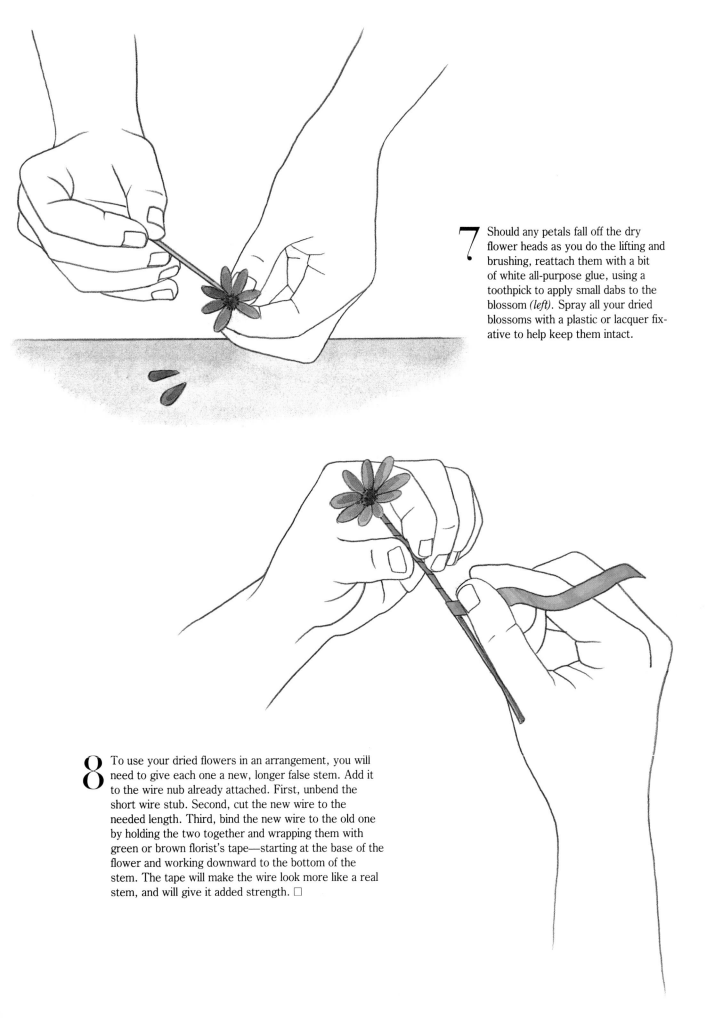

7 Should any petals fall off the dry flower heads as you do the lifting and brushing, reattach them with a bit of white all-purpose glue, using a toothpick to apply small dabs to the blossom *(left)*. Spray all your dried blossoms with a plastic or lacquer fixative to help keep them intact.

8 To use your dried flowers in an arrangement, you will need to give each one a new, longer false stem. Add it to the wire nub already attached. First, unbend the short wire stub. Second, cut the new wire to the needed length. Third, bind the new wire to the old one by holding the two together and wrapping them with green or brown florist's tape—starting at the base of the flower and working downward to the bottom of the stem. The tape will make the wire look more like a real stem, and will give it added strength. □

PRESSING FLOWERS AND FOLIAGE FOR BEAUTY THAT LASTS

One easy method of preserving plants—and a method that takes up very little space—is pressing. You can make a press yourself, or buy one. For best results, the plant material should be naturally flat. Most leaves press very well, as do thin-walled flowers. Foliage preserved by pressing can be used in a standard arrangement or in a flower picture *(pages 70-71)*. Pressed flowers are suitable only for flower pictures.

Material for pressing should be well formed and free of dew and raindrops. The best time to collect specimens is on a sunny afternoon following at least a day without rain.

Both flowers and foliage must be kept flat while they dry. You can press the drying material between the pages of an old telephone book or in a flower press. If you have a lot of material to work with, a flower press is recommended because it is more durable and exerts more even pressure.

Arrange the plant material between sheets of absorbent paper such as blotting paper or newsprint. Avoid paper that has a noticeable texture, as its design may become imprinted on the drying flowers or foliage.

It is also important to make sure that one layer of specimens does not imprint its surface patterns on others above and below it. To prevent this in a flower press, insert dividers of cardboard between the layers of blotting paper. If you are using a telephone book, allow at least 10 pages between insertions of plant materials.

To ensure that the drying leaves and flowers remain flat in the phone book, place another heavy book or object on top. In a flower press, pressure is maintained by tightening the corner wing nuts.

Drying time varies with plants, but most specimens should be dry in a week or two.

Pressed pansies, ageratum and ferns lie on a sheet of blotting paper. Pressing takes about a week, and the plant materials can be pressed either full-face, like the pansies and the ferns, or in profile, like the ageratum.

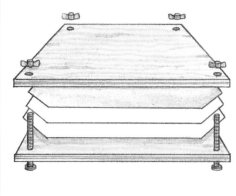

A HOMEMADE PRESS

A simple but reliable flower press consists of two pieces of sturdy plywood, four threaded bolts and four wing nuts. The two pieces of plywood match in size and shape. Both pieces have matching holes drilled through the four corners. Four bolts go through the holes from the underside of one plywood board, and the wing nuts are attached on the upper side of the other board. Layers of blotting paper and cardboard lie between the two plywood boards, and the pressure can be adjusted by simply tightening the wing nuts.

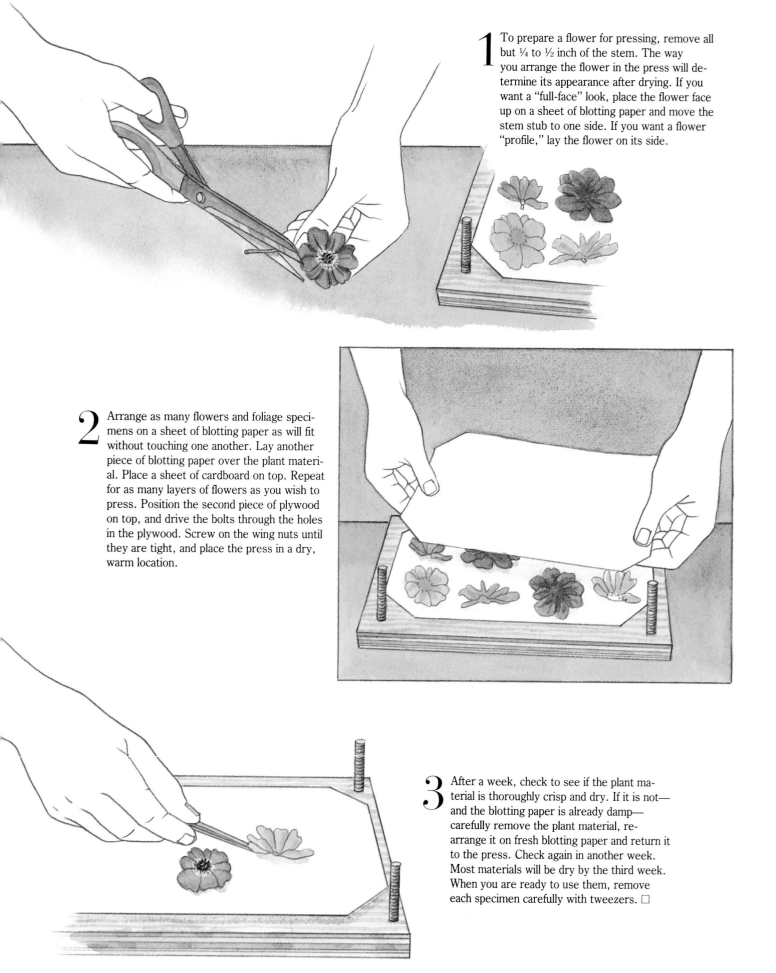

1 To prepare a flower for pressing, remove all but ¼ to ½ inch of the stem. The way you arrange the flower in the press will determine its appearance after drying. If you want a "full-face" look, place the flower face up on a sheet of blotting paper and move the stem stub to one side. If you want a flower "profile," lay the flower on its side.

2 Arrange as many flowers and foliage specimens on a sheet of blotting paper as will fit without touching one another. Lay another piece of blotting paper over the plant material. Place a sheet of cardboard on top. Repeat for as many layers of flowers as you wish to press. Position the second piece of plywood on top, and drive the bolts through the holes in the plywood. Screw on the wing nuts until they are tight, and place the press in a dry, warm location.

3 After a week, check to see if the plant material is thoroughly crisp and dry. If it is not—and the blotting paper is already damp—carefully remove the plant material, rearrange it on fresh blotting paper and return it to the press. Check again in another week. Most materials will be dry by the third week. When you are ready to use them, remove each specimen carefully with tweezers. □

SEEDPOD CLEANING AND STORAGE

The seedpods of many plants provide attractive shapes and textures not found in flowers and foliage. If collected and dried, such pods will enhance any arrangement. They go especially well with autumn and winter designs.

It is easy enough to start your own seedpod collection. Instead of removing all faded flowers from your plants, let a few remain on their stalks, and allow the plants to go to seed.

Most seedpods should be left on the plant until leaves and stems start turning brown. The only exceptions are pods that split open when mature, like milkweed pods; these must be harvested while they are still green.

Check periodically to make sure that the maturing seedpods are in no danger of being damaged by wind, rain or frost. Collect on a dry day before the pods fade or become overripe. If the pods have already opened, shake them to remove the seeds.

Although some seedpods dry completely on the plant, it is a good idea to finish drying all your pods indoors as a precaution against mold. After they are dry, clean them gently in soap and water—to get rid of dirt and insects—and air-dry them again.

If you wish, you can bleach some of the darker pods to give them a softer look. Finish with a light coat of sealant to preserve their appearance.

Properly preserved seedpods will last indefinitely. When they become dirty over time, simply swish them around in some soapy water, rinse and dry thoroughly.

Integrated with dried flowers and grasses in this autumn-colored basket are the long, ribbed pods of okra (upper left), a prickly milkweed pod (center), a dark round poppy pod (lower left) and an array of leaflike yucca pods (lower right).

1 To collect seedpods, cut them from the plant along with a generous length of stem; if any pods are open, shake them to release the seeds. Strip all foliage from the stem. To dry, tie the pods together in bunches and hang them in a well-ventilated area, or lay them flat in a box *(above)*. Turn the pods every few days so that they dry evenly.

2 Once dry, most pods should be gently swished in soapy water to remove all traces of dirt and insect residue. (Skip this step with fragile and fluffy seed heads such as clematis.) Harder seed-pods, like love-in-a-mist and magnolia, will benefit from scrubbing with a soft brush. Rinse the pods thoroughly in clear water and dry again.

3 You can lighten dark pods by bleaching. In a large glass container, mix 1 teaspoon of bleach to 1 quart of water; soak the pods 15 to 20 minutes. The pods should be fully submerged; you may have to hold down air-filled pods that tend to float. After bleaching, rinse the pods in clean water and dry them thoroughly again.

4 Store the dried pods in a covered box along with a few mothballs or an insecticidal strip until you are ready to use them. Even if you plan to use them right away, it is a good idea to store the pods for at least a few days; this will kill any insects that might otherwise hatch inside the pods after they have been incorporated in an arrangement.

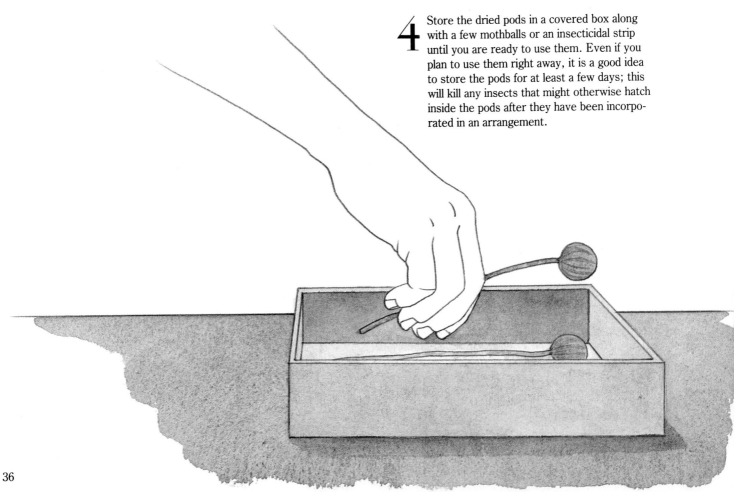

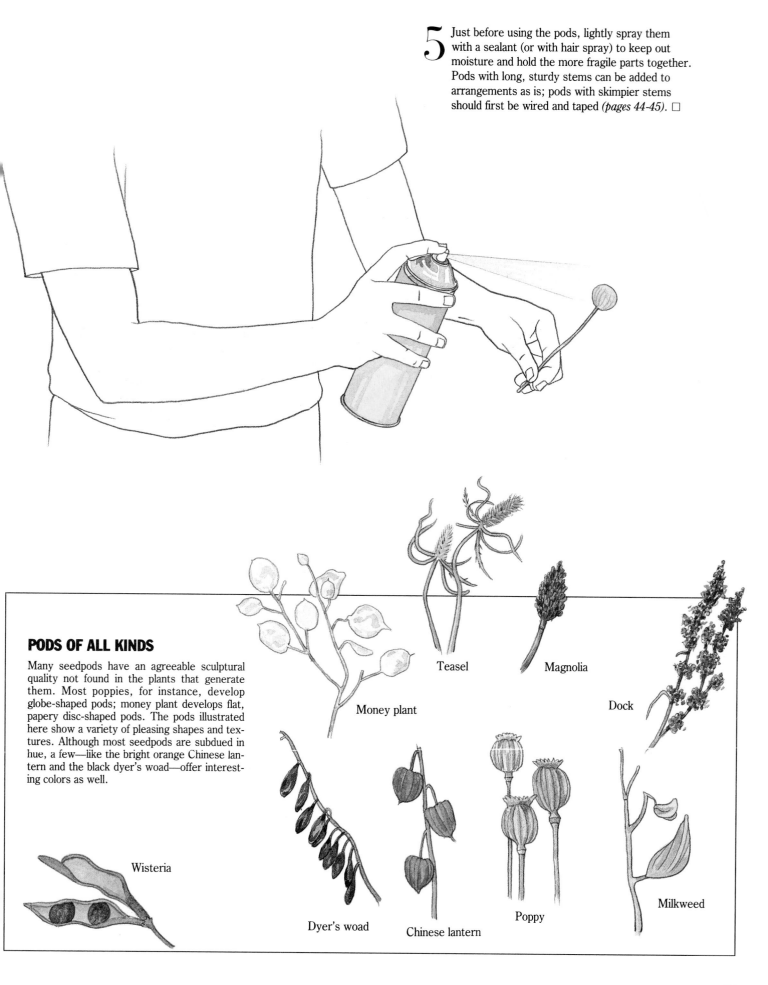

5 Just before using the pods, lightly spray them with a sealant (or with hair spray) to keep out moisture and hold the more fragile parts together. Pods with long, sturdy stems can be added to arrangements as is; pods with skimpier stems should first be wired and taped *(pages 44-45)*. □

PODS OF ALL KINDS

Many seedpods have an agreeable sculptural quality not found in the plants that generate them. Most poppies, for instance, develop globe-shaped pods; money plant develops flat, papery disc-shaped pods. The pods illustrated here show a variety of pleasing shapes and textures. Although most seedpods are subdued in hue, a few—like the bright orange Chinese lantern and the black dyer's woad—offer interesting colors as well.

Money plant

Teasel

Magnolia

Dock

Wisteria

Dyer's woad

Chinese lantern

Poppy

Milkweed

37

A GLYCERINE TREATMENT TO PRESERVE FOLIAGE

For branches and leaves, which if dried incorrectly tend to turn brown, crumbly and desiccated, there is a special technique of preservation that makes it possible to add them to dried flower arrangements for a full and shapely look. The trick is to keep the foliage *moist*—by packing its tissues with the oily, non-drying substance called glycerine. If soaked in a glycerine solution, as shown below and opposite, foliage stays fresh and pliable almost indefinitely. And the glycerine helps leaves take on rich hues of gray-green, red, gold, beige, silver—different from the colors on the growing plants, but all handsome colors in dry arrangements.

The liquid glycerine, which can be bought in drugstores and (more cheaply) at chemical supply houses, needs to be combined with very hot water so that the two mix completely. The ends of any woody branches you have chosen to preserve should be plunged into the solution immediately; the heat helps their tissues absorb the glycerine. For softer-stemmed cuttings, the solution should be allowed to cool. How long the branches need to stay in the mixture depends on the type of plant involved. It can take six weeks for the glycerine to impregnate tough, fibrous branches. With other plant material, it may be only six days. The indication of readiness is that the leaves have completely changed color.

The glycerine method works with foliage from most deciduous and evergreen trees and with some ferns. The branches you select should, of course, be handsome to begin with, and they should be cut in midsummer when the foliage is mature yet still drawing sap. Spring growth is too tender and will wilt; fall foliage is too dry to absorb the glycerine. Also, the cut branches ought to be no more than 2 feet in length. If they are longer than that, the glycerine will not be able to reach all the leaves.

Summer branches of oak leaves preserved in glycerine take on a warm, woodlike hue. The glycerine enables the foliage to maintain its flexibility and makes it easy to arrange in a variety of ways.

GLYCERINATING SINGLE LEAVES

Large individual leaves, such as those from a magnolia, can also be preserved with glycerine. Immerse the leaves in a bowl about half full of a mixture of 1 part glycerine to 1 part water. Put the bowl in a cool, dark corner until the leaves have wholly changed color. When that has occurred, remove the leaves, rinse them with soapy water and pat them dry. Wire the leaves if necessary to make artificial branches *(pages 44-45)* and use them in a dried arrangement.

1 For preserving leaves that are attached to branches, make a solution of 1 cup glycerine to 2 cups of near-boiling water. Stir to make sure the two mix thoroughly. Do not heat the glycerine; it is combustible. Pour the solution into a sturdy heatproof jar or a vase until there are about 5 inches of the liquid in the bottom.

2 Strip the leaves from the bottom 4 or 5 inches of the branches. With woody branches, hammer the lower ends until they splinter. This helps them absorb the glycerine. (Softer woods need no pounding.) Place as many branches in the jar or vase as will fit without crowding. Leave the container in a cool, shaded, well-ventilated spot.

3 Check the foliage every few days. When it has fully changed color, remove it from the solution right away; too much glycerine can wilt the tissues. Rinse the stem ends with soapy water and pat them dry, and wipe any drops of glycerine from the leaves. The foliage is now ready for use — and can be used again year after year if dusted and washed from time to time. □

SKELETONIZING LEAVES FOR DELICATE BEAUTY

Lovely additions to flower arrangements are leaves that, with their green and perishable parts removed, are reduced to intricate, lacy networks of veins. These phantom leaves—people used to call them angels' wings—can provide an ethereal background for other, brighter materials in bouquets. They can do the same in collages of dried flowers—the pressed flower pictures *(pages 70-71)* that can be made from pressed blossoms and foliage. These skeleton leaves can also be bleached to emphasize their diaphanous quality.

The best leaves for skeletonizing are tough, glossy ones because they have ribs and veins sturdy enough to hold together after the fleshy green of the leaves is gone. Magnolia leaves are ideal; excellent, too, are leaves from oaks and maples. Always choose leaves in perfect condition; any damage will ruin the final effect. Leave some stem on each leaf.

There are two ways to skeletonize leaves. The quick method is to boil them for half an hour in a quart of water containing a teaspoon of baking soda and immediately rub off the fleshy parts. But boiling is risky; it is easy to ruin the leaves. The safer way is simply to soak the leaves, as shown at right. It takes several weeks—and the slowly rotting leaf material can cause an unpleasant odor. But the method is reliable and the soaking leaves can be placed at a distance, in a garden shed or a far corner of the garage.

Once the fleshy material has softened, it can be removed easily and the skeleton leaves can be dried and pressed flat. For pressed-flower-and-foliage pictures, the skeletonized leaves can be used as is. For use in regular arrangements, they will need stems made of wire and florist's tape *(pages 44-45)*. Despite its fragile appearance, the gossamer foliage will survive the rigors of being wired, and of being moved about until the perfect spot in a bouquet is found.

A pair of large magnolia leaves, skeletonized by having their fleshy substance removed through soaking, reveal the lacy patterns of their veins. Such ghostly leaves can add a fairylike aura to dried arrangements and to pressed flower pictures.

1 Fill a pail with water and drop in the best of your collected leaves. Do not crowd them; they should not stick together. Put the pail in an out-of-the-way place for up to four weeks. Check after two weeks to see if the green parts have begun to soften.

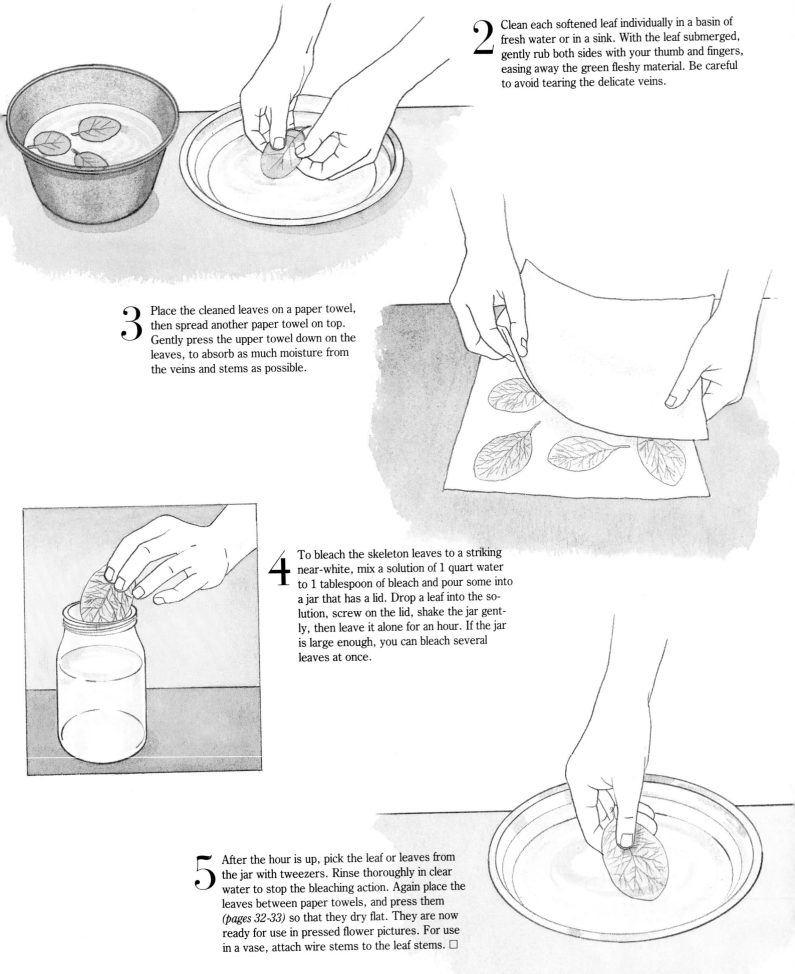

2 Clean each softened leaf individually in a basin of fresh water or in a sink. With the leaf submerged, gently rub both sides with your thumb and fingers, easing away the green fleshy material. Be careful to avoid tearing the delicate veins.

3 Place the cleaned leaves on a paper towel, then spread another paper towel on top. Gently press the upper towel down on the leaves, to absorb as much moisture from the veins and stems as possible.

4 To bleach the skeleton leaves to a striking near-white, mix a solution of 1 quart water to 1 tablespoon of bleach and pour some into a jar that has a lid. Drop a leaf into the solution, screw on the lid, shake the jar gently, then leave it alone for an hour. If the jar is large enough, you can bleach several leaves at once.

5 After the hour is up, pick the leaf or leaves from the jar with tweezers. Rinse thoroughly in clear water to stop the bleaching action. Again place the leaves between paper towels, and press them *(pages 32-33)* so that they dry flat. They are now ready for use in pressed flower pictures. For use in a vase, attach wire stems to the leaf stems. □

41

QUICK DRYING
WITH A MICROWAVE

Microwave ovens are unexpectedly useful for drying flowers and foliage. They shorten the drying time from weeks to minutes, and both blossoms and leaves generally retain more of their natural colors than they do when dried in slower ways.

The one drawback is that flower stems shrivel when microwaved and need to be removed ahead of time. This means the dried blooms must later be wired to artificial stems *(pages 44-45)*—but *after* they have been microwaved, not before, as metal is unsafe in a microwave oven. It also means it is impractical to microwave tiny, delicate flowers, which will fall apart without their stems. But there are scores of large flowers that microwave well, from roses and daisies to large dahlias, peonies and chrysanthemums.

The specimens you cut for drying should be first-rate. After you have collected them, you will need some silica gel to aid in drying and a microwave-safe container—a cardboard box or a plastic dish—that has a lid and is deep enough to hold the plant material and a layer of the gel. The cooking time depends on the power of your microwave, the density of the plant material and its moisture content. Start with the oven set on high for one minute. If the results are too dry, try a second batch at 30 seconds. Heavy flowers such as roses may need three minutes. Dry only one kind of bloom or leaf at a time because the drying period varies from one species to another. Take notes on which blooms take how long—and keep experimenting until you have found the ideal times for your plants and your own microwave.

A yellow carnation that has been dried in a microwave oven rests on a bed of silica gel. The high-speed action of the oven allows large-blossomed flowers—which would shrivel if dried slowly—to retain much of their original shape and color.

1 To dry flowers or leaves in a microwave oven, first remove the stems. Pour 1 inch of silica gel into a safe container. Arrange the plant material on top of the gel; do not let them touch each other. Cover them with more gel, using a soft paintbrush to sweep particles into crevices.

2 Place the open container in your micro-wave oven. If you are using a cardboard box, put it on top of a plastic dish as shown so that moisture can escape through the bottom of the box. Start the oven on high with the timer set on one minute. You may wish to rotate the container after 30 seconds to ensure even drying.

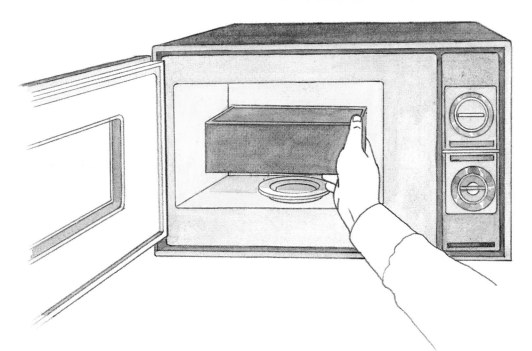

3 When the minute is up, remove your container from the oven. Cover the container with a lid left open a crack. The lid will help prevent the silica gel from absorbing moisture from the air, and the opening will let the flowers or leaves inside continue to "cook" as the heat slowly escapes.

4 After a half-hour cooling period, set the lid aside, remove the leaves or flowers and brush off the silica gel. If the plant material is not dry to the touch, put it back in the gel and heat it for another 30 seconds. Often the thicker parts of a flower, such as the calyx, take longer to dry than the thin petals. In such cases, push only the calyx into the gel before microwaving again. □

43

WIRED STEMS
FOR LENGTH AND STRENGTH

Because stems become very brittle when they lose moisture, they are usually removed before flowers are dried. The dried flowers can then be fitted with flexible artificial stems made of florist's wire. This procedure, known as wiring, makes it possible to construct complex arrangements out of the most fragile materials.

Wiring is also useful for lengthening the short stems of leaves and of seedpods like pine cones, and for reinforcing soft-stemmed fresh flowers that are to be incorporated into garlands. The wire can be curved or shaped at will to follow the contours of the garland.

Similarly, floppy-stemmed flowers like tulips may be wired for greater strength and rigidity in bouquets. But keep in mind that wiring shortens the vase life of fresh flowers, so wire only if necessary.

As illustrated on the opposite page, wiring methods vary greatly according to the kinds of materials to be wired.

You can buy florist's wire in spools and in precut lengths at garden centers and floral supply houses. The wire comes in a variety of thicknesses known as gauges, which are identified by number. The higher the number, the thinner the wire.

Always use the thinnest wire that will get the job done. For most purposes, wire of medium thickness—20 or 22 gauge—should be sufficient. Very fine wire, such as 34 gauge, is sometimes used to attach a handful of delicate flower heads to a stem that has been crafted of thicker wire.

To keep your arrangement as natural-looking as possible, cover all wire stems with green or brown florist's tape *(page 31)*. Rolls of this stretchy, sticky tape are available at craft stores.

The vivid yellow and orange strawflowers in this arrangement have weak stems. Unobtrusive wiring helps them keep their heads above a background of eucalyptus, statice, yarrow and tansy.

FLOWER SPIKES

To stiffen a flower spike, work wire around two or three blossoms *(left),* then bend the wire into a hairpin curve. Pull the wire down to secure it, and wind both ends around the stem.

STEM STUBS

To lengthen a flower or a leaf that has only 1 inch of stem, lay a length of wire parallel to the stem stub and wrap the stem and the wire together with florist's tape.

LEAVES WITHOUT STEMS

To give a stem to a leaf that has none, pierce the leaf near the base with one end of a length of wire; then bring the wire through and bend it to form a double thickness, and twist the strands together.

HOLLOW STEMS

To strengthen the hollow stem of a flower such as allium when it is to be used fresh, and to lengthen the stem of a dried poppy seedpod *(right),* push a length of wire up into the stem through the bottom opening.

WEAK STEMS

To reinforce the stem of a delicate dried flower such as a pansy or a cornflower or of a skeletonized leaf, create a ring of wire for the flower or leaf to lean on, then twist the ends of the wire around the stem.

FLOPPY STEMS

To make a drooping tulip stand straight, cut a piece of wire that is longer than the stem. Insert the tip into (but not through) the calyx, or base, of the flower, then twist the rest of the wire around the stem. □

4
MAKING ARRANGEMENTS

T he most striking floral arrangements display an imaginative combination of flowers, foliage and container. But arranging flowers requires equal parts skill and imagination. Understanding the effects created by different materials—from the graceful look provided by long, thin branches to the delicate, airy quality that sprays of small flowers give—is the first step toward combining them in an attractive arrangement. And mechanics are important, too, whether you are choosing an appropriate container, wiring stems to extend their length, or cutting a piece of floral foam that will accommodate the flowers you intend to use. The more you know about the plants and the tools involved, the more creatively you can use them.

This chapter will guide you through all phases of making floral arrangements. It begins with the basic techniques—how to put materials together—and continues by showing how different elements, such as flowers and foliage, define the piece. Later pages show how to use shape and dimension to give the arrangement a sense of order. Another section shows how to use style—formal or informal, traditional or contemporary—to achieve the effect you want. Finally, the chapter will take you through the process of arranging flowers and foliage in various ways—in containers, in a hand-tied bouquet, in a garland, in a wreath and in a pressed picture.

THE BASICS OF ARRANGING FLOWERS AND FOLIAGE

Yellow lilies and purple and white delphiniums add both color and height to this traditional autumn arrangement, which includes hydrangeas, dahlias, chrysanthemums, rose hips and some wisps of delicate foliage. Some of the lower, heavier blooms arch downward, unifying the arrangement with its container.

Flower arranging, like other arts, thrives on originality and invention. But as in other creative endeavors there are some basic principles—in this case, a few commonsensical do's and don'ts—that make success easier and also help the imagination take wing.

The most basic of all is making sure the arrangement is going to be the right size for its container. This means gathering enough flowers and foliage of sufficient length to make the finished arrangement one and a half or even two times as tall as the vase—or as wide if you are using a bowl that is broader than it is high. Any smaller than that and the arrangement will look skimpy; much larger and it will seem top-heavy.

A corollary to this rule is to let some of your flowers flow down over the rim of the container. This will integrate the arrangement with the container and also avoids a slapdash look, as though the plant materials had just been bunched together and stuck willy-nilly into the vase.

Equally important is avoiding top-heaviness by placing the large blooms and ones with dark, warm colors toward the bottom of the arrangement. Big, substantial-looking blossoms are the main focus of the arrangement, and unless situated near the base they will seem to be floating in air in defiance of the law of gravity.

All arrangements look best if they combine large flowers with small ones, dark with light, stiff vertical shapes with soft curving ones. The best methods of integrating these various elements are shown in the box on top of the opposite page and in the drawings below it and on the following two pages. The drawings also detail how to make arranging easy by using floral foam, a sort of Styrofoam that florists employ. The flowers being arranged are fresh ones, but the same principles of design apply to dry flower materials—for which there is even a special dry foam that makes the minor but fascinating art of arranging easy.

AN ARRANGEMENT
AND ITS PARTS

Good flower arrangements almost always include three elements that work together. First there are the *line* materials *(shown in green at left)* that reach upward and outward, giving an arrangement its vertical and horizontal structure. Excellent line materials are long-stemmed flowers and foliage, cattails and just-budding branches. *Mass* materials *(shown in red)* are the eye-catching clusters of large blooms—peonies, dahlias, open roses and hundreds more—that form the focus of an arrangement and provide much of its color. Filling in the gaps between mass and line elements are the *fillers (shown in purple)*—small clustered flowers, catkins, ferns and grasses.

1 Start by cutting a block of floral foam to fit your vase or bowl. If you are using fresh flowers, soak the foam in water. It should rise a couple of inches above the container's rim so you can insert stems at various angles. Secure it to the container if necessary with crisscrossed strips of sticky florist's tape.

2 Cover the foam with green plant material. For a fresh arrangement this can be sprigs of fern, as shown at right, or other foliage. Insert the sprigs at all angles; in the finished arrangement the foam should be completely hidden. With a dried arrangement, use dried sheets of sphagnum moss or handfuls of Spanish moss, and secure it to fit the foam with plant pins.

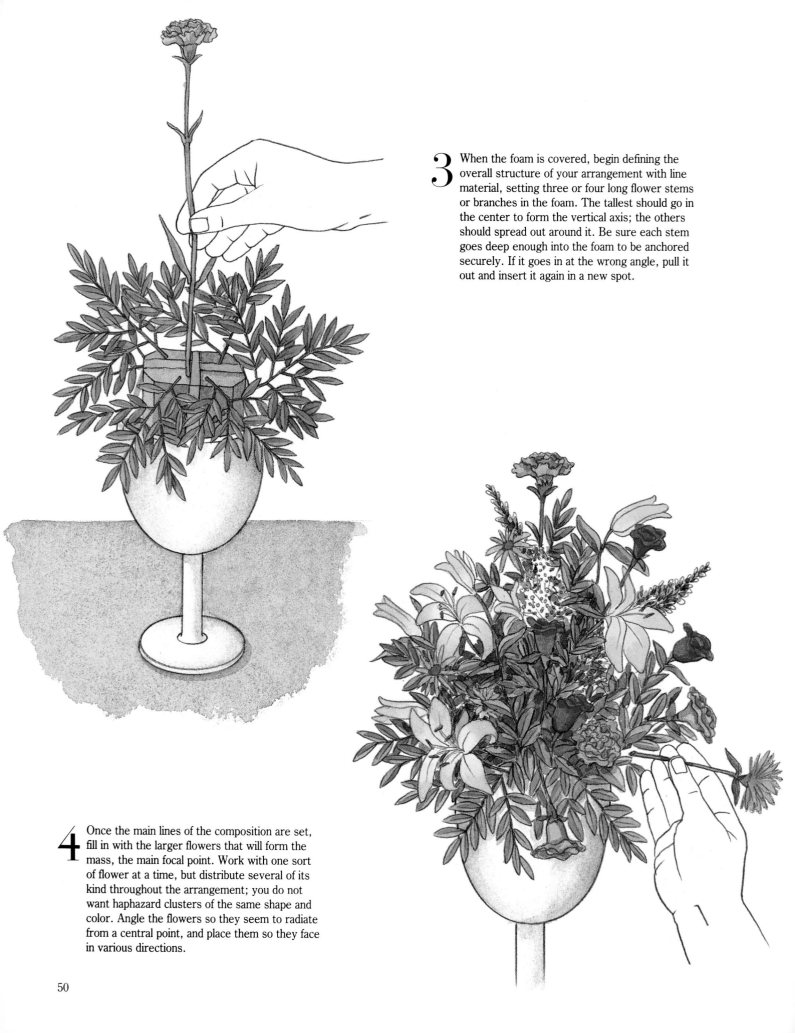

3 When the foam is covered, begin defining the overall structure of your arrangement with line material, setting three or four long flower stems or branches in the foam. The tallest should go in the center to form the vertical axis; the others should spread out around it. Be sure each stem goes deep enough into the foam to be anchored securely. If it goes in at the wrong angle, pull it out and insert it again in a new spot.

4 Once the main lines of the composition are set, fill in with the larger flowers that will form the mass, the main focal point. Work with one sort of flower at a time, but distribute several of its kind throughout the arrangement; you do not want haphazard clusters of the same shape and color. Angle the flowers so they seem to radiate from a central point, and place them so they face in various directions.

5 Insert some flowers so that they are recessed, to create a sense of depth. Be sure, though, that no two flowers of the same height are next to each other, which gives a crowded effect; trim the stems as necessary. No flower should extend much beyond the outline, and do not jam blooms together; fewer blossoms are better than too many.

6 After the main elements of the arrangement are in place, fill in any gaps with light, lacy filler materials. The filler provides a finished look but it should be used sparingly or the arrangement will look overstuffed. A fresh arrangement should be watered daily to keep the foam moist. A floral preservative in the water will keep the flowers crisp longer. □

DIFFERENT SHAPES FOR DIFFERENT PLACES

Not every spot in a house can accommodate the tall, traditional style of flower arrangement shown on the previous pages. A broad arrangement will not fit on a narrow shelf, and a tall one is not suitable as a dinner-table centerpiece because it obstructs the diners' views of one another and hinders conversation.

But there are many sorts of arrangements, of various sizes and shapes, that will look right on shelves and in corners, on end tables and dressers. Four of the basic designs —rounded, triangular, vertical and horizontal —are shown and described here and on the next pages. A couple of them not only have distinctive outlines, but also are almost flat in the rear and are meant to be seen from just one side. In all cases, though, the same principles apply. Line elements defining the shape come first, then the larger blooms that provide the mass of color, and finally delicate fillers to close any gaps.

A rounded or domed arrangement is ideal for a coffee table or similar spot that is not close to a wall and can be viewed from all sides. A low horizontal arrangement serves well as a centerpiece on a dining table or as decoration for a buffet. Vertical ones are made to order for limited spaces—on occasional tables in corners, where they can soar upward without spilling outward into the room. Flat-backed triangular arrangements similarly belong against a wall, perhaps sitting on a mantelpiece or a narrow entryway table, providing a maximum of color and symmetry while taking up a minimum of space.

Their splashy blooms set off by delicate baby's breath and ferns, yellow and white chrysanthemums arranged in a rounded design look both elegant and rustic in a wicker basket. The large blooms, facing in all directions, make the arrangement equally effective when viewed from any side.

THE ALL-AROUND ARRANGEMENT

The essence of this design is symmetry and roundness, so begin by sticking your tallest flower straight up in the middle of the florist's foam in your container *(below, left)*. Follow this with four more stems of about equal length, placing them in the sides of the foam at twelve, three, six and nine o'clock *(below, center and right)*. When the lines are established, fill in with more flowers, big ones for color and mass, smaller blooms and foliage for filler and variety.

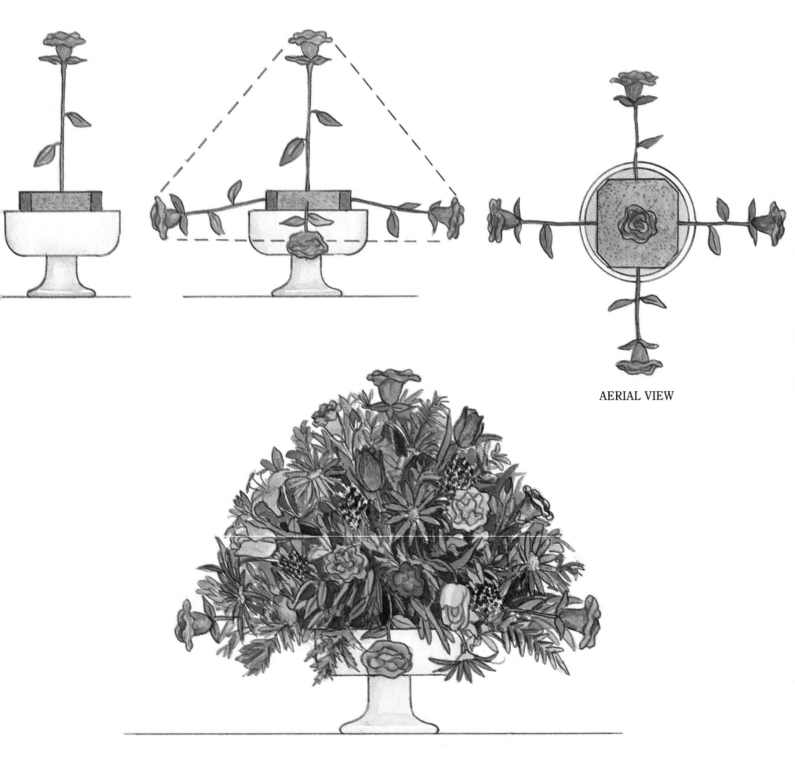

AERIAL VIEW

THE SHALLOW TRIANGLE

To establish the symmetrical shape of a triangular arrangement, place the tallest flower in the center rear of the foam, angling it backward to give the design some depth. Then put a large bloom in the center front, angling it downward and letting it protrude 5 inches or so over the container's rim, to serve as the focal point. To complete the outline of the triangle, place two more flowers at the sides, again angled downward. When you have the structure set, fill in with more blooms.

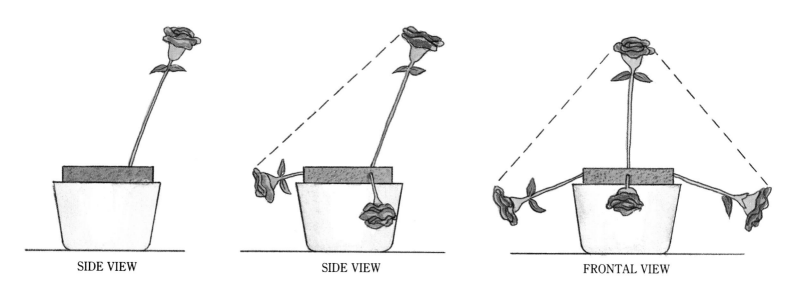

SIDE VIEW   SIDE VIEW   FRONTAL VIEW

THE SPREADING HORIZONTAL

A horizontal arrangement should be two to three times as wide as it is high or deep. Establish the width with two pieces of line material such as evergreen branches, ferns, or spiky flower heads of snapdragon or larkspur. Add short pieces of the same material, to form a cross, and angle them down over the container's rim. Fill in with more foliage and some flowers. The arrangement, although low, should mound at the central focal point.

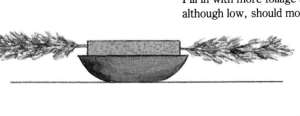

AERIAL VIEW

THE GRACEFUL VERTICAL

Line is the crucial element here. It is established with a single tall, spiky flower such as a hollyhock, larkspur or delphinium. Add a couple of shorter uprights, to enhance and give visual support to the first. All colorful mass material—and it should be used sparingly—goes lower down, as shown in the finished arrangement at far right. A couple of blossoms and leaves can stray over the rim of your tall container, but not too far or they will spoil the vertical lines. ☐

STYLES FROM EAST AND WEST

Besides varying in their basic shapes *(pages 52-55)*, flower arrangements differ considerably in style. Generally speaking, there are three main styles *(opposite)*. Each projects its own special mood or feeling, goes best with a particular sort of interior decoration—and has its own unique history. The full arrangement with its opulent mass of blooms is essentially Western, and dates back to the European Renaissance. The line arrangement that uses only a few flowers while emphasizing natural shapes originally came from Japan. Most recent is the line-mass style, a combination of the other two. It became the fashion in Europe and America after the Western discovery of Japanese art in the late 19th century.

When choosing which style to follow, consider the decor of the room you want to put the arrangement in. The old-style European arrangement looks best, to most people's taste, with traditional furniture—the furniture patterned on antique English and French designs. Japanese-inspired line arrangements seem most at home with the uncluttered look of modern furniture. The in-between line-mass sort of arrangement, its open outline combined with patches of bright blooms, tends to look less imposing than the other two and fits handsomely in an informal setting—a family room, say, or a glassed-in porch.

Whatever style you decide to follow, remember that the tone of the finished arrangement will depend in part on the container. Baskets and rough clay pots are clearly informal. A glass, silver or porcelain vase, by contrast, adds to an arrangement's formality. In short, let your decor—and your mood—determine what sort of design to make, and what container you put it in. And the occasion. You might use a brown glazed bowl for an everyday dining room bouquet but change to a cut glass container when having a dinner party.

Tulips and forsythia branches set in a shallow dish form a graceful, spare line arrangement with a distinctly Oriental flavor. The branches both form the basic structure and give the design its sense of vitality and movement.

A MASS ARRANGEMENT

The old-fashioned European-style arrangement should be solid, substantial and packed with flowers, its outline filled in, its many blooms contained and framed by line materials *(right)*. Traditionally such arrangements were large and included many sorts and colors of flowers. The size may be scaled down to match a small room, and only two or three different flowers need be employed, but the arrangement should be kept dense.

A LINE-MASS ARRANGEMENT

Borrowing key elements from the older European arrangement and Japanese forms, line-mass designs can be vivid and exuberant, the static quality of densely packed blooms being enlivened by a free, imaginative use of line materials. Usually the larger blooms are kept low and centralized while the taller, thinner line elements spring away to the sides and top. To be effective, though, such an arrangement ought to give an impression of having some structure and balance; the one pictured above, despite its open areas, forms an irregular triangle.

A LINE ARRANGEMENT

Oriental designs use fewer components than either of the other styles and depend for much of their effect on the artful use of intriguingly shaped line elements—tall but narrow flowers, gnarled branches, cattails, stiff grasses. Large blooms should be used sparingly and kept low so that they do not confuse or obstruct the subtle interplay of the stems and branches as they curve and bend to give the arrangement energy and movement and suggest the look of plants growing naturally outdoors in wind and rain. □

GARLANDS
FOR FESTIVE OCCASIONS

A garland is a flexible rope of flowers and foliage that makes an attractive decoration for a holiday or a special event. Hang it over a mantelpiece or a doorway, encircle a tablecloth, coil it around a banister—you can create a garland to fit any setting or season.

Making a garland is not difficult. But it takes time because each flower and branch of foliage must be wired individually. This allows you to position the material so that each piece faces in the desired direction.

You can use fresh or dried materials or a combination of both. Keep in mind that all fresh materials must be naturally long-lasting and well conditioned since a garland cannot be watered.

The base that holds the garland together can be anything strong and flexible, such as heavy string (dyed green for appearance) or heavy florist's wire. About 6 to 8 inches of the string should be left uncovered at each end, to use for tying the garland to a mount when you are ready to display it.

A garland's fullness comes from its foliage; this is wired on first. Always select branches with long stems since these are the easiest to wire. Once the foliage foundation is in place, add flowers, seedpods, nuts, berries. See pages 44-45 for different ways to wire flowers.

Your choice of material will determine the mood of the garland. Winter garlands often feature branches of fragrant evergreens together with berries and dried seedpods. A fall garland might include autumn leaves, ornamental grasses and chrysanthemums. In spring and summer, you might combine asparagus fern or heather branches with white daisies and pink roses.

A garland containing fresh flowers will last anywhere from a few days to a week, depending on what is in it and where it is displayed. For best results, construct a fresh garland no more than a day or two before you display it.

In a springtime garland forming a graceful curve on a sun-dappled stair railing, lavender chrysanthemums and baby's breath stand out against a foundation of Sprenger fern. Lavender ribbon bows add a formal touch.

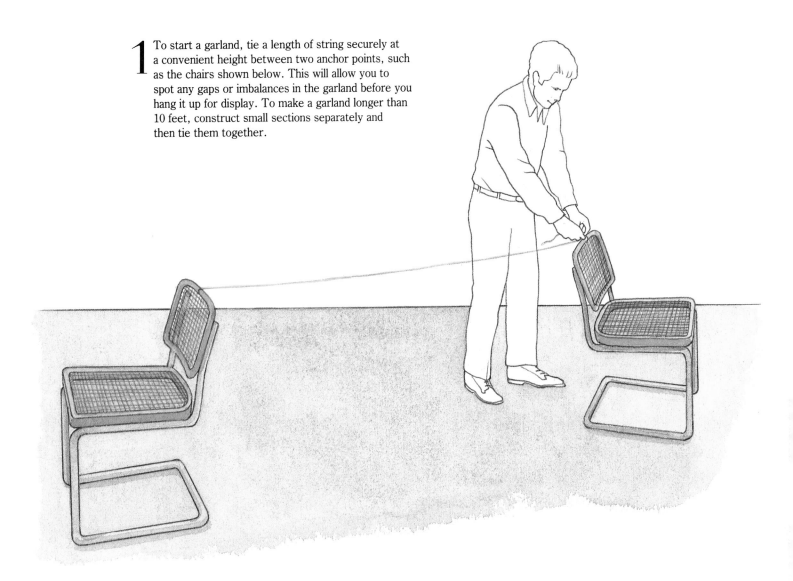

1 To start a garland, tie a length of string securely at a convenient height between two anchor points, such as the chairs shown below. This will allow you to spot any gaps or imbalances in the garland before you hang it up for display. To make a garland longer than 10 feet, construct small sections separately and then tie them together.

2 Begin by placing the first branch of foliage on the string, about 6 to 8 inches from one end of the string. Wrap flexible florist's wire around a 3- or 4-inch length of both stem and string.

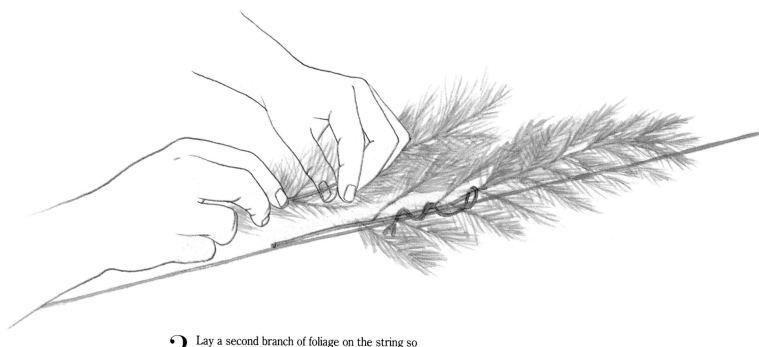

3 Lay a second branch of foliage on the string so that it overlaps half of the first branch, with the stems pointing in the same direction; wire the stem of the second branch to the string. Continue overlapping branches in this way until the string is entirely covered.

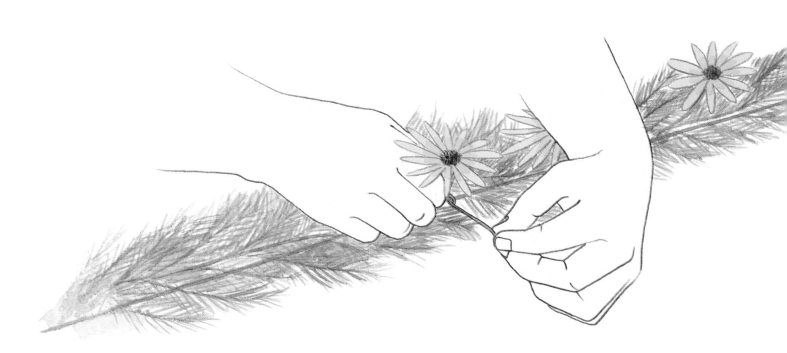

4 Wire the principal flowers in the design at intervals from one end of the garland to the other. Lay each flower in position and secure it to the string with several turns of wire (above). Attach all specimens of a particular kind of flower to the garland before adding other kinds, to make sure you have them distributed evenly.

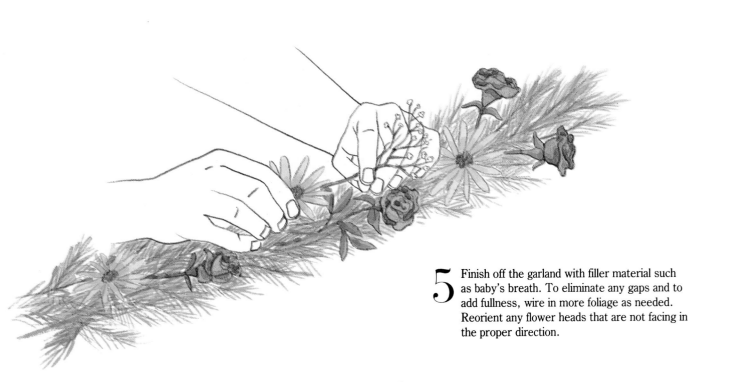

5 Finish off the garland with filler material such as baby's breath. To eliminate any gaps and to add fullness, wire in more foliage as needed. Reorient any flower heads that are not facing in the proper direction.

6 If the garland is made with fresh flowers and you do not intend to hang it for a day or two, keep it in a cool, dark place, like a basement, until you are ready to display it. Mist it with water once or twice a day. If possible, continue misting daily after you hang the garland. □

A HAND-TIED BOUQUET FOR A SPECIAL GIFT

Bouquets of freshly cut flowers that you have selected, arranged and tied yourself make unusual presents for friends. By following a few basic principles of design, you can achieve a pleasing effect with virtually any kind of material.

The simplest bouquet features one kind of flower laid against a spray of foliage. Bold flowers like anthurium, which tend to overshadow any other flowers they are put with, work well in such a bouquet. More subtly hued blooms can be combined with others of varied shapes and textures to create interesting mixed bouquets.

The foliage most commonly used in bouquets is fern, but for variety you can experiment with branches of eucalyptus, leafy birch, even blades of ornamental grass. Remove all foliage from the part of the stem that will be submerged in water.

Assemble your bouquet in graduated layers according to size, with the tallest stems forming the backdrop of the arrangement and progressively shorter ones in front. Distribute different flowers evenly so that you have a pleasing harmony of shapes and colors.

The size of individual blossoms should also be taken into account. Exceptionally large flowers, which look "heavy," belong at the bottom of the arrangement. Fine-textured filler, such as baby's breath or statice, may be used throughout the bouquet.

To tie the bouquet together, use a length of household twine or waterproof florist's ribbon. Even if you use twine for strength, you can dress up the bouquet by adding a simple bow knot of ribbon flanked by streamers.

The flowers in this abundant bouquet seem almost to explode from the clear glass vase. Cream-colored tulips and lilies share the focus with sweet-smelling lilac and freesia.

1 Begin your bouquet by laying the tallest
material—the foliage backdrop—on a flat surface. Spread the foliage in a fan shape,
crossing the stems at a point where you will
later tie the bouquet; leave at least 6 inches
of stems below this point. Remove any leaves
from the bottom 6 inches.

2 Place a layer of flowers, one by one, on top
of the fan of foliage. Arrange the flowers so
that the longest stems are in the middle of
the fan, with their tops just below the top of
the foliage *(below)*. Since odd numbers of
flowers look better than even numbers, start
with a layer of three or five tall flowers.

3 Continue to lay down flowers, reducing the height of each layer as you work toward the bottom of the bouquet. Each layer should contain more than one kind of flower. Be sure to tuck some foliage between the various layers of flowers as well as in the front of the bouquet. If you are using filler flowers like baby's breath, intersperse them throughout the arrangement.

4 When the design is complete, slip a length of twine or florist's ribbon around the place where all the stems intersect and secure it with a knot. The knot should be just tight enough to hold all the material together without deforming the fan shape. Remove all foliage below the knot. If you wish, add an attractive ribbon bow and streamers.

5 Using sharp florist's shears, even off any stem ends that protrude from the base of the bouquet. This will ensure that all the stems meet the water when the bouquet is placed in a vase. Keep the bouquet standing in water until you are ready to present it. □

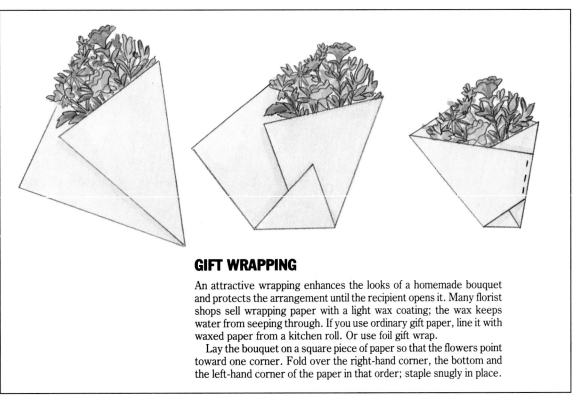

GIFT WRAPPING

An attractive wrapping enhances the looks of a homemade bouquet and protects the arrangement until the recipient opens it. Many florist shops sell wrapping paper with a light wax coating; the wax keeps water from seeping through. If you use ordinary gift paper, line it with waxed paper from a kitchen roll. Or use foil gift wrap.

Lay the bouquet on a square piece of paper so that the flowers point toward one corner. Fold over the right-hand corner, the bottom and the left-hand corner of the paper in that order; staple snugly in place.

A WREATH
FOR ANY TIME OF YEAR

Dried blossoms of strawflowers, yarrow, statice, celosia, globe amaranth and lamb's-ears contribute patches of color to this potpourri wreath.

A wreath is built up on a circular form. The easiest ones to work on are made of Styrofoam or straw, but forms are also made of wire. All three kinds come in a variety of sizes, generally from about 10 to 20 inches in diameter. They are available at craft stores, which also carry the plant pins and floral picks you will need. Plant pins, which look like hairpins with sharpened prongs, are used to secure the two-dimensional plant materials to the wreath form. A floral pick resembles a giant toothpick with a small piece of wire attached to the blunt end; you loop the wire around a small bunch of flowers and push the sharp end of the pick into the form.

You can make a wreath from only one kind of material, as in the traditional Christmas holly wreath, or you can create a potpourri effect by mixing many different kinds of plant materials, with or without a clear focal point. Fresh plants—such as trimmings from evergreens and sprigs of winter berries—make handsome outdoor wreaths. Or combine fresh wormwood, lamb's-ears or dusty miller with dried flowers and foliage. Before using fresh plants, let them partially dry in a dark place for several weeks. Be extra-generous when adding fresh plant material to a wreath, because it will shrink as it ages.

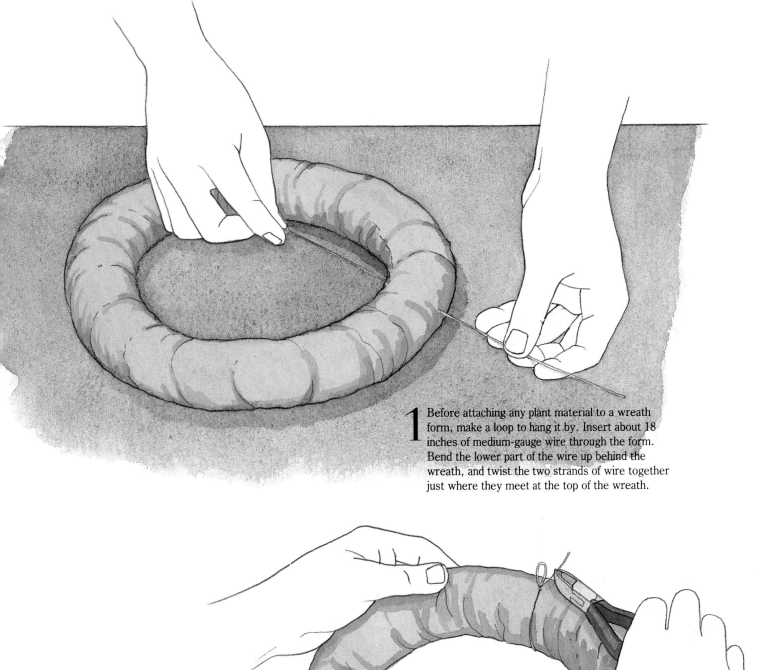

1 Before attaching any plant material to a wreath form, make a loop to hang it by. Insert about 18 inches of medium-gauge wire through the form. Bend the lower part of the wire up behind the wreath, and twist the two strands of wire together just where they meet at the top of the wreath.

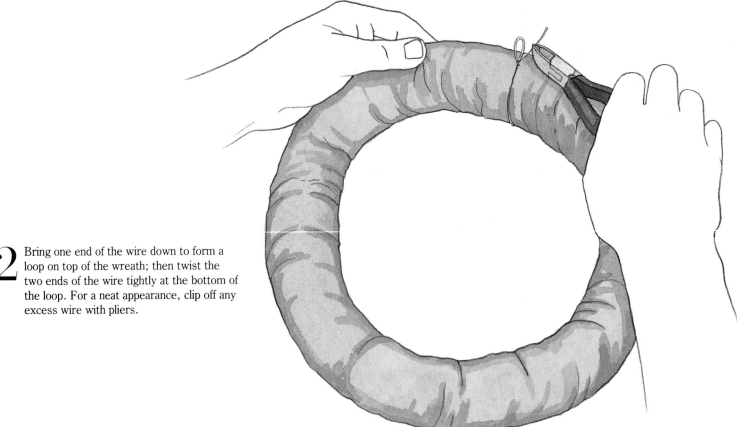

2 Bring one end of the wire down to form a loop on top of the wreath; then twist the two ends of the wire tightly at the bottom of the loop. For a neat appearance, clip off any excess wire with pliers.

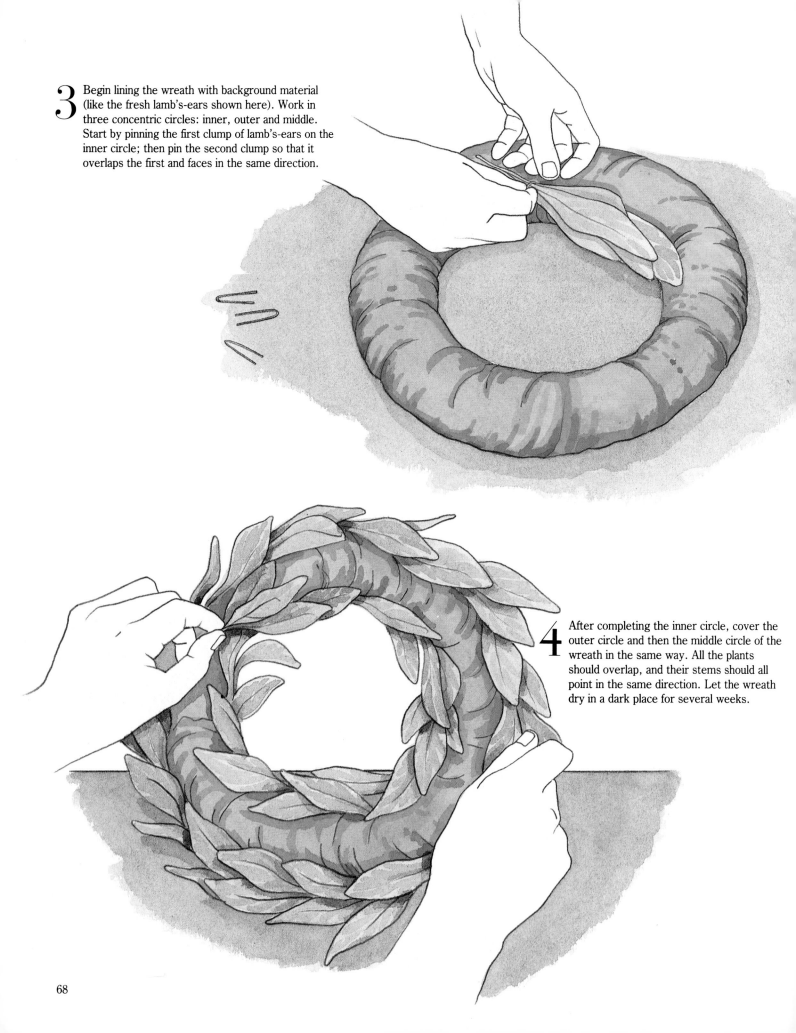

3 Begin lining the wreath with background material (like the fresh lamb's-ears shown here). Work in three concentric circles: inner, outer and middle. Start by pinning the first clump of lamb's-ears on the inner circle; then pin the second clump so that it overlaps the first and faces in the same direction.

4 After completing the inner circle, cover the outer circle and then the middle circle of the wreath in the same way. All the plants should overlap, and their stems should all point in the same direction. Let the wreath dry in a dark place for several weeks.

When the clumps of lamb's-ears are dry, add the decorative material. To insert small bunches of flowers, use floral picks that come with thin wire attached to the blunt end. First tie together three to five flowers by wrapping the thin wire around the flower stems and the shaft of the pick; then push the pointed end of the pick into the wreath.

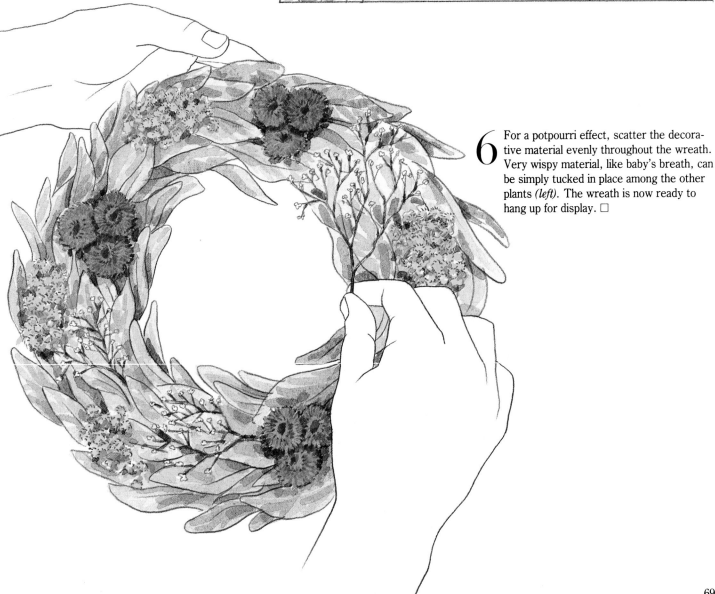

6 For a potpourri effect, scatter the decorative material evenly throughout the wreath. Very wispy material, like baby's breath, can be simply tucked in place among the other plants *(left)*. The wreath is now ready to hang up for display. □

PRESSED FLOWER PICTURES: DESIGNS THAT LAST

Aflower picture is a two-dimensional dried flower arrangement preserved in a picture frame. If the flowers and foliage are properly pressed and carefully mounted, they will last for years. To avoid mismatches, choose the frame first and design the arrangement to fit the frame. Avoid fancy frames that can overpower the delicate harmonies of flowers and foliage; for most designs, a simple rectangle or oval of wood—with a tightly fitting glass front and sturdy cardboard backing—is best.

Preparing the arrangement requires only a pair of tweezers, a little glue (optional), a supply of pressed plant materials and some time. Traditional flower pictures are arranged in triangular, vertical, round or crescent shapes. But don't hesitate to experiment with other designs that please your eye, such as attractive "sampler" patterns that show off a variety of leaves or unusually shaped flowers.

As background, choose a sheet of paper or fabric whose color and texture complement your arrangement. Neutral colors are the most versatile. Ordinary blotting paper goes with almost anything. Silk is the usual fabric for traditional designs; coarse-textured canvas is appropriate for bold, modern arrangements. Other possibilities include matting board, felt and linen.

Lay the dried plant materials on the background piece by piece. (For information about line, mass and filler and how to incorporate them into a design, see pages 48-51.) When you are satisfied with the arrangement, you can glue each piece in place with a small drop of white glue; put the drops on the strongest parts of the flowers and foliage—such as the stem ends and leafstalks.

In an asymmetrical composition built around two large dried blossoms—a reddish brown cosmos and a bicolored coreopsis mounted on a sheet of white paper—an elegant flower picture captures the essence of a late-summer meadow.

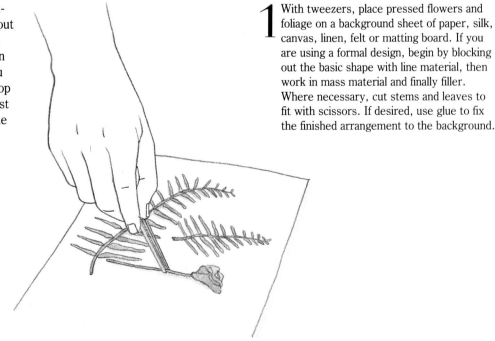

1 With tweezers, place pressed flowers and foliage on a background sheet of paper, silk, canvas, linen, felt or matting board. If you are using a formal design, begin by blocking out the basic shape with line material, then work in mass material and finally filler. Where necessary, cut stems and leaves to fit with scissors. If desired, use glue to fix the finished arrangement to the background.

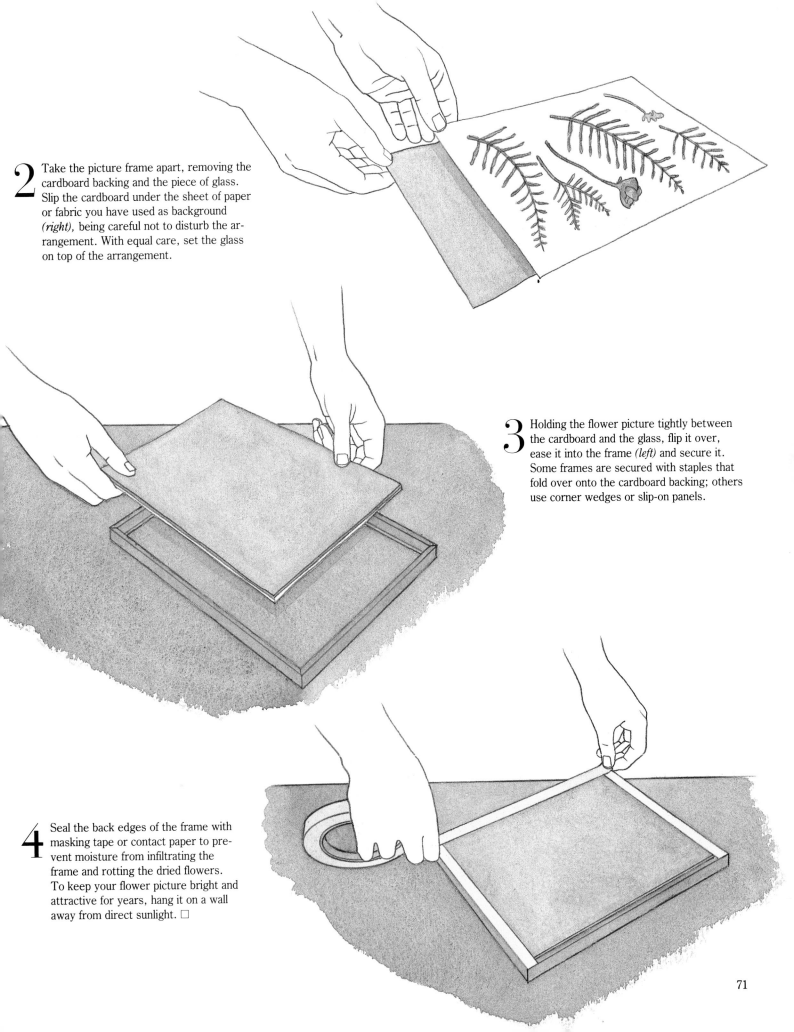

2 Take the picture frame apart, removing the cardboard backing and the piece of glass. Slip the cardboard under the sheet of paper or fabric you have used as background *(right),* being careful not to disturb the arrangement. With equal care, set the glass on top of the arrangement.

3 Holding the flower picture tightly between the cardboard and the glass, flip it over, ease it into the frame *(left)* and secure it. Some frames are secured with staples that fold over onto the cardboard backing; others use corner wedges or slip-on panels.

4 Seal the back edges of the frame with masking tape or contact paper to prevent moisture from infiltrating the frame and rotting the dried flowers. To keep your flower picture bright and attractive for years, hang it on a wall away from direct sunlight. □

5
WORKING IN TANDEM WITH NATURE

Because cut flowers are displayed indoors and seen at close range, the slightest flaws are readily apparent—all the more reason to be especially attentive to their needs as they grow. Attending to daily and seasonal chores—such as watering, weeding and mulching—is an important part of growing flowers worthy of indoor display. Knowing how to solve the occasional crisis, such as an infestation of insects, will also increase the odds of your growing near-perfect specimens.

Information included in this chapter will guide you in the year-round care of a cutting garden. The opening pages show two climate maps: a zone map that can be used to determine which perennials will survive the winter in the climate of the area where you live, and a frost-date map, which will help you to know when it is safe to plant annuals in your area. By comparing the maps with information contained in the Dictionary of Plants, you can give the best possible care to individual species. A month-by-month maintenance checklist has been included to serve as a guide for regular tasks that you can perform to keep your cutting garden in shape. This checklist is also compiled according to zones; consulting the part of the list for the zone in which you live will tell you when it is best to plant, fertilize and harvest in your area. A section on pests and diseases will help you to diagnose such problems, and to cure them, as well. The final section, Tips and Techniques, contains a number of simple but unusual suggestions on caring for, and using, the plants you grow.

CLIMATE MAPS FOR PERENNIALS AND ANNUALS

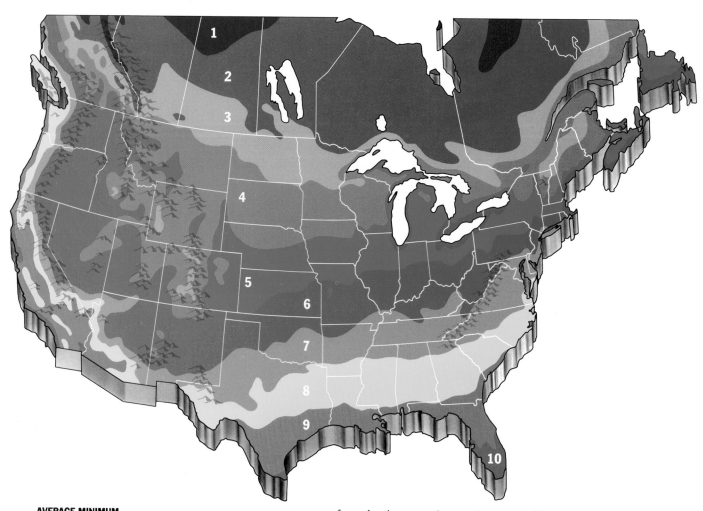

**AVERAGE MINIMUM
WINTER TEMPERATURES**

ZONE 1:
below −50°

ZONE 2:
−50° to −40°

ZONE 3:
−40° to −30°

ZONE 4:
−30° to −20°

ZONE 5:
−20° to −10°

ZONE 6:
−10° to 0°

ZONE 7:
0° to 10°

ZONE 8:
10° to 20°

ZONE 9:
20° to 30°

ZONE 10:
30° to 40°

Before planting a cutting garden, you will need to determine what plants will grow well there and when to plant them. This means knowing something about the local climate, as well as the climatic preferences of individual plants. Perennials must be hardy in your area: that is, able to endure the normal extremes of winter weather. For annuals and tender bulbs that last the season only, timing is crucial; you should know the best time to plant so as to avoid damaging frosts while taking full advantage of the growing season. The Zone Map and the Last Frost Date Map, used in combination with the Dictionary of Plants, will guide you in your planting.

The Zone Map *(above, left)* shows the 10 climatic zones, based on average minimum winter temperature, into which the United States and Canada are divided. Zone 1 is the coldest; Zone 10, the warmest. By first determining in which zone you live and then consulting the dictionary for a particular plant's hardiness range—the zones in which it normally thrives—you can tell whether that plant is a good choice for your area. Some plants cannot stand freezing temperatures; others require cold temperatures; still others require exposure to cold in winter, but cannot withstand very deep freezes. A plant that is hardy in Zones 4 to 8, for example, will not survive if the temperature falls below −30° F, yet it requires temperatures of 10° to 20° F during winter to stimulate its normal growing cycle.

Keep in mind that the zone information is based on averages, and that temperatures vary from year to year. Remember, too, that your garden may be situated in a microclimate that differs from the zone average. If the site is low-lying, chances are it will be colder than average; if the garden is located on a sunny southern slope or near a wall that traps heat, it will probably be warmer than average. Consult your local weather bureau, agricultural extension service or garden center for more advice.

The Last Frost Date Map *(above, right)* may be used to determine planting times for annuals and tender bulbs. It shows the average dates of the last spring frost. In Region A, freezing temperatures may not disappear until well into June; some areas of Regions H and I may never experience frost at all. As with the Zone Map, the regions are determined by averages. Last frost dates vary from year to year, so it is a good idea to keep abreast of local weather forecasts at planting time.

Tender annuals and bulbs cannot be planted until all danger of frost has passed. Half-hardy annuals are best planted after the last frost in spring, but will survive cool temperatures and will usually survive an unexpected late, light frost. Hardy annuals will survive light frost and can be planted as soon as the soil can be worked in spring—about four to six weeks before the last frost. Consult the dictionary to determine when it is safe to plant individual species in your area.

AVERAGE LAST FROST DATES

REGION A
June 10 or after

REGION B
May 20—June 10

REGION C
May 10—May 20

REGION D
May 1—May 10

REGION E
April 10—May 1

REGION F
March 20—April 10

REGION G
March 1—March 20

REGION H
January 30—March 1

REGION I
January 30 or before

A CHECKLIST FOR MAINTENANCE MONTH BY MONTH

	ZONE 1	ZONE 2	ZONE 3	ZONE 4	ZONE 5
JANUARY/FEBRUARY	• Study seed and plant catalogs and place orders for spring • Clean, sharpen and oil garden tools • Sketch a design for the cutting garden • Press heaved plants back into the soil • Check winter mulch and add more if necessary • Refrigerate seeds that need cold treatment • Cut tree and shrub branches for forcing	• Study seed and plant catalogs and place orders for spring • Clean, sharpen and oil garden tools • Sketch a design for the cutting garden • Press heaved plants back into the soil • Check winter mulch and add more if necessary • Refrigerate seeds that need cold treatment • Cut tree and shrub branches for forcing	• Study seed and plant catalogs and place orders for spring • Clean, sharpen and oil garden tools • Sketch a design for the cutting garden • Press heaved plants back into the soil • Check winter mulch and add more if necessary • Refrigerate seeds that need cold treatment • Cut tree and shrub branches for forcing	• Study seed and plant catalogs and place orders for spring • Clean, sharpen and oil garden tools • Sketch a design for the cutting garden • Press heaved plants back into the soil • Check winter mulch and add more if necessary • Refrigerate seeds that need cold treatment • Cut tree and shrub branches for forcing	• Study seed and plant catalogs and place orders for spring • Clean, sharpen and oil garden tools • Sketch a design for the cutting garden • Press heaved plants back into the soil • Check winter mulch and add more if necessary • Refrigerate seeds that need cold treatment • Cut tree and shrub branches for forcing
MARCH/APRIL	• Sow annual and perennial seeds indoors • Cut tree and shrub branches for forcing	• Sow annual and perennial seeds indoors • Cut tree and shrub branches for forcing	• Sow annual and perennial seeds indoors • Cut tree and shrub branches for forcing	• Sow annual and perennial seeds indoors • Plant bare-root and container-grown perennials, trees and shrubs • Set stakes for tall perennials • Cut tree and shrub branches for forcing	• Sow annual and perennial seeds indoors • Remove winter mulch • Prepare site and soil for the cutting garden • Test pH and adjust if necessary • Perform spring cleanup • Plant bare-root and container-grown perennials, trees and shrubs • Set stakes for tall perennials • Cut tree and shrub branches for forcing
MAY/JUNE	• Remove winter mulch • Perform spring cleanup • Prepare site and soil for the cutting garden • Check and adjust pH • Sow annual and perennial seeds outdoors • Move indoor-started and purchased seedlings outdoors • Plant bare-root and container-grown perennials, trees and shrubs • Plant summer bulbs • Divide, transplant perennials • Set stakes for tall plants • Fertilize as necessary • Weed the cutting garden • Apply summer mulch • Water as necessary • Check for insects, diseases • Disbud plants to encourage large blooms • Cut flowers and foliage for fresh or dried arrangements	• Remove winter mulch • Perform spring cleanup • Prepare site and soil for the cutting garden • Check and adjust pH • Sow annual and perennial seeds outdoors • Move indoor-started and purchased seedlings outdoors • Plant bare-root and container-grown perennials, trees and shrubs • Plant summer bulbs • Divide, transplant perennials • Set stakes for tall plants • Fertilize as necessary • Weed the cutting garden • Apply summer mulch • Water as necessary • Check for insects, diseases • Disbud plants to encourage large blooms • Cut flowers and foliage for fresh or dried arrangements	• Remove winter mulch • Perform spring cleanup • Prepare site and soil for the cutting garden • Check and adjust pH • Sow annual and perennial seeds outdoors • Move indoor-started and purchased seedlings outdoors • Plant bare-root and container-grown perennials, trees and shrubs • Plant summer bulbs • Divide, transplant perennials • Set stakes for tall plants • Fertilize as necessary • Weed the cutting garden • Apply summer mulch • Water as necessary • Check for insects, diseases • Disbud plants to encourage large blooms • Cut flowers and foliage for fresh or dried arrangements	• Prepare site and soil for the cutting garden • Check and adjust pH • Sow annual and perennial seeds outdoors • Move indoor-started and purchased seedlings into the garden • Plant bare-root and container-grown perennials, trees and shrubs • Plant summer bulbs • Divide, transplant perennials • Set stakes for tall annuals and perennials • Fertilize as necessary • Weed the cutting garden • Apply summer mulch • Water as necessary • Check for insects, diseases • Disbud plants to encourage large blooms • Cut flowers and foliage for fresh or dried arrangements	• Sow annual and perennial seeds outdoors • Move indoor-started and purchased seedlings into the garden • Plant bare-root and container-grown perennials, trees and shrubs • Plant summer bulbs • Divide, transplant perennials • Set stakes for tall annuals and perennials • Fertilize as necessary • Weed the cutting garden • Apply summer mulch • Water as necessary • Check for insects, diseases • Disbud plants to encourage large blooms • Cut flowers and foliage for fresh or dried arrangements

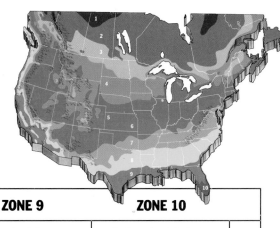

ZONE 6	ZONE 7	ZONE 8	ZONE 9	ZONE 10	
• Study seed and plant catalogs and place orders for spring • Clean, sharpen and oil garden tools • Sketch a design for the cutting garden • Press heaved plants back into the soil • Check winter mulch and add more if necessary • Refrigerate seeds that need cold treatment • Cut tree and shrub branches for forcing	• Study seed and plant catalogs and place orders for spring • Clean, sharpen and oil garden tools • Sketch a design for the cutting garden • Press heaved plants back into the soil • Check winter mulch and add more if necessary • Refrigerate seeds that need cold treatment • Cut tree and shrub branches for forcing	• Study seed and plant catalogs and place orders for spring • Clean, sharpen and oil garden tools • Sketch a design for the cutting garden • Refrigerate seeds that need cold treatment • Sow annual and perennial seeds indoors • Prepare site and soil for the cutting garden • Test pH and adjust if necessary • Plant bare-root and container-grown perennials, trees and shrubs • Set stakes for tall perennials • Cut tree and shrub branches for forcing	• Study seed and plant catalogs, place orders for spring • Clean, sharpen and oil tools • Sketch a design for the cutting garden • Refrigerate seeds that need cold treatment • Prepare site and soil for the cutting garden • Test and adjust pH • Perform spring cleanup • Sow annual and perennial seeds indoors and outdoors • Plant bare-root and container-grown perennials, trees and shrubs • Divide, transplant perennials • Set stakes for tall perennials • Fertilize as necessary • Weed the cutting garden • Water as necessary • Check for insects, diseases • Cut tree and shrub branches for forcing	• Study seed and plant catalogs, place orders for spring • Clean, sharpen and oil tools • Sketch a design for the cutting garden • Refrigerate seeds that need cold treatment • Prepare site and soil for the cutting garden • Test and adjust pH • Perform spring cleanup • Sow annual and perennial seeds indoors and outdoors • Plant bare-root and container-grown perennials, trees and shrubs • Divide, transplant perennials • Set stakes for tall perennials • Fertilize as necessary • Weed the cutting garden • Water as necessary • Check for insects, diseases • Cut tree and shrub branches for forcing	**JANUARY/FEBRUARY**
• Sow annual and perennial seeds indoors • Remove winter mulch • Prepare site and soil for the cutting garden • Test pH and adjust if necessary • Perform spring cleanup • Fertilize as necessary • Plant bare-root and container-grown perennials, trees and shrubs • Set stakes for tall perennials • Cut tree and shrub branches for forcing	• Sow annual and perennial seeds indoors • Remove winter mulch • Prepare site and soil for the cutting garden • Test pH and adjust if necessary • Perform spring cleanup • Fertilize as necessary • Plant bare-root and container-grown perennials, trees and shrubs • Set stakes for tall perennials • Cut tree and shrub branches for forcing	• Perform spring cleanup • Sow annual and perennial seeds outdoors • Move indoor-started and purchased seedlings into the garden • Plant bare-root and container-grown perennials, trees and shrubs • Plant summer bulbs • Divide, transplant perennials • Set stakes for tall annuals and perennials • Fertilize as necessary • Weed the cutting garden • Apply summer mulch • Water as necessary • Check for insects, diseases • Disbud plants to encourage large blooms • Cut flowers for fresh or dried arrangements	• Sow annual and perennial seeds outdoors • Move indoor-started and purchased seedlings into the garden • Plant bare-root and container-grown perennials, trees and shrubs • Plant summer bulbs • Divide, transplant perennials • Set stakes for tall annuals and perennials • Weed the cutting garden • Apply summer mulch • Water as necessary • Check for insects, diseases • Disbud plants to encourage large blooms • Cut flowers for fresh or dried arrangements	• Sow annual and perennial seeds outdoors • Move indoor-started and purchased seedlings into the garden • Plant bare-root and container-grown perennials, trees and shrubs • Plant summer bulbs • Divide, transplant perennials • Set stakes for tall annuals and perennials • Weed the cutting garden • Apply summer mulch • Water as necessary • Check for insects, diseases • Disbud plants to encourage large blooms • Cut flowers for fresh or dried arrangements	**MARCH/APRIL**
• Sow annual and perennial seeds outdoors • Move indoor-started and purchased seedlings into the garden • Plant bare-root and container-grown perennials, trees and shrubs • Plant summer bulbs • Divide, transplant perennials • Set stakes for tall annuals and perennials • Fertilize as necessary • Weed the cutting garden • Apply summer mulch • Water as necessary • Check for insects, diseases • Disbud plants to encourage large blooms • Cut flowers and foliage for fresh or dried arrangements	• Sow annual and perennial seeds outdoors • Move indoor-started and purchased seedlings into the garden • Plant bare-root and container-grown perennials, trees and shrubs • Plant summer bulbs • Divide, transplant perennials • Set stakes for tall annuals and perennials • Fertilize as necessary • Weed the cutting garden • Apply summer mulch • Water as necessary • Check for insects, diseases • Disbud plants to encourage large blooms • Cut flowers and foliage for fresh or dried arrangements	• Plant bare-root and container-grown perennials, trees and shrubs • Set stakes for tall perennials • Weed the cutting garden • Water as necessary • Check for insects, diseases • Disbud plants to encourage large blooms • Cut flowers and foliage for fresh or dried arrangements	• Plant bare-root and container-grown perennials, trees and shrubs • Set stakes for tall perennials • Weed the cutting garden • Water as necessary • Check for insects, diseases • Disbud plants to encourage large blooms • Cut flowers and foliage for fresh or dried arrangements	• Plant bare-root and container-grown perennials, trees and shrubs • Set stakes for tall perennials • Weed the cutting garden • Water as necessary • Check for insects, diseases • Disbud plants to encourage large blooms • Cut flowers and foliage for fresh or dried arrangements	**MAY/JUNE**

	ZONE 1	ZONE 2	ZONE 3	ZONE 4	ZONE 5
JULY/AUGUST	• Sow perennial seeds outdoors • Weed the cutting garden • Water as necessary • Check for insects, diseases • Disbud plants to encourage large blooms • Prepare a compost pile • Cut flowers and foliage for fresh or dried arrangements • Preserve leaves with glycerine • Pick leaves to skeletonize • Collect seedpods for drying	• Sow perennial seeds outdoors • Weed the cutting garden • Water as necessary • Check for insects, diseases • Disbud plants to encourage large blooms • Prepare a compost pile • Cut flowers and foliage for fresh or dried arrangements • Preserve leaves with glycerine • Pick leaves to skeletonize • Collect seedpods for drying	• Sow perennial seeds outdoors • Weed the cutting garden • Water as necessary • Check for insects, diseases • Disbud plants to encourage large blooms • Prepare a compost pile • Cut flowers and foliage for fresh or dried arrangements • Preserve leaves with glycerine • Pick leaves to skeletonize • Collect seedpods for drying	• Sow perennial seeds outdoors • Weed the cutting garden • Water as necessary • Check for insects, diseases • Disbud plants to encourage large blooms • Prepare a compost pile • Cut flowers and foliage for fresh or dried arrangements • Preserve leaves with glycerine • Pick leaves to skeletonize • Collect seedpods for drying	• Sow perennial seeds outdoors • Weed the cutting garden • Water as necessary • Check for insects, diseases • Disbud plants to encourage large blooms • Prepare a compost pile • Cut flowers and foliage for fresh or dried arrangements • Preserve leaves with glycerine • Pick leaves to skeletonize • Collect seedpods for drying
SEPTEMBER/OCTOBER	• Move tender plants to a cold frame • Water as necessary • Lift summer bulbs • Collect autumn leaves for pressing • Collect berried branches • Clean up leaves and other debris • Cut back tops of frost-killed plants • Apply winter mulch • Turn off water; drain hose	• Move tender plants to a cold frame • Water as necessary • Lift summer bulbs • Collect autumn leaves for pressing • Collect berried branches • Clean up leaves and other debris • Cut back tops of frost-killed plants • Apply winter mulch • Turn off water; drain hose	• Move tender plants to a cold frame • Lift summer bulbs • Plant spring-flowering bulbs • Water as necessary • Collect autumn leaves for pressing • Collect berried branches • Clean up leaves and other debris • Cut back tops of frost-killed plants • Apply winter mulch • Turn off water; drain hose	• Move tender plants to a cold frame • Lift summer bulbs • Plant spring-flowering bulbs • Water as necessary • Collect autumn leaves for pressing • Collect berried branches • Clean up leaves and other debris • Cut back tops of frost-killed plants • Apply winter mulch • Turn off water; drain hose • Cut flowers and foliage for fresh or dried arrangements • Pick leaves to skeletonize	• Move tender plants to a cold frame • Lift summer bulbs • Plant spring-flowering bulbs • Prepare site and soil for fall planting • Divide, transplant perennials • Sow perennial and hardy annual seeds outdoors • Plant bare-root and container-grown perennials, trees and shrubs • Water as necessary • Collect autumn leaves for pressing • Collect berried branches • Clean up leaves and other debris • Cut flowers and foliage for fresh or dried arrangements • Pick leaves to skeletonize • Collect seedpods for drying
NOVEMBER/DECEMBER				• Collect berried branches • Clean up leaves and other debris	• Collect berried branches • Cut back tops of frost-killed plants • Clean up leaves and other debris • Water as necessary • Turn off water; drain hose • Apply winter mulch

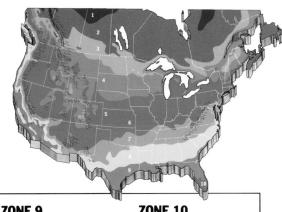

ZONE 6	ZONE 7	ZONE 8	ZONE 9	ZONE 10	
• Sow perennial seeds outdoors • Weed the cutting garden • Water as necessary • Check for insects, diseases • Disbud plants to encourage large blooms • Prepare a compost pile • Cut flowers and foliage for fresh or dried arrangements • Preserve leaves with glycerine • Pick leaves to skeletonize • Collect seedpods for drying	• Sow perennial seeds outdoors • Weed the cutting garden • Water as necessary • Check for insects, diseases • Disbud plants to encourage large blooms • Prepare a compost pile • Cut flowers and foliage for fresh or dried arrangements • Preserve leaves with glycerine • Pick leaves to skeletonize • Collect seedpods for drying	• Weed the cutting garden • Water as necessary • Check for insects, diseases • Disbud plants to encourage large blooms • Prepare a compost pile • Cut flowers and foliage for fresh or dried arrangements • Preserve leaves with glycerine • Pick leaves to skeletonize • Collect seedpods for drying	• Weed the cutting garden • Water as necessary • Check for insects, diseases • Disbud plants to encourage large blooms • Prepare a compost pile • Cut flowers and foliage for fresh or dried arrangements • Preserve leaves with glycerine • Pick leaves to skeletonize • Collect seedpods for drying	• Weed the cutting garden • Water as necessary • Check for insects, diseases • Disbud plants to encourage large blooms • Prepare a compost pile • Cut flowers and foliage for fresh or dried arrangements • Preserve leaves with glycerine • Pick leaves to skeletonize • Collect seedpods for drying	**JULY/AUGUST**
• Move tender plants to a cold frame • Lift summer bulbs • Plant spring-flowering bulbs • Prepare sites and soil for fall planting • Divide, transplant perennials • Sow perennial and hardy annual seeds outdoors • Plant bare-root and container-grown perennials, trees and shrubs • Water as necessary • Collect autumn leaves for pressing • Collect berried branches • Clean up leaves and other debris • Cut flowers and foliage for fresh or dried arrangements • Pick leaves to skeletonize • Collect seedpods for drying	• Move tender plants to a cold frame • Lift summer bulbs • Plant spring-flowering bulbs • Prepare sites and soil for fall planting • Divide, transplant perennials • Sow perennial and hardy annual seeds outdoors • Plant bare-root and container-grown perennials, trees and shrubs • Water as necessary • Collect autumn leaves for pressing • Collect berried branches • Clean up leaves and other debris • Cut flowers and foliage for fresh or dried arrangements • Pick leaves to skeletonize • Collect seedpods for drying	• Move tender plants to a cold frame • Lift summer bulbs • Prepare sites and soil for fall planting • Divide, transplant perennials • Sow perennial and hardy annual seeds outdoors • Plant bare-root and container-grown perennials, trees and shrubs • Water as necessary • Collect berried branches • Clean up leaves and other debris • Cut flowers and foliage for fresh or dried arrangements • Pick leaves to skeletonize • Collect seedpods for drying	• Prepare sites and soil for fall planting • Divide, transplant perennials • Sow annual and perennial seeds outdoors • Plant bare-root and container-grown perennials, trees and shrubs • Water as necessary • Collect berried branches • Cut flowers and foliage for fresh or dried arrangements • Pick leaves to skeletonize • Collect seedpods for drying	• Prepare sites and soil for fall planting • Divide, transplant perennials • Sow annual and perennial seeds outdoors • Plant bare-root and container-grown perennials, trees and shrubs • Collect seedpods for drying • Collect berried branches • Water as necessary • Cut flowers and foliage for fresh or dried arrangements • Pick leaves to skeletonize • Collect seedpods for drying	**SEPTEMBER/OCTOBER**
• Collect berried branches • Cut back tops of frost-killed plants • Clean up leaves and other debris • Water as necessary • Turn off water; drain hose • Apply winter mulch	• Plant spring-flowering bulbs • Collect berried branches • Cut back tops of frost-killed plants • Clean up leaves and other debris • Water as necessary • Turn off water; drain hose • Apply winter mulch	• Plant spring-flowering bulbs • Divide, transplant perennials • Plant bare-root and container-grown perennials, trees and shrubs • Sow annual and perennial seeds outdoors • Water as necessary • Collect autumn leaves for pressing • Collect berried branches • Cut flowers and foliage for fresh or dried arrangements • Cut back tops of frost-killed and withered plants • Clean up leaves and other debris • Turn off water; drain hose	• Plant spring-flowering bulbs • Divide, transplant perennials • Plant bare-root and container-grown perennials, trees and shrubs • Sow annual and perennial seeds outdoors • Water as necessary • Collect autumn leaves for pressing • Collect berried branches • Cut flowers and foliage for fresh or dried arrangements • Clean up leaves and other debris • Cut back withered perennials; remove faded annuals	• Plant spring-flowering bulbs • Divide, transplant perennials • Plant bare-root and container-grown perennials, trees and shrubs • Sow annual and perennial seeds outdoors • Water as necessary • Collect autumn leaves for pressing • Collect berried branches • Cut flowers and foliage for fresh or dried arrangements • Clean up leaves and other debris • Cut back withered perennials; remove faded annuals	**NOVEMBER/DECEMBER**

WHAT TO DO WHEN THINGS GO WRONG

PROBLEM	CAUSE	SOLUTION
Leaves, growing tips and flower buds turn black, and flower buds may not open. Any flowers that open are streaked in brown. Flowers and leaves are covered with a gray to brown fuzzy growth.	Botrytis blight, a fungus disease that is most prevalent in damp, cool, cloudy weather.	Remove and discard any infected plant parts and spray with fungicide to prevent the spread of the disease. Water on sunny mornings so that the leaves do not remain wet. Ensure good air circulation by spacing and thinning plants.
Leaves do not grow properly, or they turn yellow and wilt. Stems turn black and collapse. In time, the entire plant wilts and dies and can be easily pulled from the ground. Examining the roots shows that they are soft, wet and darkened.	Root rot and stem rot, soilborne fungus diseases.	To prevent these diseases, ensure that the soil drains well. Cut back and discard any infected plant parts, or, if the case is severe, remove the plant and its surrounding soil. Drench the soil with a fungicide before replanting to control the spread of the disease.
Leaves develop brown or yellow streaks, mottled areas or spots, and they may curl or become misshapen. Plant growth may be stunted.	One of several viral diseases, including mosaic virus.	Remove damaged leaves. Infections sometimes do little damage, and symptoms often disappear by themselves. There are no chemical controls for viruses, but aphids, which spread the diseases, can be controlled with insecticides.
Young seedlings, especially those started indoors, suddenly topple over and die.	Damping-off, a soilborne fungus disease that attacks roots and stems.	Drench seed flats with a fungicide before sowing seeds indoors. Use only sterile, soil-less medium that has not been used before. Do not overwater or crowd seedlings. Ensure that the garden soil drains well.
New growth is distorted and stunted and leaves suddenly turn yellow. Flower buds may be deformed and may not open; flowers that open lack color. Annuals and perennials in the daisy family are the primary, but not the only, plants affected.	Aster yellows, a disease caused by a bacteria-like organism, which is spread by leafhoppers.	Remove and discard infected plants. Control leafhoppers with an insecticide and keep the garden well weeded to eliminate their breeding sites. Do not plant the same type of plant in the same spot.
Plants cease to grow, turn yellow, wilt and die. A cross section of an infected stem shows dark brown spots or streaks.	Wilt, a disease caused by soilborne fungi or bacteria.	Remove and discard infected plants. There are no chemical controls, except professional soil treatment, which may be needed in severe cases.

PROBLEM	CAUSE	SOLUTION
Leaves are covered with irregular spots that are dark brown, sometimes with purple borders and black centers. Eventually, entire leaves turn brown and look scorched. Purplish lesions are often found along the stems, and growth is often stunted.	Anthracnose, a fungus disease that is most prevalent in warm, wet weather.	Remove and discard any infected leaves. Spray with a fungicide to prevent the spread of the disease.
The undersides of the leaves are coated with a gray or tan fuzzy growth that resembles tufts of cotton. Leaves eventually turn yellow and fall from the plant.	Downy mildew, a fungus disease.	Remove and discard infected leaves. Spray with a fungicide to prevent the spread of the disease. Water in the morning so that the leaves do not remain wet during the night. Cut back frost-killed annuals and perennials in the fall and remove weeds and fallen leaves from the garden.
Upper leaf surfaces are flecked or streaked in yellow or white and appear bleached. Leaf edges may curl; leaves may develop blisters.	Air pollution and smog.	Providing shade for plants when the weather is hot and humid will make them less susceptible to damage from pollution. In high-risk areas, choose pollution-resistant plants.
Tan, brown, purple, red or black spots that are round or irregular in shape appear on leaves and are often surrounded by yellow halos. As the spots increase in number and size, entire leaves turn yellow, die and fall from the plant.	Leaf spot, a fungal or bacterial disease that is spread by wind, water, insects or garden tools.	Remove and discard infected leaves as soon as they appear. Spray with a fungicide to prevent the disease from spreading. To prevent it from recurring, water plants in the morning so that the foliage does not remain wet during the night. Cut back and discard frost-killed annuals and perennials in the fall and keep the garden weed-free to eliminate sites where fungi or bacteria can overwinter.
Small yellow spots develop on upper leaf surfaces, and an orange to brown powder appears on lower leaf surfaces. Leaves may wilt and die, and plant growth may be slowed.	Rust, a fungus disease that is most prevalent when nights are cool and humid.	Remove infected leaves and spray with a fungicide to prevent the disease from spreading. Water plants in the morning so that the leaves do not remain wet during the night. Cut back frost-killed annuals and perennials in fall and keep the garden free of weeds and fallen leaves.
Leaves, stems and flower buds are coated with a dusty white or gray powder. Leaves become distorted and eventually turn yellow and drop from the plant. Flowers may also be deformed.	Powdery mildew, a fungus disease that is most prevalent when days are warm and nights are cool and humid.	Remove infected leaves and spray the plant with a fungicide to prevent the spread of the disease. Powdery mildew may be eradicated with a sulfur spray, but do not use this treatment in temperatures above 80° F, since it will burn the leaves. Water plants in the morning so that the leaves do not remain wet during the night. Ensure good air circulation by spacing plants. Remove all frost-killed plants and plant debris from the garden in the fall.

PROBLEM	CAUSE	SOLUTION
Leaves turn dull and become yellow, reddish or bronze colored. Tiny black specks are visible on the undersides of the leaves. Flower buds and flowers become discolored and dry up. In severe infestations, leaves wither and fall, and webbing appears around the flower buds and the leaves.	Spider mites, tiny pests that may be red, black, green, yellow, pink or white and that suck plant juices from the leaves.	Keep plants well watered, especially during hot, dry periods, and spray the undersides of the foliage with water. Treat with an insecticidal soap or a chemical miticide. Spray trees and shrubs with horticultural oil in early spring to smother the eggs. Ladybugs, too, will control mite infestations.
Small holes appear in leaves, flower buds and flowers, and in time, entire leaves or blossoms may be eaten. Egg clusters may be visible on tree trunks.	Caterpillars, the wormlike larvae of butterflies and moths, which range in size from less than 1 inch to several inches long.	Hand-pick and destroy caterpillars if the infestation is small. Control a severe infestation with a chemical insecticide or with *Bacillus thuringiensis* (Bt), a bacterium that kills caterpillars but does not damage plants, birds, animals or flying insects. Bt can be applied before infestations occur. Scrape egg clusters off tree trunks in late winter to help control caterpillar populations in spring.
Growth is stunted, and leaves curl, become distorted and may wilt and turn yellow. Flower buds and flowers are deformed. A shiny, sticky substance appears on the leaves and stems, which may eventually become coated with a sooty black powder.	Aphids, 1/8-inch semi-transparent insects that may be green, yellow, black, red or brown, and that suck plant juices from buds, leaves and stems. Aphids also transmit a variety of diseases.	Small clusters of aphids can be knocked off plants with a strong stream of water. Treat severe infestations with an insecticidal soap or with a chemical insecticide. Spray trees and shrubs with horticultural oil in early spring to smother eggs. Ladybugs will also control aphid populations.
Large holes appear in leaves, especially those close to the ground. Entire small plants may be consumed. Telltale shiny, silvery streaks appear on plants and along the ground.	Snails and slugs—shell-less snails—which are brown, grow up to 3 inches long and appear at night.	Trap snails and slugs with saucers of beer or inverted grapefruit halves or with commercial bait set in the garden at dusk. Bait will need to be reapplied after rain or watering.
Plant growth is stunted and growing tips die back. Leaves turn yellow, wilt and fall from the plant. White cottony patches and round or oval shells that may be black, brown, gray, green or white appear on the stems and the leaves.	Scales, insects with hard or soft shells that grow up to 3/8 inch long.	Prune away any infested stems. Spray weekly with insecticidal soap or with a chemical insecticide until the insects disappear. Spray trees and shrubs with horticultural oil in early spring to smother eggs.
Foliage turns yellow, leaf margins may curl, and growth slows or stops altogether. When plants are disturbed, a cloud of small white flying insects appears.	Whiteflies, white, 1/16-inch insects that appear in colonies on the undersides of the leaves.	Whiteflies are attracted to yellow; place sticky yellow cards in the garden to attract and trap them. Keep the garden well weeded to eliminate the insects' breeding sites. If the infestation is severe, spray with an insecticidal soap, an organic insecticide or a chemical insecticide.

82

PROBLEM	CAUSE	SOLUTION
Leaves are marked with white, light green or yellow serpentine trails. Leaves eventually turn brown and die.	Leaf miners, the larvae of beetles, flies or moths that tunnel through the leaves eating the leaf tissue. Insects range in length from 1/8 to 1/4 inch long.	Remove severely infested leaves and spray the plant with a systemic chemical insecticide as symptoms appear. Cut annuals and perennials to the ground in fall and discard them, and keep the garden weed-free to eliminate the insects' breeding sites.
Plants suddenly turn yellow and wilt. Examining the roots reveals that they are damaged or deformed and have knots and swellings.	Nematodes, microscopic worms that live in the soil and attack plant roots. Since they are too small to be seen, only a laboratory test can confirm their presence.	Remove and discard infested plants and the surrounding soil. Do not replant the garden with the same type of plant for three years. Plant marigolds to repel nematodes. If the infestation is severe, seek professional soil treatment.
Plant growth is stunted, and foliage becomes speckled with white or yellow-brown spots.	Leafhoppers, wedge-shaped, gray or green winged insects that grow up to 1/5 inch long, suck sap from the leaves and spread diseases.	A strong stream of water may knock insects off the plants, but will not kill them. Control their numbers with an organic or a chemical insecticide, and keep the garden weed-free.
A bubbly white substance appears along the stems at leaf joints. Plant growth may be stunted.	Spittlebugs, 1/4-inch tan or brown insects that excrete the white froth to protect themselves as they feed.	Control small infestations by washing the insects off the plants with water. Spray plants with insecticidal soap or a chemical insecticide when the infestation is severe. Cut annuals and perennials to the ground in the fall and dispose of the cuttings.
Leaves develop small patches of white, yellow or brown around their margins, or they take on a dull, silvery appearance and then wilt and dry up. Flower buds darken and may not open; if they do, the petals will have brown edges.	Thrips, slender, winged insects that are barely visible to the eye. They suck plant juices from leaves and flowers.	Remove infested flower buds and growing tips; completely remove and destroy severely infested plants. Spray plants with an insecticidal soap or a systemic chemical insecticide.
Round, oblong or irregularly shaped holes appear in leaves and flower petals, and eventually, entire leaves and petals may be eaten.	Japanese, cucumber, Colorado potato, Asiatic garden, blister and other beetles. They range in size from 1/4 to 3/4 inches long, have hard shells and are of varied colors.	For a small infestation, pick beetles off by hand. If the infestation is severe, treat with an insecticide. Beetle traps have limited effectiveness. The larvae of Japanese beetles may be controlled with milky spore as long as no other insecticides are used. Since beetles often breed in weeds, keep the garden weed-free.
Upper leaf surfaces are covered with small yellow spots. In time, the foliage may turn entirely yellow, wilt and fall from the plant. Flower buds appear deformed and may not open; if they open, flowers are deformed.	Plant bugs, insects of varying colors up to 1/4 inch long.	Spray with an organic or a chemical insecticide as soon as signs of damage appear. Cut annuals and perennials to the ground after the first frost and discard the cuttings. Remove all weeds and plant debris from the garden, since they provide hibernation sites for insects.

TIPS AND TECHNIQUES

A PRESCRIPTION FOR BRITTLE FLOWERS

If in the drying process your flowers become too brittle to shape or arrange without breaking, wave them through the mist of a humidifier until they are pliable. Mist produced by a humidifier is fine enough to moisten flowers slightly, and it will not saturate them the way a hand mister or spray bottle might. Steam from a boiling teakettle works nearly as well, but you must be careful not to burn yourself as you wave the flower through the steam. Once dampened, flowers can be arranged in the shape you choose, and they will retain that shape when the mist has dried.

KEEPING DRIED FLOWERS INSECT-FREE

Moths, weevils and other insects can damage stored flowers just as they do stored food and clothing. But you can protect dried flowers by storing them with dried lavender, thyme, mint and rosemary, which naturally repel insects, and do it without the strong and unpleasant odor that mothballs give off. To keep enough of these natural repellents on hand, you may want to set aside space for them when you plan your cutting garden.

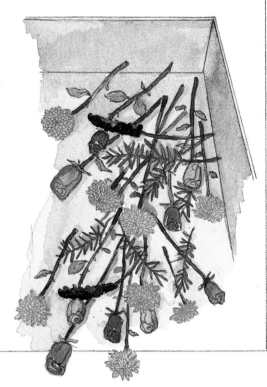

NATURAL CONTAINERS

The container is a crucial part of any display, and choosing the right one may be a creative act in itself. Anything that has a cavity that will hold water or floral foam is a potential vase, and some of the most often overlooked containers are the natural ones: fresh fruits such as bright red and yellow apples, pineapples with their spiny, geometrically patterned skin, and vegetables such as orange pumpkins, green winter squash and variegated gourds. By carefully carving a vaselike hole in one of these fruits or vegetables and inserting a florist's vial to hold water, you can create a colorful, original container.

NOVEL CAKE DECORATIONS

Cakes are often decorated with flowers fashioned from frosting, and creating lifelike imitations is no easy task. Yet real flowers will serve as well. Crystallized flowers, or freshly cut blossoms that have been brushed with egg white, sprinkled with extra-fine sugar and allowed to dry, make elegant additions to cakes, and they are certainly as beautiful as their artificial counterparts. The best flowers for this purpose are the edible ones: roses, marigolds, violets, freesias and cherry blossoms. Mint leaves can be used to add a touch of greenery. Whatever flowers or leaves you do choose, make sure that they haven't been sprayed with an insecticide or other potentially harmful substance.

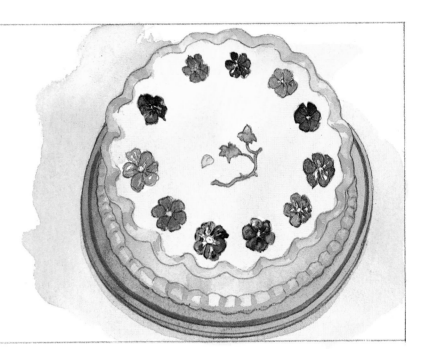

FLOATING BLOSSOMS

The broken heads of fresh flowers that you may have intended to use in tall arrangements can be floated singly on water in a clear-glass bowl, a goblet or a snifter to create an attractive, if short-lived, centerpiece. The large, dramatic blossoms of fresh roses, peonies, water lilies and magnolias make especially dramatic single-flower displays. In a large bowl, several blooms can be floated randomly for a casual yet elegant effect. Flowers with small blossoms, such as zinnias and marigolds, can be tied together to form a floating bouquet. To use a floating arrangement for a party, condition the blossoms as you would any fresh flowers, and wait until the last minute to place them in water.

DRIED FLOWER UPKEEP

Because dried flower displays last much longer than fresh ones, they accumulate more dust and dirt. Although they are quite delicate, most preserved flowers can be cleaned. Glycerinated foliage is the easiest, since it can be wiped off with a damp cloth. But air-dried materials can be ruined by dampness. The safest way to remove dust and dirt from dried flowers and foliage is with a soft paintbrush or a feather. If spiders have built webs on your flowers, gently twist the strands around a pencil or small stick to remove them.

6
DICTIONARY OF PLANTS

Flower arranging involves more than having an eye for shape and color. It requires knowing something about the individual plants themselves—how to grow, harvest, preserve and condition them once they have been cut, as well as how to set them off to their best advantage in an arrangement. Grouping fresh flowers may involve problems of mechanics as well as aesthetics. Some flowers last longer than others, some have weak stems that may need support, and some may open or close depending on the time of day or the amount of light they receive. Preserved materials, too, have their idiosyncrasies: some can be easily arranged once dried, others are brittle and require delicate handling, and still others can stand only with the support of wired stems. All these variables are best considered before you begin arranging.

The Dictionary of Plants describes more than 150 genera, including the species and varieties that are especially suitable for cutting and arranging indoors. Each entry contains plant descriptions and information on how to cultivate individual species to achieve the best results. A section on cutting and conditioning tells you what to do once the flowers are ready to be harvested— whether you intend to use them fresh or dried. A section entitled "Uses" gives suggestions on how the plants may be used in particular kinds of arrangements. In many cases, you may be able to use not only the blossoms, but also the seed heads and foliage of a given plant. The Uses section, however, has been included to provide ideas; it is in no way intended to limit your imagination when it comes to arranging plant materials.

ABELMOSCHUS ESCULENTUS

ACACIA DECURRENS

ACANTHUS MOLLIS

Abelmoschus (ab-el-MOS-kus)
Gumbo, lady's-finger

Genus of tropical annuals and perennials. Leaves are large and alternate with veins that are arranged palmately. Flowers are large and funnel-shaped.

Selected species and varieties. *A. esculentus,* okra, is an annual with stout, erect stems that grows up to 7 feet tall. Leaves are 12 inches or more in width and lobed or divided. Flowers are up to 3 inches across and yellow with reddish centers. Blooms are followed by slender, ribbed, curved pods that are up to 8 inches long. Tender pods are used as vegetables.

Growing conditions. Okra needs full sun and warm weather. Soil should be fertile and slightly acid to neutral. Because seeds germinate poorly, plant a dozen seeds for every foot of length in a row. Later, thin so that plants are 12 to 18 inches apart.

Uses. Okra seedpods can be used dried in wreaths or garlands. When used whole, the pods provide a conical shape and unusual texture; when split along the seams, they provide a feathery look.

Harvesting and preparing. Pick okra seedpods while they are still green, or the plant will stop producing them. Toward the end of the growing season, let some pods mature on the plant to produce a variety of sizes. Air-dry the pods whole, or split them at the seams before drying.

Acacia (a-KAY-sha)
Acacia, mimosa, wattle

A genus of 800 species of shrubs and trees found throughout the tropics and subtropics. Leaves are usually twice-compound; leaflets are small and numerous. Some species have no leaves; instead, they have lance-shaped flattened leafstalks that resemble leaves. Some have thorns. Flowers are small and grouped into finger-shaped or globular spikes or racemes; they are usually yellow and bloom in spring. Dried pods resemble twisted pea pods. Zones 8-10.

Selected species and varieties. *A. armata,* kangaroo thorn, is a spreading shrub. Leaves are sharp, pointed and undivided. Flowers occur in globular heads on drooping branchlets. *A. decurrens,* green wattle, is an evergreen shrub or a small tree. Bark is olive green to dark gray. Leaflets are ½ inch long in pairs of 16 to 70. Flower heads are ¼ inch across, golden yellow, globelike and arranged in racemes. Seedpods are 3 to 4 inches long. Zones 9 and 10.

Growing conditions. Kangaroo thorn and green wattle need sun and plenty of water. They grow quickly but are short-lived. Prune after the plant has finished blooming.

Uses. Fresh-cut, flowering acacia branches provide color and an arching line to arrangements of fresh flowers. When dried, the flowering branches retain much of their color and are attractive in dried arrangements. The flowers alone can be used in pressed flower designs.

Harvesting and preparing. To use fresh, hammer the stem ends before conditioning. To air-dry, tie small branches in bunches and hang upside down. Larger branches will maintain a more graceful shape if they are allowed to stand upright in a container with a small amount of water.

Acanthus (a-KAN-thus)
Bear's breech

A perennial or small shrub with large, broadly lobed, sometimes spiny leaves. Flowers are showy, white or purplish, and occur in long, erect spikes. Zones 8 and 9.

Selected species and varieties. *A. mollis* grows 3 to 4 feet tall. Leaves are basal, heart-shaped, nonspiny, hairy on their upper surfaces and about 2 feet long. Flower spikes appear in August and have white or pink blooms with deeply toothed bracts.

Growing conditions. Full sun is necessary for profuse flowering. Soil should be deep, fertile and well drained. In cooler areas, mulch with branches of evergreen or salt hay in winter. Propagate from seed or by division in early fall or spring.

Uses. The spiky flowers of bear's breech provide line in tall arrangements, whether fresh or dried. The large, heart-shaped leaves add texture to the base of fresh bouquets. The seed heads can be used in dried arrangements.

Harvesting and preparing. To use the flowers fresh, sear the stem ends before conditioning normally. To use the leaves fresh, sear the ends of the leafstalks and then submerge the entire leaf in cool water. To use the seed heads, pick after the top buds flower and the stem tips start to harden, and air-dry by hanging or laying stalks on their sides.

Acer (AY-ser)
Maple, box elder

Genus of deciduous trees and some shrubs having leaves that may be simple and lobed or compound. Flowers appear in racemes in spring, before or with the leaves. Fruits are small, flattened winged nuts called samaras. Zones 3-9.

Selected species and varieties. *A. platanoides*, Norway maple, is a fast-growing tree that reaches 65 feet and has smooth bark and a rounded form. Leaves are five-lobed, bright green in summer and turn yellow in fall. Roots are shallow; branches are dense and provide heavy shade. Zones 4-7. *A. saccharum*, sugar maple, rock maple, attains a height of 120 feet and has a rounded form. Leaves are similar to those of Norway maple, but they turn red, scarlet, orange or yellow in the fall. Zones 4-8.

Growing conditions. Norway and sugar maples are easy to grow and they adapt well to ordinary garden soil. For best results, soil should be fertile and reasonably moist. Mulch with wood chips or shredded bark.

Uses. Freshly cut spring branches can be used as filler in mixed arrangements of spring flowers; branches preserved in glycerine can be used in fresh or dried summer arrangements. Dried branches of fall leaves make colorful bouquets by themselves. Individual leaves can be skeletonized and used to provide texture in dried arrangements. Clusters of dried seeds can also be used in dried arrangements.

Harvesting and preparing. Cut branches in spring when the leaves are beginning to emerge and sear the stem ends before conditioning normally. For long-lasting, flexible leaves, cut branches in summer and place the stem ends in a glycerine solution. Dry branches of autumn leaves by standing them upright in a container with a small amount of water. Pick clusters of winged seeds before they fall, and air-dry by placing them on a wire mesh.

Achillea (ak-i-LEE-a)
Yarrow, milfoil

Genus of perennials with medicinally fragrant leaves that are ferny and divided or toothed. Flower heads are small and numerous, and often occur in flat-topped clusters. Blooms appear from June or July until frost. Zones 3-10.

Selected species and varieties. *A. filipendulina*, fernleaf yarrow, grows 3 feet tall. Flowers are yellow or mustard-colored and 5 inches across. Zones 4-10. 'Coronation Gold' is a cultivar similar to the species, but the flower heads are only 3 to 4 inches across. Zones 4-10. *A. millefolium*, common yarrow, grows about 2 feet tall and has white, rose or bright red flowers. 'Cerise Queen' is 18 inches tall and has 2- to 3-inch cherry-red flower clusters. 'Fire King' grows 2 feet tall and has clusters of bright pink flowers with white centers, and light green leaves. Blooms appear in middle to late summer. Zones 3-10. 'Red Beauty' grows from 18 to 24 inches tall. Flowers are 2 to 3 inches across, open to a rose-red color and fade to pink and nearly white as they mature.

Growing conditions. Yarrow grows well in full sun and sandy, well-drained soil; it is highly drought-resistant. Propagate by division in spring and early fall, or from seed; when propagated from seed, plants will not bloom until the second year. Space plants 12 to 15 inches apart.

Uses. Used fresh, both fernleaf and common yarrow are brightly colored and long-lasting, and make excellent mass flowers. When dried, fernleaf yarrow retains excellent shape and color, and is appropriate in a mixed dried arrangement.

ACER SACCHARUM

ACHILLEA MILLEFOLIUM 'FIRE KING'

ACONITUM NAPELLUS

AGAPANTHUS ORIENTALIS

AGERATUM HOUSTONIANUM

Harvesting and preparing. Pick fernleaf yarrow when the flowers are open and the inner and outer rays are flat. Air-dry by hanging upside down. If left too long on the plant, the flowers will turn brown.

—

Aconitum (ak-o-NY-tum)
Monkshood, wolfsbane

Clump-forming perennial plant with leaves that are usually veined and lobed. Flowers are showy, blue or purple, and appear in summer or autumn, followed by the seed heads. All parts of the plant—flowers, leaves and stems—are poisonous. Zones 3-8.

Selected species and varieties. *A. napellus,* golden monkshood, helmet flower, garden wolfsbane, is an erect, slender, 3-foot-tall plant with leaves divided into narrow segments. Flowers are violet, 1¼ to 1½ inches long and resemble a helmet.

Growing conditions. Monkshood prefers partial shade and a rich organic soil that retains moisture. Fertilize each spring. Stake when necessary and water during dry periods. In areas where winters are cold, mulch with a loose insulating material such as straw. Propagate from seed or by division.

Uses. Used fresh, monkshood is a colorful, long-lasting flower that gives line to mixed arrangements. Used in a pressed design, it provides color and an unusual helmet-like shape. The seed heads can be used in either fresh or dried mixed arrangements.

Harvesting and preparing. Separate blossoms into individual flowers to press. To use seed heads, allow blossoms to remain on the plant, harvest the seed heads when they appear, and use fresh or hang to air-dry.

—

Adam's needle see *Yucca*
African daisy see *Arctotis*
African lily see *Agapanthus*
African marigold see *Tagetes*

Agapanthus (ag-a-PAN-thus)
Agapanthus, African lily, lily-of-the-Nile

Genus of evergreen and deciduous plants that grow 2 feet tall. Leaves form at the base of the plant and are slightly succulent or leathery, linear or strap-shaped, and arching. Flowers are blue or white and occur in round heads of about 30 blossoms. Zones 8-10.

Selected species and varieties. *A. africanus* has leathery evergreen leaves that are 1½ feet long. Twenty blue to deep blue-violet flowers are arranged in shapely umbels reaching 10 to 20 inches in height. Zones 9 and 10. *A. orientalis* is similar but has softer, more reflexed leaves and 40 to 100 blue flowers. Zones 9 and 10.

Growing conditions. Soil should be fertile, loamy and consistently moist. Good drainage is essential. Fertilize at the beginning of each growing season. Agapanthus can be grown north of Zone 8 if planted in wooden tubs; its expanding roots will break earthenware pots. Bring the plant indoors before the first frost and let it go dormant over the winter; keep it nearly dry, in an area that receives some light, at a temperature of 45° F. Increase water and temperature in the spring. Propagate by dividing the tuberous roots. Plant so that the crown is just beneath the soil surface.

Uses. Used by itself, fresh agapanthus makes a striking bouquet with its large clusters of flowers. Individual flower heads can be dried for mixed dried arrangements or pressed for use in flat designs. The seed heads can also be used in mixed dried arrangements.

Harvesting and preparing. Preserve individual flowers in silica gel, dry them in a microwave or press them. Air-dry seed heads by standing them upright in a container; this will allow them to retain their shape.

—

Ageratum (aj-er-AY-tum)
Ageratum, flossflower, pussyfoot

Genus of annuals, subshrubs and shrubs that grow 6 to 18 inches tall. Leaves are usually serrated, opposite, and ovate or lanceolate. Flower heads are blue, purple, rose or white, and may be solitary or occur in puffy clusters.

Selected species and varieties. *A. houstonianum,* garden ageratum, grows to 14 inches tall. Leaves are heart-shaped and form at the base of the plant. Garden ageratum has blue, lilac- or lavender-colored flowers that are 5/16 inch across. 'Bavaria' is a tall cultivar with 20-inch stems and flower heads of pale blue, tipped in deeper blue.

Growing conditions. Ageratum grows in full sun to partial shade and needs fertile, porous soil. It is easily propagated from seed or from cuttings. Set plants 10 inches apart.

Uses. Fresh garden ageratum adds color to a low mixed arrangement; 'Bavaria' adds height and line to a tall arrangement or a bouquet. Both retain good color when dried.

Harvesting and preparing. Air-dry flowers by placing the ends of the stems in a container with a small amount of water.

—

Ajuga (a-JOO-ga)
Bugleweed

A low-growing annual or perennial with green leaves that are usually toothed and sometimes deeply lobed. Flowers are clustered on spikes and are white, blue or red. Zones 2-10.

Selected species and varieties. *A. reptans,* carpet bugle, grows 6 inches tall and has half-prostrate stems. Flowers are blue or purplish. Zones 3-10. 'Burgundy Glow' has tricolored foliage. New growth is bright burgundy; aging leaves become creamy white and dark pink. 'Silver Beauty' grows to 4 inches tall. Leaves have gray-green edges and are spattered with cream. Flowers are blue.

Growing conditions. Bugleweed grows well in sun or partial shade. It is easily cultivated in ordinary garden soil. 'Silver Beauty' tolerates deep shade. Propagate from seeds in spring, from root cuttings or by division.

Uses. The unusually colored leaves of 'Burgundy Glow' and 'Silver Beauty' make these cultivars useful in fresh arrangements. Both the leaves and the flowers can be used in pressed designs.

Harvesting and preparing. For a variety of colors, cut some leaves of 'Burgundy Glow' when young, and some after they have matured.

—

Albizia (al-BIZ-ee-a)
Mimosa, silk tree

A deciduous tree or shrub with alternate leaves and numerous small leaflets. Blooms occur on spikes with tassel-like heads; they are white, greenish yellow or pink, and are followed by flat seedpods. Zones 8 and 9.

Selected species and varieties. *A. julibrissin* grows 40 feet high and spreads widely. Foliage is lacy and the flowers are pomponlike, varying in color from pale pink to rosy pink. Flowers appear in profusion for a month or more during July and August. Pods are flat, brown and papery, and hang for a long time after opening. When the wind blows, the pods rustle. Zones 7-9.

Growing conditions. Grow silk tree in full sun and ordinary but well-drained soil. Pruning is rarely necessary except to restrict the size of the tree.

Uses. Branches with long, flat dried pods may be arranged in containers with other dried materials or used in wreaths. The pressed flowers provide color and an unusual fan shape in flat designs.

Harvesting and preparing. Allow pods to air-dry naturally on the tree. Pick flowers when they are in full bloom, and press.

—

Alcea (AL-kee-a)
Hollyhock

A tall biennial or short-lived perennial that reaches 6 to 10 feet and has hairy, alternate leaves and spirelike clusters of showy flowers that appear in the second year. Blooms are 3 inches across, red, yellow, pink or white, single or double. Zones 2-10.

Selected species and varieties. *A. rosea,* garden hollyhock, sometimes grows 10 feet tall.

Growing conditions. Plant hollyhock in full sun in well-drained, reasonably fertile soil and space plants 1½ to 2 feet apart. Keep

AJUGA REPTANS

ALBIZIA JULIBRISSIN

ALCEA ROSEA

ALCHEMILLA MOLLIS

ALLIUM AFLATUNENSE

beds free of weeds, and water during dry spells. Propagate from seeds sown in June or July, or from cuttings from the root crown.

Uses. Because of their height, hollyhocks provide line in tall fresh arrangements. Colorful individual flowers can be dried and used in flower wreaths.

Harvesting and preparing. Individual flowers may be dried in silica gel or in a microwave oven. Dry whole stalks of flowers by hanging them upside down.

—

Alchemilla (al-ke-MIL-a)
Lady's mantle

Low perennial with lobed or palmately divided leaves. Flowers are small, green or yellow, loosely clustered and lack petals. Zones 3-8.

Selected species and varieties. *A. mollis* grows 2 feet tall with slightly lobed, round, gray-green leaves with soft hairs. Flowers are borne above the foliage in a feathery spray. Flowers are yellow tinged with green and bloom plentifully in early summer.

Growing conditions. Lady's mantle prefers a sunny location with well-drained soil. Propagate from seeds or by division. Lady's mantle often self-sows.

Uses. Long-lasting lady's mantle flowers make good filler in low arrangements. When dried, both flowers and leaves can be arranged in containers with other dried materials or used in wreaths.

Harvesting and preparing. To air-dry, pick the flowers when they are fully open and hang or stand them upright in an empty container. Preserve the leaves in silica gel to retain their creased shape, or press them flat.

—

Allium (AL-ee-um)

Genus of aromatic rhizomatous and bulbous plants that are used for food as well as ornament. Leaves are generally linear, hollow and 1 to 3 feet long, and some have solid three-sided leaves. Flowers are ball-shaped and bloom in the spring and summer; some are fragrant. Zones 3-9.

Selected species and varieties. *A. aflatunense* grows 2 to 4 feet tall with 4-inch-wide, strap-shaped leaves that are shorter than the flower stalks. Flowers are star-shaped, lilac-purple and occur in dense umbels that are 4 inches wide. Zones 3-8. *A. christophii,* star of Persia, has leaves that are pointed and strap-shaped with white downy undersides. Globular, uncrowded umbels almost 1 foot across have up to 80 star-shaped flowers of a metallic lilac hue and bloom in June. *A. giganteum,* giant onion, has 5-inch lilac-colored flower balls on tall stalks above basal clumps of strap-shaped leaves. Zones 5-9. *A. schoenoprasum,* chive, has 2-foot stems with pink and deep lavender blooms. *A. tuberosum,* Chinese chive, garlic chive, grows 1½ feet tall and has solid leaves that are ¼ inch wide. Flowers are ³/₁₆ inch long, fragrant and white. Blooms in late summer and early fall. Zones 4-9.

Growing conditions. Plant allium in early spring in a sunny area with rich, moist, well-drained soil. Mulch and apply liquid fertilizer the first year or two, until the plant is established. Propagate from seed, from offsets or by division. When seeded, allium blooms in the second year. Established plants need little care except for dividing bulb clumps every two years to ensure maximum bloom.

Uses. Giant onion and star of Persia are striking form flowers whose stems add strong lines to contemporary or Oriental arrangements. The more delicate chive and Chinese chive can be used as filler. Dried allium flowers retain their color well.

Harvesting and preparing. Whether the flowers are used fresh or dried, pick them when the top tubules have opened. To air-dry, slip lengths of wire through the stems to keep them rigid, and then stand the flowers upright in a container with a small amount of water. To preserve the most color, dry allium flowers in silica gel or in a microwave oven.

—

Allwood pink see *Dianthus*

Alstroemeria

(al-stre-MEER-ee-a)

Peruvian lily, lily-of-the-Incas

A summer-flowering perennial with slender stems and narrow leaves that are twisted at the base. Flowers are 2 inches long, slightly irregular, purple, red or yellow, and occur in showy terminal clusters. Zones 7-10.

Selected species and varieties. *A. aurantiaca* grows 3 feet tall and has flowers that are about 1½ inches long. Flowers bloom in spring and are yellow; the upper petals are spotted and streaked with purplish brown. The three outer petals are tipped with green. Clusters contain 10 to 30 flowers. Peruvian lily is hardy as far north as Zone 7.

Growing conditions. Peruvian lily is a sun lover, but can grow in semishady areas in fertile, sandy soil. To grow as far north as Zone 7, mulch heavily, or plant the flower in the spring, lift after blooming and store over the winter in damp sand in a cool place. Propagate by root division or by sowing seeds in sandy, peaty soil and keeping seedlings at a temperature of 60° F. Plants mature very slowly when propagated from seed.

Uses. The showy flowers and long stems of Peruvian lilies make them ideal for fresh bouquets, whether they are used alone or mixed with other long-stemmed flowers. Separate florets may be used either fresh or dried in low arrangements.

Harvesting and preparing. Preserve individual florets in silica gel or press them.

—

Alumroot see *Heuchera*

Amaranth see *Amaranthus*

—

Amaranthus (am-a-RAN-thus)

Amaranth

An annual with brightly colored foliage, alternate leaves and heavy flower spikes. Flowers are small, but they are prominent because they occur in chaffy, often brightly colored, clusters.

Selected species and varieties. *A. caudatus,* love-lies-bleeding,

tassel flower, grows to 5 feet tall and spreads broadly. Flowers occur on long, slender, drooping spikes. *A. cruentus,* prince's feather, reaches 6 feet tall. Flowers are red or purple and occur in terminal panicles of lateral spikes. *A. tricolor,* Joseph's coat, tampala, grows to 4 feet tall, has large, oval leaves of variegated green, red and yellow and is often used as a houseplant. Flowers are inconspicuous. *A. tricolor salicifolius,* fountain plant, has 7-inch-long, ⅜-inch-wide pendant leaves.

Growing conditions. Amaranth is easily grown in a sunny location in ordinary soil. Too fertile a soil may produce dull leaf color. Propagate from seed.

Uses. The colorful flower spikes of love-lies-bleeding and prince's feather may be used in fresh or dried arrangements. The colored leaves of Joseph's coat add accent to fresh arrangements.

Harvesting and preparing. To dry love-lies-bleeding and prince's feather, pick the flowers as soon as they are fully open and hang. Press both the flowers and leaves of Joseph's coat.

—

American bittersweet

see *Celastrus*

—

Ammobium (a-MO-bee-um)

Winged everlasting

Genus of tender perennials that are often treated as annuals. Plants grow to 3 feet tall with winged or angled stems and white, woolly foliage. Flowers are yellow and surrounded by collars of dry white bracts and chaffy scales.

Selected species and varieties. *A. alatum* is a 3-foot-tall bushy plant with prominently winged branches. Javelin-shaped basal leaves form a rosette. Stem leaves are smaller and fewer. Flower heads are numerous, 1½ inches across and bloom in summer. 'Grandiflora' has larger flower heads and self-sows in sandy soil.

Growing conditions. Winged everlasting needs sun but grows in any ordinary garden soil. Seeds may be sown outdoors in early spring

ALSTROEMERIA AURANTIACA

AMARANTHUS TRICOLOR SALICIFOLIUS

AMMOBIUM ALATUM 'GRANDIFLORA'

ANAPHALIS MARGARITACEA

ANEMONE × HYBRIDA

ANETHUM GRAVEOLENS

and thinned to 1 foot apart. Where winters are mild, winged everlasting is sometimes treated as a biennial; seeds sown outdoors in September will bloom the following summer.

Uses. Because the flower heads retain their true white color when dried, they make valuable additions to dried bouquets and wreaths.

Harvesting and preparing. Pick when two-thirds of the flowers on the stem are open; others will open as they dry. Hang to air-dry.

Anaphalis (a-NAF-a-lis)
Pearly everlasting

White, woolly-appearing, erect perennial with tiny hairs on the bottom sides of narrow, alternate leaves. Flowers and bracts are numerous and pearly white. Zones 3-9.

Selected species and varieties. *A. margaritacea* grows 20 inches tall, and has 4-inch leaves and ¼-inch flower heads that bloom in August.

Growing conditions. Pearly everlasting will grow in sun or shade in well-drained, sandy, fertile soil, and is drought-resistant. Plants may need some support. Cut stems to the ground after they finish flowering. Propagate by division in spring and fall, or from seed, and space plants 12 to 15 inches apart.

Uses. Because of its delicate appearance and because it lasts longer if its stems are cut short, fresh pearly everlasting is best used in a low arrangement. When the plant is dried, its color and shape are retained, making it useful in a wreath or other dried arrangement.

Harvesting and preparing. To use pearly everlasting flowers fresh, cut the stems short; this will prolong the flowers' vase life. To air-dry, pick before the flower heads open, and hang in bundles.

Anemone (a-NEM-o-nee)
Windflower

Hardy and nonhardy perennials that range in size from diminutive plants to well-branched plants 2 to 5 feet tall with compound leaves. Flowers have showy petal-like sepals that

may be red, pink, purple or white. Some species bloom in spring; others bloom in the fall. Zones 2-10.

Selected species and varieties. *A.* × *hybrida,* Japanese anemone, is a late-summer-blooming perennial with 3-foot stems. Flowers are pink or white. *A. pavonina,* peacock anemone, has 12-inch-tall stems and divided leaves. Flowers have seven to 12 sepals of scarlet with pale yellow claws and are 1½ to 2½ inches across. Zones 7-10.

Growing conditions. Windflower does well in partial shade and well-drained soil. Propagate by dividing tubers in the spring. In mild climates, plant in the fall. Plant tubers 2 inches deep and 12 to 15 inches apart.

Uses. Delicate, showy and long-lasting, windflowers make good mass flowers in fresh arrangements. When flowers are dried, their color deepens. Use the fern-like leaves in pressed designs.

Harvesting and preparing. When using windflower in fresh arrangements, leave space between the flowers, since they continue to grow and twist after being cut. Dry them in silica gel or in a microwave oven, but keep them away from humidity once dried, because they may reabsorb moisture. To preserve the leaves, press them.

Anethum (a-NAY-thum)
Dill

A small genus of aromatic annuals and biennials that grow 3 to 5 feet tall. Foliage is blue-green and lacy. Small yellow flowers occur in flattened umbels at the top of stiff, hollow stems. Seeds and fresh leaves are used to flavor food.

Selected species and varieties. *A. graveolens* is a half-hardy annual that grows 3 feet tall. Flower umbels may be 6 inches across.

Growing conditions. Dill is easily grown in full sun and well-drained, average soil. Sow seed in early spring or late summer. Dill does not survive transplanting. Thin to allow 1 to 1¼ feet between plants.

Uses. Dill's yellow flowers and lacy green foliage lend color and texture to fresh arrangements or to pressed flower designs. The dried seed heads can be used as filler when arranged in containers, or they can be used in wreaths.

Harvesting and preparing. Pick the seed heads before the seeds have darkened, and air-dry by hanging them in bunches.

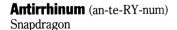

Anthemis (AN-the-mis)

Large group of annuals, biennials and perennials with fragrant, alternate, deeply cut leaves. Flower is daisylike with yellow or white rays and a yellow center. Zones 3-8.

Selected species and varieties. *A. tinctoria,* golden marguerite, is a perennial that grows to 3 feet tall. Flowers are 2 inches across. 'Kelwayi', hardy marguerite, has cut leaves and darker yellow flowers. It blooms from June until frost and has highly aromatic foliage. Zones 4-8.

Growing conditions. Golden marguerite is a sun lover and needs well-drained soil that is neutral or slightly alkaline. After it has finished blooming, cut down stems to encourage basal growth. Yearly plant division is necessary for strong growth. Propagate by division in early fall or spring, or from seed. Staking helps, since the plants are easily damaged by wind and heavy rain.

Uses. When used in fresh arrangements, golden marguerite is long-lasting; it may be used as a filler flower or grouped to form a focal point. Though the petals fade, the yellow center retains its color when dried, making it appropriate in nosegays or in wreaths.

Harvesting and preparing. Air-dry golden marguerites by hanging them in bunches.

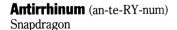

Anthurium (an-THUR-ee-um)
Tailflower, painter's palette

Genus of tropical perennials, some species of which are epiphytic. Leaves are large and green, sometimes variegated. Flowers are minute and crowded in a fleshy column called a spadix, which grows from the center of a heart-shaped waxy bract that may be red, pink, white or green. Zone 10.

Selected species and varieties. *A. andraeanum,* flamingo flow-

er, grows to 2 feet tall with dark green, leathery, oblong, heart-shaped leaves 8 inches long by 5 inches wide. The flower bract is scarlet at first, then turns green as it matures. The spadix is 3 to 5 inches long and yellowish with a white base.

Growing conditions. Flamingo flower will thrive in shade or low light with a humid atmosphere and nights of 60° F. Grow in porous, humus-rich, moist and well-drained soil. New roots should be covered with sphagnum moss as they appear on the surface. Propagate from seeds, suckers and stem cuttings.

Uses. Flamingo flowers may be grouped together or used singly in tropical or Oriental fresh arrangements, where they will last for weeks. Flamingo flowers can also be used dried, though they are somewhat brittle.

Harvesting and preparing. To condition flowers for use in fresh arrangements, place them upside down in tepid water for one hour, and then upright in cool water. To dry flamingo flowers, place the stems in a container with a small amount of water.

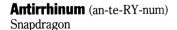

Antirrhinum (an-te-RY-num)
Snapdragon

Genus of annuals and perennials that may be as short as 9 inches or as tall as 3 feet. Leaves are alternate and lance-shaped. Flowers occur on terminal spikes; corollas are two-lipped, giving the flowers a mouthlike appearance. Flowers open from the bottom up from June to September and occur in most colors except blue. Seed heads follow on the spikes.

Selected species and varieties. *A. majus,* common snapdragon, toad's mouth, is an evergreen perennial that is generally treated as an annual and grows to 3 feet tall. Flowers are purplish red to white. 'Madame Butterfly' is a cultivar that grows 24 to 30 inches tall. Flowers are double and seem to cover the stems from top to bottom. Rocket Series grows 2½ feet tall and can withstand hot summers.

Growing conditions. Snapdragons need full sun to attain their maximum height, but they will bloom in

ANTHEMIS TINCTORIA 'KELWAYI'

ANTHURIUM ANDRAEANUM

ANTIRRHINUM MAJUS

ARCTOTIS STOECHADIFOLIA GRANDIS

ARMERIA MARITIMA

ARTEMISIA LUDOVICIANA ALBULA 'SILVER KING'

light shade. Soil should be somewhat alkaline, fertile and well drained. If plants are cut back after blooming, they will rebloom in fall. Taller plants need staking. Propagate from seeds started indoors in February. Seeds are small and should be scattered thinly and pressed in or barely covered by the sowing medium. Water carefully. Plant 6 to 12 inches apart in spring as soon as the soil can be worked. Snapdragons may also be propagated from cuttings.

Uses. Snapdragons are long-lasting, and they provide line in tall fresh arrangements. The spikes with seed heads can be used in dried arrangements, and individual flowers can be split open and used in pressed flower designs.

Harvesting and preparing. Pick seed heads once they have turned brown and air-dry by standing them upright. Split individual flowers open before pressing; they will retain color better than they would if pressed whole.

Arctotis (ark-TOH-tis)
African daisy

Genus of hairy annuals, perennials and small shrubs having alternate, toothed or deeply cut leaves on long stalks. Flower heads are blue, yellow or orange with both ray and disk flowers. Plants bloom in summer.

Selected species and varieties. *A. stoechadifolia* is a branching 2½- to 4-foot tender annual. Leaves are grayish green, up to 3 inches long and occur on ribbed stems. Flower heads are 3 inches across and have blue or violet centers and white or cream rays that are red on the undersides. *A. stoechadifolia grandis* has larger leaves and flower heads. Flower rays are grayish lavender on the bottom.

Growing conditions. African daisy needs a warm, sunny location since it opens only in full sunlight. Soil should be porous, fertile and well drained. Avoid overwatering. Propagate by starting seeds indoors and moving plants outside when night temperatures reach 50° F. Space the plants 6 to 12 inches apart. Flowers close at night.

Uses. African daisies are colorful flowers, whether used fresh or dried. Use them as mass flowers in either tall or low fresh arrangements. Dried flowers can be used in mixed bouquets or as focal points in flower wreaths.

Harvesting and preparing. To use African daisies as dried flowers, preserve them in silica gel.

Armeria (ar-MEER-ee-a)
Thrift, sea pink, ladies' cushion

An evergreen perennial that grows from 1 inch to 2½ feet tall and forms a dense basal rosette of linear, narrow leaves and stiff stalks with dense, globular flower heads. Flowers are white, pink, red or magenta. Zones 3-9.

Selected species and varieties. *A. maritima,* common thrift, grows 4 inches to 1½ feet tall. The stalks are downy.

Growing conditions. Thrift does well in a sunny location with sandy, well-drained soil. It grows well near the sea. Overwatering will cause rotting in the center of the dense mat. In cold areas, protect plants with a winter covering of evergreen branches. Propagate by division in September. Thrift can be grown from seed, but the first-year blooms will show considerable variation in quality.

Uses. Thrift may be used fresh as filler in a low arrangement, or grouped to form a focal point in a taller arrangement. Dried, it can be used in a bouquet or a wreath.

Harvesting and preparing. To retain the color and shape of blossoms when drying, pick flowers when they are almost open, and hang to air-dry.

Artemisia (ar-te-MEE-zee-a)
Sagebrush, southernwood, wormwood

Genus of annuals, perennials and low shrubs having alternate and mostly divided or dissected leaves that are grayish green to grayish silver. Flowers are yellow or white and are grown for their medicinal and aromatic qualities. Zones 3-9.

Selected species and varieties. *A. annua,* sweet Annie, grows 1 to 5 feet tall and is a sweetly fragrant annual. Leaves are pale green; flower heads are 1/12 inch wide, yellow, and bloom in loose but profuse panicles in August and September. *A. ludoviciana,* western sage, is a spreading plant about 1 to 4 feet tall. The undersides of the leaves are white and hairy. Flower heads are 1/8 inch across and grayish white. *A. ludoviciana albula* 'Silver King' is a 1- to 3-foot-tall hardy perennial with silver-gray foliage and whitish flower heads.

Growing conditions. Sagebrushes do well in sunny, dry areas; high humidity and wet soil cause rotting. Yearly division will control spreading. Propagate by root division or from seed. Sweet Annie is easily started from seed.

Uses. Sweet Annie and western sage provide line in tall fresh arrangements; they can also be used to create dried wreaths.

Harvesting and preparing. To make a wreath, pin the flower stems of sweet Annie or western sage to a wreath form and allow them to dry in place. For other dried arrangements, harvest branches at the end of the season and hang in bundles to air-dry.

Arum lily see *Zantedeschia*

Arundo (a-RUN-doh)

A tall perennial reed with broad, linear leaves and minute flowers that are clustered in huge terminal plumes. Zones 7-10.

Selected species and varieties. *A. donax,* giant reed, carrizo, grows on 20-foot erect stems. Leaves are alternate and gray-green. Flower panicles are narrow and may be erect or slightly drooping. *A. donax variegata* is similar to the species, but its leaf blades have a white stripe. Zones 8-10.

Growing conditions. Giant reed needs full sun and a soil that is deep, porous, fertile and well drained. Propagate by dividing or by placing stem cuttings in water and leaving them to develop new plants from their joints.

Uses. Giant reed may be used fresh or dried for its bold line. It is striking enough to be used by itself, but is equally appropriate for use in a tall, mixed Oriental or contemporary arrangement.

Harvesting and preparing. To air-dry giant reed, cut and place upright in an empty container.

Asclepias (a-SKLEE-pee-as)
Milkweed

Large genus of perennials with leaves that may be opposite or in whorls and usually contain a milky sap. Height ranges from 1 to 6 feet. Flowers of some species are showy. Blooms occur from July to September. Fruits are dry pods packed with seeds bearing fluffy, silky hairs. Zones 3-9.

Selected species and varieties. *A. exaltata* grows to 3 feet tall on stout stems. *A. physocarpa* reaches 6 feet tall with 2- to 4-inch leaves and stems that are woody at the base, giving the plant a shrubby appearance. *A. syriaca,* common milkweed, grows 3 to 6 feet tall and has branchless, hairy stems with thick, short-stalked leaves. Flowers are green to purple, and occur in stalked umbels. Seedpods are 3 to 4 inches long. *A. tuberosa,* butterfly weed, grows up to 3 feet tall. Leaves are alternate; flowers are 1/3 inch across and borne in showy orange heads. Sap is nonmilky. Seedpods grow erect on downpointing stalks and are 3½ to 5 inches long.

Growing conditions. Grow milkweed in full sun and average, dry garden soil. Butterfly weed will tolerate a richer soil than other milkweeds. The plants' deep roots do not allow for successful transplanting. Plants are easily propagated from seed or by division. Plants are weedy and will sprout from any portion of root left in the ground; they also spread rapidly by windblown seed.

Uses. Both milkweed and butterfly weed may be used as filler in a fresh arrangement; brightly colored butterfly weed can also be grouped and used as a focal point. The seedpods of both can be used in dried wreaths and arranged in containers.

Harvesting and preparing. Sear the stems of fresh milkweed before conditioning normally. Air-dry the seedpods by laying them on their

ARUNDO DONAX VARIEGATA

ASCLEPIAS TUBEROSA

ASPARAGUS DENSIFLORUS 'SPRENGERI'

ASTILBE × ARENDSII 'FANAL'

BACCHARIS HALIMIFOLIA

sides or by standing them upright in a container.

Asparagus (a-SPA-ra-gus)

Genus of perennial vines and shrubs. Branchlets are narrow, green and leaflike, and emerge from spreading stems. Flowers are white or yellow. Fruits are usually fleshy berries containing one to several seeds. One species is the edible vegetable. Zones 8-10.

Selected species and varieties. *A. densiflorus* has woody stems and a sprawling habit, and spreads to 3 feet. 'Sprengeri', Sprenger fern, usually has weak, hooked bristles. The berry is one-sided and coral-red. *A. setaceous,* asparagus fern, is an evergreen with fernlike, usually thornless, flat branches. Leaves are spines with reflexed tips. Creamy flowers, solitary or in twos and threes, bloom in the fall. Berries are the size of small peas and are red to purple.

Growing conditions. Sprenger and asparagus ferns do best in light shade and in fertile, well-drained soil. Propagate from seeds or cuttings, or by careful division. Before sowing, soak seeds in tepid water or file a tiny slit through the outer coat of each seed, and sow indoors in moderately moist sandy soil at 60° to 70° F.

Uses. Sprenger and asparagus ferns make good filler in fresh bouquets. Drooping Sprenger ferns may be placed around the outside edges of arrangements and allowed to spill over and disguise the sides of containers.

Harvesting and preparing. Condition normally.

Asp of Jerusalem see *Isatis*

Astilbe (a-STIL-bee)
Astilbe, false goatsbeard, spirea

Perennial with compound, fernlike leaves. Flowers bloom in dense feathery panicles of tiny white, pink or red blooms from June to August. Fruits are follicles. Zones 4-8.

Selected species and varieties. *A.* × *arendsii* grows to 3½ feet tall and has white, pink or crimson flowers. 'Fanal' is a 2-foot variety with deep red flowers and finely divided foliage tinged with red. Flowers bloom in early to middle summer. Zones 5-8. *A. chinensis* is a narrow, branching deciduous perennial that grows to 2 feet tall. Flower panicles are erect, showy, and white, rose or purple. Zones 5-8.

Growing conditions. For best results, plant astilbe in partial shade in rich, moist soil. Mulching helps the plant to retain moisture. Propagation by seed provides bloom in the second year. Plants may be divided in the fall or spring. Plant *A.* × *arendsii* 1½ to 2½ feet apart and *A. chinensis* 1 foot apart.

Uses. The feathery flowers of astilbe can be used as filler in fresh and dried arrangements; they retain their color well when dried. The dried flowers can also be used in wreaths.

Harvesting and preparing. Pick when flower clusters are two-thirds opened; then air-dry by laying the stalks on their sides. Plumes may shrink some when dried.

Baby's breath see *Gypsophila*

Baccharis (BAK-a-ris)
Sea myrtle

Large genus of shrubs that are sometimes evergreen, with leaves either alternate or lacking. Tubular flowers are white or yellow and are crowded in small heads. Fruit is a showy, cottony seed. Zones 4-10.

Selected species and varieties. *B. halimifolia,* groundsel bush, groundsel tree, is a 6- to 12-foot, many-branched shrub with coarsely toothed, short-stalked, resinous, gray-green leaves. Numerous thistlelike flower heads are borne in 3-inch-long clusters and bloom in late summer. There are both male and female plants; the female plants produce showy fruit in the fall.

Growing conditions. Sea myrtle should be grown in a sunny location in ordinary, well-drained garden soil. It is drought-resistant but will also grow in wet and saline soil.

Prune annually in early spring to remove old arching branches and to maintain density. Propagate from seeds and cuttings.

Uses. Groundsel bush flowers and berries may be used as filler in mixed, fresh or dried arrangements, or in dried wreaths.

Harvesting and preparing. To air-dry, pick the seed heads as the white puffs appear and stand them in an empty container. If left on the plant too long, the seed heads will shatter.

Bachelor's button
see *Centaurea*

Baptisia (bap-TIZ-ee-a)
False indigo, wild indigo

A hardy, upright perennial that grows in clumps, with branching stems and short-stalked leaves that usually have three leaflets. Flowers occur in terminal and lateral racemes in blue-violet, yellow or white. Fruits are oblong and inflated. Seedpods end in curved beaks. Zones 3-9.

Selected species and varieties. *B. australis* grows 3 to 6 feet tall with blue-green leaves. Flowers are indigo, 1 inch across, and bloom in erect terminal racemes 9 to 12 inches long in May and June.

Growing conditions. False indigo is easy to grow in full sun in porous, sandy soil. Remove faded flowers unless you want seeds to form. Staking may be necessary in exposed areas. Every few years, lift, divide and reset in newly spaded and fertilized ground. Apply a complete fertilizer each spring. The first hard frost kills stems to the ground. Propagate by division in early fall or spring, or from seeds sown in a cold frame or a protected area outdoors. Space plants 3 feet apart.

Uses. False indigo flowers are showy and colorful; they provide line in fresh arrangements. The plant's clusters of brown pods make striking additions to dried wreaths and garlands.

Harvesting and preparing. Allow pods to dry on the plant, or cut them when fully formed and then hang to air-dry.

Barley see *Hordeum*

Bayberry see *Myrica*

Bear's breech see *Acanthus*

Bee balm see *Monarda*

Beech see *Fagus*

Bellflower see *Campanula*

Bells-of-Ireland see *Moluccella*

Big flower see *Coreopsis*

Black-eyed Susan
see *Rudbeckia*

Blanketflower see *Gaillardia*

Blazing star see *Liatris*

Bluebells see *Eustoma*

Blue gum see *Eucalyptus*

Blue lace flower see *Trachymene*

Boneset see *Eupatorium*

Bouteloua (boo-te-LOO-a)
Grama grass, gramma

Genus of annual and perennial grasses that grow in dense clumps of rigid, slender stems, and flat or rolled narrow leaves. Flowers are few to many on spiky, one-sided racemes. Zones 4-9.

Selected species and varieties. *B. curtipendula,* sideoats gramma, grows to 32 inches tall with 35 to 50, purplish, spreading, pendulous, ¾-inch spikes borne on a slender axis 6 to 10 inches long. Each spike has five to eight spikelets. Leaf blades are ⅛ inch wide.

Growing conditions. Grama grass needs full sun and ordinary soil that is kept relatively dry. Propagate from seeds and by division in the spring.

Uses. Grama grass is useful in a fresh or dried arrangement for its line and unusual form.

Harvesting and preparing. To dry, pick before the flower spikes are fully developed; then dry by hanging upside down or by standing the stalks upright in an empty container.

Box Elder see *Acer*

BAPTISIA AUSTRALIS

BOUTELOUA CURTIPENDULA

BRIZA MAXIMA

CALENDULA OFFICINALIS

CALLISTEPHUS CHINENSIS

Briza (BREE-za)
Quaking grass, pearl grass

Genus of annual and perennial slender grasses with flat leaf blades and loose flower panicles that hang in small, often nodding, spikelets.

Selected species and varieties. *B. maxima*, large quaking grass, is an annual, erect, tufted plant that grows 1 to 2 feet tall and has smooth stems and ⅓-inch-wide leaves with rough upper surfaces. Flower panicles are 4 inches long and consist of eight ovate, 1-inch spikelets that are pale yellow, turning metallic with age. *B. minor* is an annual that grows in tufts 6 to 15 inches tall. Leaves are the same size as those of large quaking grass, but are rough on both sides. Flower panicles are 8 inches long, erect and broadly pyramidal with three-angled, ovate, greenish white, ⅛-inch spikelets.

Growing conditions. Grow quaking grass in full sun and fertile, well-drained soil. It prefers cool weather and does not survive transplanting. To propagate quaking grass, sow seeds in early spring or early fall. Thin seedlings to 3 to 4 inches apart.

Uses. Quaking grass stalks with seed clusters add motion and texture to fresh or dried arrangements, and make good filler.

Harvesting and preparing. To air-dry the seed clusters, pick when they are well developed but still green. Hang in bundles or stand upright in an empty container.

—

Broom see *Cytisus*

Broomcorn see *Sorghum*

Brown-eyed Susan see *Rudbeckia*

Bugleweed see *Ajuga*

Bull bay see *Magnolia*

Bulrush see *Typha*

Burning bush see *Euonymus*

Butterfly weed see *Asclepias*

—

Calendula (ka-LEN-du-la)
Pot marigold, field marigold

Genus of annuals and perennials with alternate, undivided, lobeless, faintly toothed leaves. Flower heads are solitary and consist of a disk of short florets surrounded by yellow, orange or cream ray florets that look like petals. They bloom from spring to frost.

Selected species and varieties. *C. officinalis*, common pot marigold, is an erect, branched annual that grows 1 to 1½ feet tall. Leaves are oblong and narrow at the base. The plant is covered with fine hairs, is slightly clammy to the touch and gives off a pungent scent when bruised. Flowers are 1½ to 4 inches across. Pot marigold petals are used as a substitute for saffron to flavor and give color to foods such as stews and puddings.

Growing conditions. Grow pot marigold in a sunny location and in moist soil. Propagate from seeds sown indoors in April. Set outside in May. In mild climates, sow seeds outdoors in spring or fall.

Uses. Brightly colored pot marigold flowers may be used as accents in fresh or dried arrangements. The dried flowers and petals can be used in potpourris.

Harvesting and preparing. To use fresh, cut the flowers before they are fully open. Preserve flowers with a drying agent to retain the most color. To use in a potpourri, air-dry the flowers by hanging them upside down.

—

Calico bush see *Kalmia*

Calla lily see *Zantedeschia*

—

Callistephus (ka-LIS-te-fus)
China aster

An erect, branched, hairy annual up to 2½ feet tall with stiff stems. Leaves are alternate, broadly oval and irregularly toothed. Flower heads are solitary, 2 to 3 inches across on long stalks with large, yellow disks and many narrow, strap-shaped ray florets that are usually violet or violet blue.

Selected species and varieties. *C. chinensis* is a tender annual with showy flowers up to 5 inches across. Colors are violet, blue, red, rose, pink, white and pale yellow.

Growing conditions. Grow china aster in full sun and in fertile, moderately moist, well-drained, neutral or slightly alkaline soil. China asters are highly susceptible to fusarium wilt. To reduce the spread of this disease, grow them in the same soil for only two to three years. Mulch soil with loose organic material. Plant away from the radiant heat of buildings and walls. Stake tall plants. Propagate from seed indoors in March; for successive blooming during the summer, sow again outdoors every two weeks until mid- or late June.

Uses. China asters are long-lasting, and may be used as mass flowers in fresh arrangements. They retain good color and shape when dried.

Harvesting and preparing. Preserve China asters with a drying agent to retain the most color.

—

Calluna (ka-LOO-na)
Heather, Scotch heather

A low-growing shrub with evergreen foliage and small, opposite leaves. The calyx of the flower is bell-shaped and extends beyond the corolla, which is also bell-shaped. Flowers bloom in late summer. Zones 3-8.

Selected species and varieties. *C. vulgaris* grows to 3 feet tall with narrow leaves that overlap each other and cover the branches; they may be hairy or hairless, and are approximately ½ inch long. Flowers are purplish pink, ⅛ inch long and bloom in one-sided racemes. 'Mullion' grows 18 inches high and has soft purplish pink to deep pink flowers.

Growing conditions. Heather grows best in an exposed location with good air circulation in a slightly acidic soil. It grows well by the seashore, on sandy banks and on slopes. To plant, add acid peat moss and coarse sand to the garden soil. Mulch and water during dry spells. Shear plants severely each spring. Propagate from softwood cuttings planted in a cold frame.

Uses. Heather may be used as filler in a fresh or dried arrangement, or as a base in a dried wreath.

Harvesting and preparing. Preserve heather in a drying agent for the best color and shape retention.

To use in a wreath, shape fresh flower stalks into wreath form, spray with acrylic sealer or unscented hair spray, and allow to air-dry.

—

Campanula (kam-PAN-u-la)
Bellflower

Large genus of perennial and annual plants having basal leaves that are often longer and broader than the stalk leaves. Flowers are large and showy, sometimes solitary and sometimes occurring in spikes. Egg-shaped seed heads follow the blossoms.

Selected species and varieties. *C. medium,* Canterbury bells, is a biennial that is treated as an annual and grows 3 to 4 feet tall. Flowers are bell-shaped and solitary, 1 inch wide, 2 inches long, white, blue or pink, and bloom in loose racemes from late spring through early summer.

Growing conditions. Plant Canterbury bells in full sun and in ordinary, fertile, well-drained soil. The plants will tolerate light shade. Stake to prevent tall plants from drooping. Propagate from seed outdoors in autumn for bloom the following late spring, and protect with evergreen mulch throughout the winter. Canterbury bells bloom six months after germination.

Uses. Canterbury bells last well in fresh arrangements. Dried, the white and pink flowers retain their color and can be used in bouquets or in wreaths; blue flowers fade to white. Seed heads can be used in mixed dried arrangements.

Harvesting and preparing. Preserve individual flowers in a drying agent. Once flowering has ceased, harvest the seed heads and air-dry by laying them on their sides.

—

Campsis (KAMP-sis)
Trumpet flower, crown plant

A deciduous, perennial, shrubby vine that climbs to 30 feet or more by aerial rootlets. Leaves are opposite and toothed. Showy, trumpetlike, orange or scarlet flowers bloom in terminal cymes or in panicles. The dry pods that follow the flowers are several inches long. Zones 4-9.

CALLUNA VULGARIS 'MULLION'

CAMPANULA MEDIUM

CAMPSIS RADICANS

CAPSICUM ANNUUM 'MASQUERADE'

CARTHAMUS TINCTORIUS

Selected species and varieties. *C. radicans,* trumpet vine, has orange flowers that are 2 inches across and 3 inches long and bloom in midsummer. Oblong fruit with two opposite ridges appears from late summer to fall. Seeds are winged. 'Flava' has yellow flowers. Underground runners can send up new plants at some distance from the main stem.

Growing conditions. Plant trumpet vine in a sunny location in fertile, moderately moist soil. It will tolerate some shade. This heavy vine needs assistance in supporting itself. In late winter or early spring, cut back all of the previous year's growth to within 2 to 3 inches of the ground and remove thin, crowded shoots. In spring, apply fertilizer to encourage strong flowering shoots. Propagate from seeds, from cuttings of green or mature wood, from root cuttings and by layering.

Uses. With its showy blossoms, trumpet flower may be used as a mass flower in a low fresh arrangement. Its curving stems can be used to add movement to a taller grouping. Dried individual flowers and seedpods may be used in mixed arrangements and in wreaths.

Harvesting and preparing. Use care in handling the leaves and flowers, since both can irritate the skin. To dry, preserve individual flowers in a drying agent.

—

Candle larkspur see *Delphinium*

Canterbury bells see *Campanula*

Cape daisy see *Venidium*

—

Capsicum (KAP-si-kum)
Pepper

Genus of perennial shrubs and annuals that reach 6 to 8 feet tall. Leaves are alternate, simple and ovate to elliptical. Flowers may be solitary or occur in twos and threes with white or green corollas that are sometimes tinged with violet. Fruit is a pod containing many seeds and may be red, orange or yellow.

Selected species and varieties. *C. annuum,* ornamental pepper, produces tiny white flowers and small fruits of various shapes and changing colors. 'Masquerade' produces long, thin peppers on 8- to 10-inch plants. *C. frutescens,* tabasco pepper, matures late and is used to flavor hot sauces. Flowers occur in pairs or as several emerging from a single node. Fruit is 2 inches long by ½ inch wide, bullet-shaped and appears from the end of July to the first frost.

Growing conditions. Pepper needs full sun and rich soil that is kept moist, especially when the plant is budding and blooming. It also needs shelter from sweeping winds. Propagate from seeds, which can be stored for a year in airtight containers in a cool place before sowing. For uniform germination, soak seeds in hot water at 190° F overnight. Start seeds indoors eight to 10 weeks before the last frost and set plants outside two to three weeks after all danger of frost is past. Young plants are tender, but older plants can endure some frost in the fall.

Uses. Peppers add color and an unusual shape to wreaths, garlands and hanging bunches.

Harvesting and preparing. Use care in handling the peppers, since they can burn the skin, eyes and nose. To air-dry, either pull up the whole plant and hang it upside down, or pick individual peppers as they ripen and lay them on a screen.

—

Cardinal flower see *Lobelia*

Carnation see *Dianthus*

Carpet bugle see *Ajuga*

Carrizo see *Arundo*

—

Carthamus (KAR-tha-mus)

A rigid, spiny-leaved annual. Flower heads are flat-topped, solitary, terminal, white, yellow or purple with leaflike collars or bracts in place of ray florets. Fruits are small, dry seeds.

Selected species and varieties. *C. tinctorius,* safflower, false saffron, grows 2 feet tall and has thistlelike flower heads about 1 inch across with red florets that are used in manufacturing silk dyes and rouge. Fruits are four-seeded and pearly white.

Growing conditions. Grow safflower in a sunny location in a fairly heavy, loamy soil. Propagate by sowing seed in early spring. Thin seedlings to about 6 inches apart.

Uses. Safflower blossoms may be used as filler in fresh arrangements; the white fruit, too, may be used for texture. Both are appropriate in wreaths and in other mixed dried arrangements.

Harvesting and preparing. To use dried, pick the stalks when some of the flowers are open, strip the leaves, except for those at the top of the stems, and hang in bundles. Air-dry the white fruit.

■

Cattail see *Typha*

■

Celastrus (see-LASS-trus)

Genus of deciduous, twining, woody, shrubby vines with alternate and simple leaves. Flowers are greenish and inconspicuous, and usually have male and female flowers on different plants; only female plants bear fruit, but male plants are required for pollination. Fruit is an orange capsule that splits open in the fall to reveal red berries.

Selected species and varieties. *C. orbiculatus,* Oriental bittersweet, spreads up to 36 feet long, has 4-inch rounded leaves and bears fruit in small, lateral clusters. Zones 5-7. *C. scandens,* American bittersweet, waxwork, fever twig, reaches 20 feet in length and has smaller leaves than above. Flowers are followed by 4-inch-long terminal clusters of fruit. Zones 3-7.

Growing conditions. Bittersweet grows in full sun and in ordinary, neutral soil that is not too wet in the winter. Prune vines heavily to prevent them from twining about living shrubs and trees. Remove deadwood in early spring and prune during the growing season to remove unwanted growth. Propagate from seeds sown in the fall, or from stem or root cuttings.

Uses. Branches with colorful ripe fruits may be arranged in containers with other fresh materials, or used to form wreaths.

Harvesting and preparing. Pick before the yellow flower panicles open; the fruit will open as it dries. Hang, or place upright in a container to dry. Shape the fresh branches into wreaths and allow them to dry in place.

■

Celosia (see-LO-see-a)

Genus of annuals and perennials with alternate, lobed or simple leaves. Minute flowers are crowded on large, dense, chaffy spikes, which may be either crested or plumed. Flowers bloom in summer.

Selected species and varieties. *C. cristata,* plumed celosia, crested celosia, cockscomb, is a 1- to 4-foot annual. Flower heads can be crested or plumed. Crested types have rounded flower heads that can be up to 1 foot across; plumed types have spiky flower heads up to 15 inches long. Colors may be solid white, yellow, purple or shades of red, or may be variegated.

Growing conditions. Celosia grows in full sun, fertile soil and plenty of moisture. Propagate from seeds sown indoors in March in peat pots and placed in the garden when all danger of frost is past, or sow seeds outdoors in early summer.

Uses. With its unusual shape, crested celosia makes a good mass flower in a fresh or dried arrangement; plumed celosia adds line and motion to a vertical arrangement. Both retain good color when dried.

Harvesting and preparing. To use dried, pick when the blossoms are at their peak and hang to air-dry.

■

Centaurea (sen-TOR-ee-a)

Genus of annuals and perennials having lobed or divided basal leaves and lance-shaped upper leaves. Flower heads contain tubular flowers that are raylike along the edges and have overlapping bracts below. They are pink, purple, blue, yellow or white.

Selected species and varieties. *C. cyanus,* bachelor's button, is a 2½-foot-tall, sprawling, hardy annual. Leaves are soft, hairy and alternate. Flowers are blue, pink or white, 1½ inches across, borne on long stalks and bloom from June to September. Some forms are double-flowered. *C. moschata,*

CELASTRUS ORBICULATUS

CELOSIA CRISTATA (CRESTED FORM)

CENTAUREA CYANUS

CHAMAEMELUM NOBILE

CHRYSANTHEMUM COCCINEUM (ROBINSON'S HYBRIDS)

sweet sultan, sultan's flower, is a 2-foot annual. The flowers are 2 inches across, solitary, white, yellow or purple, and fragrant.

Growing conditions. Bachelor's button and sweet sultan grow well in sun and in sandy, well-drained soil. Growth is rapid and plants are hardy until the first frost. Both tolerate transplanting. To prolong the blooming period, remove spent flowers to keep them from going to seed. Propagate from seeds sown in the garden after all danger of frost is past, or sown indoors in mid-April and set out at the end of May.

Uses. With its unusual shape and texture, sweet sultan makes a good filler in a tall fresh or dried arrangement. Bachelor's button can be used as a focal point in a small, fresh spring arrangement.

Harvesting and preparing. To dry sweet sultan, pick flowers within a half day of their opening and hang. Dry bachelor's button in a drying agent in order to retain the most color.

—

Chamaemelum
(kam-a-MAY-lum)
Chamomile

Low-growing perennial with leafy stems and alternate leaves. Yellow or white flowers bloom from May or June to August or September. Zones 3-10.

Selected species and varieties. *C. nobile* is a half-hardy perennial, usually grown as an annual, that spreads by creeping stems and grows to 12 inches high and wide. Foliage is lacy, finely divided and borne on stems topped with daisy-like flowers that are 1 inch across and white. The plant is apple-scented and blooms from August until frost.

Growing conditions. Chamomile does best in sun and in sandy, well-drained, slightly acid soil. It tolerates light shade. Propagate from seeds or from cuttings started indoors in early spring and transplanted to the garden after all danger of frost is past.

Uses. Use delicate chamomile blossoms as filler in fresh or dried arrangements. The dried flowers make a fragrant addition to a potpourri.

Harvesting and preparing. To dry, pick the flowers when they start to bloom and either hang them in bundles or preserve them with a drying agent.

—

Chamomile see *Chamaemelum*
Chaste tree see *Vitex*
China aster see *Callistephus*
Chinese chive see *Allium*
Chinese lantern see *Physalis*
Chive see *Allium*
Christmas fern see *Polystichum*

—

Chrysanthemum
(kri-SAN-the-mum)

Genus of annuals, perennials and small shrubs, often erect with many-branched stems that are either hairless or hairy and are sometimes slightly sticky. Leaves are alternate and lobed, and may be toothed or smooth-edged. Foliage and other parts of the plant are odoriferous when crushed. Most flower heads have disk florets encircled by rows of petal-like ray florets. Zones 3-10.

Selected species and varieties. *C. coccineum,* painted daisy, pyrethum, is a 2-foot unbranched perennial with thin, fernlike leaves. Flower heads are 3 inches across and have yellow disk flowers and white, pink or red ray flowers. Zones 3-9. Robinson's Hybrids grow from 18 to 24 inches tall. Flowers are single, pink, rose or crimson. Zones 3-9. *C. maximum,* shasta daisy, grows 2 feet tall and has simple, rigid stems. The flower is solitary, 2⅜ inches across and has a yellow disk and white ray flowers. Zones 4-10. 'Alaska' is a hardy perennial having blooms that are 4 inches across. Zones 4-9. Double fringed types grow from 24 to 30 inches tall and have blooms that are 4 to 5 inches across and white. The number of petals varies. 'T. E. Killen' has two rows of petals and a crested center. Others, such as 'Aglaya', have fluffy double blooms consisting of many rows of lacelike fringed petals.

C. × morifolium, florist's chrysanthemum, has grayish, hairy leaves and flowers that are 1 to 6 inches in diameter. Florist's mums come in a wide range of colors, except blue, and a variety of forms (single, double, pompon, quill, spider). Zones 5-10. Incurved types have broad, mature ray florets that curve inward to form large, round blooms. Spider types have fine to coarse ray florets that are long and tubular. Tips show definite coils and hooks. The disk flower is not apparent. Double types may have more than five rows of ray florets with flat disk flowers. Ray flowers may or may not be at right angles to the stem and may hide the disk flower. *C. parthenium,* feverfew, is a 1- to 3-foot leafy perennial with strongly scented foliage. Blooms are ¾ inch across, numerous and have many white rays. Zones 5-8.

Growing conditions. Chrysanthemums grow well in sun and ordinary, well-drained soil. Fertilize regularly. Pinch out tips of the stems to induce branching when the plants are 4 inches tall. Stop pinching in midsummer. Cut old stems down to the ground after the plant has finished blooming. In northern climates, use a light winter mulch. Propagate by division, from cuttings or from seeds.

Uses. Chrysanthemums last up to two weeks in fresh arrangements or in vases of loose flowers. When dried, they add color to mixed autumn arrangements, bouquets, wreaths and garlands. Use feverfew blossoms as filler in low or vertical fresh arrangements.

Harvesting and preparing. Dry chrysanthemums by hanging or by standing them upright in a container; preserve individual flower heads in a drying agent. To air-dry feverfew blossoms, pick flowers when they are fully developed but before they turn creamy, and hang in bundles.

Cirsium (SER-see-um)
Thistle, plume thistle

Genus of spiny annuals, biennials and perennials with alternate or basal leaves that are irregularly toothed or lobed. Outer edges have strong prickles. Flowers are tubular and armed with spiny bracts, may be solitary or clustered on the ends of branches, and are white, yellow, red or purple. They bloom from July to September.

Selected species and varieties. *C. japonicum* is a 3-foot biennial that is grown as a hardy annual. Flowers are purple or rose-colored and 1½ inches across.

Growing conditions. Thistle grows in full sun to partial shade and in average, moist soil. Propagate from seeds sown in early spring. Space plants 2 feet apart.

Uses. Thistles may be used in either fresh or dried arrangements as filler flowers; they may also be used in wreaths.

Harvesting and preparing. Wear heavy-duty gloves when handling thistle to protect hands from the spines. To air-dry, pick as soon as the plume begins to show, wire the stem and stand it in an empty container. If thistle is picked later, the color will be pale and the seeds will disperse.

Clarkia (KLAR-kee-a)
Godetia, farewell-to-spring

A graceful annual with alternate leaves and showy racemes of rose to purplish flowers.

Selected species and varieties. *C. amoena,* satin flower, summer's darling, is a 1- to 3-foot hardy annual that is coarse and sprawling. Flower spikes are loose and have 1- to 2-inch flowers that may be lavender-red, red, salmon, pink or white. Petals are satiny and may be single or double. There are dwarf varieties of satin flower.

Growing conditions. Satin flower does well in full sun, cool nights and a fairly light soil. Grow where winters are mild and summers are not hot and humid. Plants bloom better if planted densely. Propagate from seeds sown outdoors in May, and thin the seedlings to 10 inches apart. Seeds may also be sown from late summer through fall.

Uses. Satin flowers may be used fresh in tall arrangements for line, and in lower arrangements to create focal points. They can also be used in pressed flower designs.

Harvesting and preparing. Cut satin flowers when the buds at the top of the plant open.

CIRSIUM JAPONICUM

CLARKIA AMOENA

CONSOLIDA AMBIGUA

CONVALLARIA MAJALIS

COREOPSIS LANCEOLATA

Clove pink see *Dianthus*

Cockscomb see *Celosia*

Coneflower see *Echinacea; Rudbeckia*

—

Consolida (kon-SO-li-da)
Larkspur

An annual having narrow, divided leaves and showy flowers that bloom in spikes.

Selected species and varieties. *C. ambigua,* rocket larkspur, is a hardy 1- to 2-foot annual with horizontally spreading branches. Flower spikes are violet, pink, rose or blue, and bloom from June to August. Fruits are podlike, hairy follicles with black seeds. *C. orientalis* grows erect, reaching 3½ feet tall, and has deeply lobed leaves. Flowers are purplish violet. Seeds are red-brown and occur in hairless follicles. *C. regalis* grows 4 feet tall with two to three linear, lobed leaves. Flowers are deep blue, pink or white.

Growing conditions. Larkspur likes a sunny, sheltered site and rich soil. Mulch with dried grass clippings to keep roots cool when plants reach 12 to 18 inches tall. Cut dead flower spikes back to a point just above a strong leaf. In mild climates, propagate by sowing seeds in the fall; elsewhere, seeds can be sown in early spring, even before the last frost. Larkspur does not transplant well. Space plants 2 feet apart.

Uses. Larkspurs provide good line in tall fresh or dried arrangements. Shorter lengths of larkspur may be used as filler in centerpieces or other small arrangements. The dried seed heads, too, can be used in bouquets and wreaths.

Harvesting and preparing. To dry the flowers, pick when the spikes are four-fifths open, then hang individually. Once dried, keep in a nonhumid atmosphere to prevent the flowers from reabsorbing moisture. Pick green seed heads just as they form and hang in bundles to dry.

—

Convallaria (kon-va-LAR-ee-a)
Lily-of-the-valley

A rhizomatous perennial that grows 8 inches tall and has two large, oval basal leaves. Flowers are white, bell-shaped and borne in one-sided racemes. Zones 4-8.

Selected species and varieties. *C. majalis* has ¼- to ½-inch fragrant, waxy flowers that bloom from mid-May to mid-June and are followed by orange berries.

Growing conditions. Lily-of-the-valley does best in full or partial shade and moist, fertile soil. Foliage dies to the ground in late summer. Propagate by dividing the rhizomes.

Uses. Lilies-of-the-valley may be used alone or mixed with other flowers in fresh spring bouquets. Both leaves and flowers may be used in small dried arrangements or pressed designs.

Harvesting and preparing. Preserve flower sprays by laying them on their sides in silica gel or by drying in a microwave oven. Preserve leaves by placing the stem ends in a glycerine solution.

—

Coral bells see *Heuchera*

—

Coreopsis (kor-ee-OP-sis)
Coreopsis, tickseed

Genus of annuals and perennials having leaves that are generally opposite, often lobed or dissected, but sometimes entire. Flower heads are composed of disk flowers and showy ray flowers, usually yellow, but sometimes purple or pink, and may be solitary or occur in branched clusters. They bloom in summer and fall. Zones 4-10.

Selected species and varieties. *C. grandiflora,* big flower, is a short-lived perennial that grows to 2 feet. Flower heads are orange-yellow, 3 inches across and bloom from mid-June to late July. *C. lanceolata,* lance coreopsis, grows 2 to 3 feet tall. Leaves are entire and appear mainly at the base of the plant. Flowers are 2½ inches across, yellow and grow on long stalks. *C. verticillata,* threadleaf coreopsis, reaches 18 to 30 inches tall and has fernlike leaves and 2-inch, dark yellow flower heads.

Growing conditions. Coreopsis does best in a sunny location and in sandy, acid soil. Tall plants need staking. Threadleaf coreopsis is drought-resistant. Propagate from seeds, from cuttings taken in summer, or by division in spring or fall.

Uses. Coreopsis is long-lasting and brightly colored, and can be used as a mass flower in a high or low, fresh or dried arrangement. The leaves and flowers of threadleaf coreopsis are especially attractive when pressed.

Harvesting and preparing. Preserve the flower heads in silica gel or dry them in a microwave oven.

—

Corn lily see *Gladiolus*

—

Cornus (KOR-nus)
Dogwood

Genus of deciduous shrubs and trees that have undivided, lobeless, opposite or alternate leaves. Flowers bloom in spring and are followed by fruit in fall. Zones 3-9.

Selected species and varieties. *C. florida,* flowering dogwood, is a 40-foot tree with horizontal branches. Flowers are small, yellow and surrounded by four large, notched white bracts. Red berries appear in clusters in fall. Zones 5-9. 'Rubra', red flowering dogwood, has red or pink bracts. Zones 5-9.

Growing conditions. Plant dogwood in partial shade in any good, moist garden soil. It will tolerate sun. Mulch and water regularly. Propagate from seeds or cuttings.

Uses. When used fresh, flowering dogwood branches provide line in Oriental and horizontal arrangements. The flowers and leaves may be used in pressed designs. Branches of autumn leaves and red berries make colorful additions to seasonal bouquets.

Harvesting and preparing. Cut branches in spring when blossoms appear, or cut before the buds have opened for forcing indoors. Cut autumn branches when the berries and leaves have arrived at their peak colors. Preserve branches of leaves by placing stem ends in a glycerine solution. Dry the flowers in silica gel, in a microwave oven or press them.

Cortaderia (kor-ta-DEER-ee-a)

A tall, reedlike grass with basal leaves that form massive clumps. Individual plants are male or female. Flowers bloom in large, plumelike panicles. Zones 8-10.

Selected species and varieties. *C. selloana,* pampas grass, grows 8 to 12 feet tall and has many rough, margined, long and narrow leaves. Flower spikes are 1 to 3 feet long and silvery or pale pink. The female plant has white or pinkish silky hairs; the male plant is hairless.

Growing conditions. Pampas grass grows in full sun and in fertile, well-drained soil. It will tolerate dry soil. Remove dead material from the center of the clump. Cut plants to the ground in late winter. Leaf edges are razor sharp. Propagate by root division.

Uses. Pampas grass may be used to add texture, motion and line to a vertical or an Oriental fresh or dried arrangement.

Harvesting and preparing. Pick pampas grass while the seed heads are still green and tight; while drying, they will continue to develop, but will not shatter and drop seeds as they would if picked later. Air-dry by placing stem ends in a container with 1 inch of water. For flexibility, preserve pampas grass by standing the stalks in a glycerine solution. The stalks may also be bleached.

—

Cosmos (KOS-mos)

Genus of annuals and perennials with opposite leaves that are usually pinnate. Flower heads are showy, radiate, solitary or in panicles, and the ray flowers are white, rose, purple, yellow or orange.

Selected species and varieties. *C. bipinnatus,* common cosmos, is an annual that grows to 10 feet tall. Leaves are pinnate. Flower heads are 3 to 4 inches across; the disk flower is yellow and the ray flowers are white, pink or crimson. 'Sensation Mix' is a 4-foot plant with large single blooms having rounded petals and yellow centers. *C. sulphureus* is an annual that grows 7 feet tall and has yellow disk flowers and yellow or orange ray flowers that are 3 inches across. There are many flowering cultivars.

CORNUS FLORIDA 'RUBRA'

CORTADERIA SELLOANA

COSMOS BIPINNATUS 'SENSATION MIX'

CYTISUS × PRAECOX

DAHLIA HYBRID

Growing conditions. Cosmos requires sun, warm weather and sandy soil; if the soil is too rich, plants will grow too tall and produce few flowers. Stake the taller plants. Propagate from seeds. In the north, sow seeds indoors in early spring. Cosmos blooms two months after sowing.

Uses. Cosmos make good cut flowers, and may be grouped alone in vases or used as accent flowers in tall fresh summer arrangements. They may also be used dried in wreaths or other arrangements, and can be pressed.

Harvesting and preparing. Preserve cosmos flowers in a drying agent; once they have dried, keep them away from moisture since they tend to reabsorb it.

Crabapple see *Malus*
Crown plant see *Campsis*

Cytisus (SIT-i-sus)
Broom

Genus of nonspiny and spiny, deciduous and evergreen flowering shrubs and small trees. Leaves are compound and have three leaflets. Flowers are solitary or they occur in small clusters of yellow, purple or white. Fruit is a flat pod. Zones 5-10.

Selected species and varieties. *C.* × *praecox,* Warminster broom, has vertical deciduous stems with flowers that are cream and yellow. It blooms in early May. *C. scoparius,* Scotch broom, grows 5 to 6 feet tall with a dense mass of ascending branches that remain green all winter. Flowers are yellow and bloom in mid-May. 'Carla' grows 5 to 6 feet tall and has pink and crimson flowers lined with white.

Growing conditions. Broom grows well in a sunny site in acid, well-drained and good, but not too rich, soil. Broom is difficult to transplant. Prune the plant when flowers fade. Scotch broom is extremely invasive. It has taken over thousands of acres of land in California and the Northwest. Propagate from seeds, from greenwood cuttings, and by layering and grafting. Space plants 3 to 5 feet apart.

Uses. The flowering branches of broom will lend line to tall or Oriental, fresh or dried arrangements. Scotch broom remains green year round, and it may be used as background foliage in an arrangement with three sides. When dried, it turns gray.

Harvesting and preparing. Air-dry broom by hanging or by standing it upright in a small amount of water in a container.

Daffodil see *Narcissus*
Dagger fern see *Polystichum*

Dahlia (DAL-ya)

A tender, tuberous-rooted perennial that is mostly unbranched and has opposite or whorled leaves. Flower heads are radiate and have two rows of bracts.

Selected species and varieties. There are hundreds of dahlia cultivars. Among them are medium to tall plants with long-stemmed blossoms, and dwarf plants from 1 to 12 inches tall that bloom from early summer to frost. Flowers range from 2-inch, ball-shaped pompons to 12-inch, multipetaled blossoms with curled, quill-like petals. Colors are white, pink, lavender, yellow, orange, red and maroon in monochromes and bicolors.

Growing conditions. Plant dahlias in full sun and moist soil; space them 2 to 3 feet apart and use 2 to 3 inches of deep mulch. Stake tall plants. To develop large blooms, pinch side shoots and retain only the main stalk. Propagate by dividing tubers or from cuttings. In the fall, after frost has killed the top growth, carefully dig up the tubers; bury them in sand, sawdust or vermiculite; and store them in a cool, dry place over winter.

Uses. Dahlias may be used as mass flowers in low or tall, fresh or dried arrangements. They may also be used in wreaths to provide colorful focal points.

Harvesting and preparing. To use dahlias fresh, sear the stem ends and then condition in the normal manner. Preserve the flowers in silica gel or dry them in a microwave oven. They should be kept in a dry atmosphere to prevent them from reabsorbing moisture.

—

Daucus (DAW-kus)

Genus of annuals and biennials with pinnate leaves and tiny white flowers borne in umbels. Zones 3-9.

Selected species and varieties. *D. carota,* Queen Anne's lace, wild carrot, is a 3-foot, branched, taprooted annual or biennial with fernlike pinnately compound leaves. The flower umbel is compound, generally flattened on top and white with a single, deep red flower in the center. Flowers bloom from July to September and are followed by cuplike seed heads.

Growing conditions. Queen Anne's lace grows in the sun and in sandy soil. The plant may become invasive if it is allowed to drop its seeds; to control spreading, remove faded flowers before they go to seed. Propagate Queen Anne's lace from seeds sown outdoors.

Uses. Queen Anne's lace flowers may be used as mass or filler flowers in fresh arrangements. Dried flowers can be used in wreaths or in pressed designs, and the dried seed heads contribute a deep brown color to mixed arrangements.

Harvesting and preparing. Preserve the flower heads with a drying agent, or air-dry by laying them on mesh. Keep the flowers dry to prevent them from reabsorbing moisture. Allow the seed heads to dry naturally on the plant.

—

Delphinium (del-FIN-ee-um)

A hardy, stately perennial with palmate leaves and soft, brittle stems. Flowers occur in various shades of blue and purple. Zones 3-10.

Selected species and varieties. *D. elatum,* candle larkspur, common delphinium, has 4- to 6-foot upright stalks covered with 2-inch, single or double purple flowers followed by small seed heads. Pacific Hybrids can reach 6 to 8 feet tall. Plants are erect, massive and dense, with single and double flowers that come in a variety of colors. *D. grandiflorum chinensis,* Siberian larkspur, is a perennial with finely cut and branched foliage. Flowers are blue and 1½ inches wide.

Growing conditions. Delphiniums need sunshine for at least half the day; they prefer well-drained, rich soil that is neutral to slightly alkaline. Delphiniums benefit from a light sprinkling of lime over the surrounding soil in early spring. Plants require staking. When leaves turn yellow, cut the plants back to their bases and feed with mixed fertilizer to encourage new shoots and fall blooming. Plants die or lose vigor after two to three years. Apply winter mulch after the ground freezes. Propagate from seeds, spacing plants 2 feet apart.

Uses. Delphiniums provide line in vertical fresh arrangements, and they provide color in mixed pink and blue country bouquets. The dried flowers and seed heads can be arranged in containers with other dried materials or used in wreaths.

Harvesting and preparing. To use the flower fresh, pick before its top buds have opened. To use dried, pick when half the stem is in flower and half is in bud; then hang each stalk separately. Stems can also be dried upright in a container with a small amount of water. Individual flowers can also be preserved in silica gel. To preserve the seed heads, cut after the petals fall and before the seeds turn dark brown and split; air-dry by laying the stalks with seed heads on their sides.

—

Devil-in-a-bush see *Nigella*

—

Dianthus (dy-AN-thus)
Pinks

Genus of annuals, biennials and evergreen perennials having narrow, grasslike, opposite leaves. Flowers have a pungent fragrance, are solitary or borne in clusters of pink, rose, white and yellow, and bloom in June. Zones 3-10.

Selected species and varieties. *D. × allwoodii,* allwood pink, grows 4 to 20 inches tall with bluish green foliage that forms a tuft. Zones 4-8. *D. barbatus,* sweet William, is a 2-foot perennial treated as a biennial. Flowers occur in brightly colored terminal clusters of pink, red and white with variations. Dou-

DAUCUS CAROTA

DELPHINIUM ELATUM

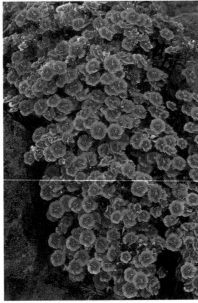

DIANTHUS CHINENSIS

DICTAMNUS ALBUS 'PURPUREUS'

DIGITALIS PURPUREA

DIPSACUS FULLONUM

ble flowers are available. Zones 6-10. *D. caryophyllus,* carnation, clove pink, grows 1 to 3 feet tall and bears 12 to 18 highly fragrant flowers. Zones 8-10. 'Chabaub Giant Mix' grows from 15 to 20 inches tall and blooms over a long period. 'Grenadin Mix' is a 2-foot plant with double flowers. *D. chinensis,* Chinese pink, Indian pink, is a 1½-foot-tall annual with 1-inch-wide, white, red or lilac-colored flowers that grow in loose clusters.

Growing conditions. Pinks like full sunshine, well-drained, slightly alkaline soil and cool summers. Where winters are severe, plants should have a light cover of pine boughs after the ground freezes. Propagate from seeds sown in a cold frame in late summer or from stem cuttings taken in midsummer.

Uses. Allwood pink, carnation and Chinese pink make good filler flowers in fresh spring bouquets. Sweet William may be used as a mass flower in a fresh or dried arrangement.

Harvesting and preparing. To retain shape and color, preserve flowers in silica gel or dry in a microwave oven.

Dictamnus (dik-TAM-nus)
Gas plant, dittany

A somewhat woody perennial with dark green, glossy foliage and white to rose flowers that grow in spiky racemes. Blooms occur in June or July, and are followed by star-shaped seedpods. Zones 2-9.

Selected species and varieties. *D. albus* grows 3 feet tall and emits a strong-smelling inflammable oil. Both the plant and its seedpods are poisonous. 'Purpureus' has pinkish purple flowers.

Growing conditions. Gas plant grows well in full sun and well-drained, fertile soil. It tolerates relatively dry soil. Space plants 2½ feet apart. Propagate from seeds sown outdoors in fall. Plants started from seed will not bloom for 3 or 4 years. Collect seed as pods just turn brown, since pods will burst and scatter the seeds. Gas plants do not respond well to division.

Uses. Gas plant flowers can be used in fresh bouquets, and they last well in water. The seedpods

can be used in dried arrangements; they were once used as small candle holders.

Harvesting and preparing. To dry the seedpods, cut them and hang in bundles.

Digitalis (di-ji-TAL-is)
Foxglove

Summer-flowering perennial or biennial with alternate, simple leaves that occur in basal rosettes in young plants. Flowers are showy, one-sided racemes of purple, yellow, brown or white, often spotted or streaked inside. They bloom from late spring to summer and are followed by seed heads. Zones 4-10.

Selected species and varieties. *D. purpurea* is a 2- to 4-foot-tall biennial with 2-inch drooping bell-shaped flowers on erect spikes. Excelsior Hybrids are early-blooming varieties that reach 5 feet tall and have large pink, rose, purple, cream, yellow and white flowers growing all around the stem.

Growing conditions. Foxglove grows best in a moist, shady area and in rich, well-drained soil. Space plants 1½ feet apart. Propagate from seeds sown in early spring so that plants will have have time to grow strong enough to endure winter. Renew biennials each year by sowing seeds in August.

Uses. Foxglove stems with blossoms can be used in tall fresh arrangements. Stems with seed heads are appropriate in dried arrangements.

Harvesting and preparing. To use the stalks of seed heads, pick when the seed heads have formed, remove the foliage and hang to dry.

Dill see *Anethum*

Dipsacus (DIP-sa-kus)
Teasel

Genus of prickly or spiny biennials and perennials. Leaves are basal or opposite, simple to pinnately cut and often united at their bases. Flowers are crowded in dense terminal heads, each head having spiny bracts at its base. The seed head is incurved and spiny. Zones 3-9.

Selected species and varieties.
D. fullonum grows 6 feet tall and has leaves that are simple, lanceolate and 12 inches long. Stems are prickly. The flowers are pale purple, ½ to ⅔ inch long, and grow densely crowded on 4-inch heads. They bloom from summer to fall.

Growing conditions. Teasel grows well in a sunny location in any reasonably fertile, well-drained soil. It needs little attention. The plant should be picked before seeds drop to prevent its becoming invasive. Propagate from seeds sown in early summer or midsummer. Teasel may be transplanted in the fall.

Uses. Teasel's unusual seed heads add texture to wreaths and other dried arrangements.

Harvesting and preparing. Use heavy gloves when picking teasel to protect the hands from the seed heads' sharp spikes. To preserve the silvery color of the stems and heads, pick when still in flower. Remove the leaves and scrape the spines from the stem with a knife. Hang to air-dry. Teasel flowers may also be left to dry naturally on the plant, where they will turn a pale tan color.

—

Dittany see *Dictamnus*

Dock see *Rumex*

Dogwood see *Cornus*

Dusty miller see *Senecio*

Dutch iris see *Iris*

Dwarf feather top
see *Pennisetum*

Dyer's woad see *Isatis*

—

Echinacea (ek-i-NAY-see-a)
Purple coneflower

A coarse, rough, hairy perennial having large, alternate, simple leaves and black, pungent roots. Flower heads are solitary with drooping ray flowers and cone-shaped, purple disk flowers. Flowers bloom in middle to late summer. Zones 3-9.

Selected species and varieties.
E. purpurea grows 3 feet tall. Lower leaves are ovate to broadly lanceolate and coarsely toothed; leaves are narrower on the upper stem.

Flower heads are 6 inches across and have rose-purple ray flowers and coppery or orange-brown disk flowers. 'Bravado' grows 4 feet tall with lavender-pink 4- to 4½-inch flower heads. The petals remain flat and do not droop. Zones 4-9. 'White Luster' has pure white, drooping ray flowers and greenish-coppery disk flowers. Zones 4-9.

Growing conditions. Coneflower is drought-resistant and will thrive in full sun to partial shade; it tolerates wind. Soil should be a well-drained, sandy loam. Plants grown in soil that is too rich or too moist tend to become floppy and need staking. Water during extended dry spells. Every four to five years, dig up, divide and replant in deeply spaded and newly fertilized soil. Propagating by seed may yield plants not true to type. Division is the most reliable method of propagation. Space plants 18 to 24 inches apart.

Uses. Coneflowers make long-lasting cut flowers, and their shuttlecock forms add interest to fresh arrangements. Coneflowers can be used as mass flowers in fresh groupings. The cones, or seed heads, are appropriate in wreaths and other dried arrangements.

Harvesting and preparing. Coneflowers dry well in silica gel or in a microwave oven. Cones without petals may be air-dried.

—

Echinops (EK-i-nops)
Globe thistle

Genus of annuals, biennials and perennials with alternate leaves that are prickly-toothed or lobed. Flower heads are globular and have dense, spiny bracts that are usually metallic blue or white and bloom in summer. Zones 3-9.

Selected species and varieties.
E. ritro, small globe thistle, grows 3 to 4 feet tall with leaves that are white and felty underneath. Flower heads are blue, 1½ to 2 inches across and bloom from July to September. 'Taplow Blue' has flower heads that are up to 3 inches across. The flower balls are steel blue in color and bloom in midsummer.

Growing conditions. Globe thistle prefers sun, but will tolerate partial shade. It grows well in rich,

ECHINACEA PURPUREA

ECHINOPS RITRO 'TAPLOW BLUE'

ERYNGIUM ALPINUM

EUCALYPTUS POLYANTHEMOS

moist, well-drained soil and requires plenty of space. Small globe thistle may have to be staked. Propagate by dividing clumps in spring. Blooms will appear in the second year. Propagating from seed is not reliable.

Uses. Globe thistles provide color and an unusual shape when used as filler in both fresh and dried mixed arrangements. They can also be used in wreaths.

Harvesting and preparing. When picking globe thistles, wear gloves to protect hands from the bristles on the leaves. Pick as soon as the globes are deep gray-blue and before the flower buds open; allow some leaves to remain on the stems. Hang to air-dry.

◼

Edelweiss see *Leontopodium*
English lavender see *Lavandula*

◼

Eryngium (e-RIN-jee-um)
Eryngo

Bold-appearing perennial with simple leaves that are generally either cut or lobed, and usually spiny-edged. Flowers are small, white or blue, occur in dense bracted heads and bloom in summer. They are followed by the seed heads. Zones 4-8.

Selected species and varieties. *E. alpinum* grows 2½ feet tall and has soft, basal foliage. Upper leaves and stems are bluish or whitish. Flower heads are steel blue in color, cylindrical and ¾ inch to 1½ inches long. *E. amethystinum* grows 1½ feet tall and has blue flowers. *E. maritimum,* sea holly, reaches 1 foot tall. Leaves are stiff, ovate and three-lobed with coarse, spiny teeth. Flower heads are pale blue and 1 inch long.

Growing conditions. *E. alpinum* favors meadows and other grassy areas. Space plants 1½ feet apart. Sea holly thrives in full sun and well-drained, sandy soil of moderate to low fertility. It tolerates salt spray. Space sea holly plants 1 foot apart. Do not transplant either species, since both have long taproots. In cold areas, mulch in winter with evergreen branches. Fertilize each spring to stimulate strong growth.

Propagate from seeds and from root cuttings. Seeds may not always produce "true" plants. Division is not recommended because of the long taproot.

Uses. Eryngo flowers are long-lasting when used in fresh arrangements; they can also be used dried. The seed heads of eryngo add interest to wreaths and other dried arrangements.

Harvesting and preparing. Since flowers on the same stalk bloom and fade at different times, pick individual flower heads before they open completely. Hang or wire the stems and stand them upright to dry. Allow the seed heads to dry naturally on the plant.

◼

Eryngo see *Eryngium*

◼

Eucalyptus (yew-ka-LIP-tus)
Eucalyptus, gum tree

Large genus of fast-growing, shallow-rooted evergreen trees and shrubs. Leaves are usually alternate, without marginal teeth, and are often variable on the same plant. Flowers are white, yellow or red, and may be solitary or appear in umbels. Fruit is a top-shaped capsule that varies in size depending on the species. Zones 8-10.

Selected species and varieties. *E. globulus,* blue gum, can reach 200 feet tall with a smooth, bluish white bark that peels off in fall. Aromatic leaves are alternate and sickle-shaped or lanceolate. The leaves on young plants are glaucous white; on mature plants they are lustrous dark green. Flowers are solitary but insignificant. Fruit is top-shaped and 1¼ inches wide. Zones 9 and 10. *E. polyanthemos,* silver dollar gum, redbox, grows 50 to 60 feet tall and has low branches. It often sheds bark. Juvenile trees have opposite, orbicular, glaucous leaves that are almost silvery with light reddish margins and veins; mature trees have lance-shaped leaves. Flowers bloom in umbels of six to eight blossoms. Fruits are ½ inch wide.

Growing conditions. Eucalyptus does well in a sunny location with well-drained, ordinary soil. It tolerates drought, heat and flooding.

Uses. Eucalyptus branches may be used fresh or dried to add height and motion to line arrangements.

Harvesting and preparing. To use fresh, hammer and sear the stem ends of immature branches that bear fruit before conditioning normally. Preserve branches in a glycerine solution; they will turn gray-brown, but will remain flexible. Branches may also be air-dried, but they will become brittle.

Euonymus (yew-ON-i-mus)
Spindle tree

Large genus of deciduous and evergreen trees, shrubs and vines with opposite, stalked and mostly smooth leaves. Flowers are small and inconspicuous, green, white or yellow, appear in cymes in the leaf axil, and bloom in spring or summer. Fruits are pink-, crimson-, scarlet- or orange-lobed capsules that appear from midsummer to fall. Zones 3-10.

Selected species and varieties. *E. alatus* 'Compactus', dwarf winged euonymus, burning bush, grows 6 to 10 feet tall and wide. It is densely branched and has small corky ridges or wings running the length of the branches. Dark green 1- to 3-inch leaves turn brilliant red in the fall, and small orange fruits appear. *E. americana,* strawberry bush, wahoo, grows 4 to 6 feet tall. Leaves are 1 to 3 inches long and turn red in the fall. Flowers are greenish purple, ⅓ inch across and insignificant. Fruit is pink to scarlet and splits open in the fall to reveal orange seeds. Zones 6-9. *E. atropurpurea,* eastern wahoo, burning bush, is a deciduous shrub or small tree that reaches 24 feet tall. Leaves are 5 inches long, elliptical, finely serrated and turn pale yellow to red in the fall. Fruit is crimson, four-lobed and ⅝ inch across. The fruit and all other parts of the shrub are poisonous. Zones 4-9.

Growing conditions. Spindle tree grows well near the sea, in sun or partial shade, and in ordinary soil. Propagate spindle tree from stratified seeds sown in the spring or from softwood cuttings.

Uses. The showy color of the leaves and berries in autumn makes strawberry bush and burning bush useful in fresh or dried seasonal arrangements. Autumn leaves retain good color when pressed, and can be used in pressed flower and foliage designs.

Harvesting and preparing. To use fresh, hammer the ends of branches before conditioning normally. Preserve branches by placing the stem ends in a glycerine solution.

Eupatorium
(yew-pa-TOR-ee-um)
Boneset

Genus of perennials and shrubs with opposite leaves that are sometimes whorled or alternate. Tubular flowers are purple to rose or white, and they occur in flat-topped clusters. Zones 2-9.

Selected species and varieties. *E. maculatum,* Joe-Pye weed, smokeweed, is 6 feet tall with whorled, coarse, 10- to 12-inch-long leaves. Flowers are fragrant and purple. Joe-Pye weed blooms from July to October. Zones 3-9. *E. perfoliatum,* thoroughwort, is 5 feet tall with 8-inch, opposite, lanceolate leaves. Flowers are white and bloom from midsummer to fall. Zones 3-10.

Growing conditions. Joe-Pye weed and thoroughwort grow in ordinary, moist soil that is slightly alkaline. Propagate by division in the spring or fall, or from seeds or cuttings.

Uses. The long stems, color and fragrance of Joe-Pye weed and thoroughwort make them especially appropriate in tall fresh arrangements. When dried, the flowers retain their color, scent and shape, and may be used in mixed dried bouquets or wreaths. The iridescent, starry calyx can also be used in wreaths or other dried arrangements.

Harvesting and preparing. To use the flowers dried, pick before the center flower in each cluster opens up, remove the leaves and hang to dry. Pick the calyx once the center feathers fall out, and hang to air-dry.

EUONYMUS ALATUS 'COMPACTUS'

EUPATORIUM PERFOLIATUM

EUSTOMA GRANDIFLORUM

FAGUS GRANDIFOLIA

FORSYTHIA × INTERMEDIA 'SPECTABILIS'

Eustoma (yew-STO-ma)
Bluebells, prairie gentian

Genus of annuals, biennials or short-lived perennials with rosettes of basal foliage and stem leaves that are undivided, toothless, stemless and often stem-clasping. Flowers are bell-shaped, white or blue, solitary or in clusters, and bloom in spring or early summer.

Selected species and varieties. *E. grandiflorum,* lisianthus, Texan bluebell, is a 2- to 3-foot-tall annual. Leaves are opposite and oblong. Flowers are 2 to 3 inches wide, pale purple with dark purple spotting at their bases, and form in branched clusters. Available cultivars have pink, white or lavender-colored flowers; some are dwarf varieties. Blooms occur in summer.

Growing conditions. Grow lisianthus in full sun to partial shade in neutral or slightly alkaline, moist, well-drained soil. Propagate from seeds sown indoors early and transplanted outdoors after the last frost. Lisianthus is sometimes treated as a biennial; well-established seedlings can be wintered in a cold frame. Space plants 6 to 8 inches apart.

Uses. Lisianthus is a showy, long-lasting flower that may be used in a mixed low or horizontal fresh arrangement. Individual flowers may be used in taller dried arrangements if their stems have been wired; they are also appropriate in wreaths.

Harvesting and preparing. Dry individual flowers in silica gel or in a microwave oven.

—

Fagus (FAY-gus)
Beech

Genus of tall, spreading, deciduous trees with smooth, light gray bark and alternate, toothed leaves. Male flowers have heads that are round and drooping. Female flowers occur in spikes, sometimes below the male flowers. Fruits are triangular nuts enclosed in a prickly rosette of bracts. Zones 3-9.

Selected species and varieties. *F. grandifolia,* American beech, grows to a height of 90 feet and can spread 60 feet in width. Leaves are ovate to oblong, smooth, hairless, 5 inches long with nine to 15 pairs of veins. Leaves turn yellow in fall. Zones 4-9.

Growing conditions. American beech grows well in full sun, moist, loamy limestone soil and lots of space.

Uses. The gray-branched foliage may be used fresh or dried in a large, contemporary, summer or autumn arrangement. Beechnuts may be used in cone wreaths or in other dried arrangements.

Harvesting and preparing. To use the branches fresh, hammer the ends before conditioning normally. Preserve branches in a glycerine solution during July and August; they will turn a deep green and then a deep brown. Remove when they reach the desired shade. Dry branches of autumn leaves in a container with a small amount of water. Gather the beechnuts in the fall and wire them.

—

False goatsbeard see *Astilbe*

False indigo see *Baptisia*

False saffron see *Carthamus*

False sunflower see *Heliopsis*

Farewell-to-spring see *Clarkia*

Fennel flower see *Nigella*

Feverfew see *Chrysanthemum*

Fever twig see *Celastrus*

Field marigold see *Calendula*

Flag see *Iris*

Flamingo flower see *Anthurium*

Flax see *Linum*

Fleur-de-lis see *Iris*

Flossflower see *Ageratum*

Flowering dogwood see *Cornus*

—

Forsythia (for-SITH-ee-a)

Erect or spreading deciduous shrub having opposite leaves that are simple or three-parted and stalked. Showy yellow flowers occur in clusters of one to six in the leaf axil. The flower is a four-lobed calyx with the corolla below and split into four strap-shaped lobes that resemble four separate petals. Flowers bloom in spring before or with unfolding leaves. Fruit is a woody cap with winged seeds. Zones 3-9.

Selected species and varieties.
F. × intermedia, border forsythia, grows up to 10 feet tall and has stiff, upright branches that arch slightly. Leaves are 5 inches long, oblong or ovate, sometimes three-parted and usually toothed. Flowers are 1½ inches long and vary in shades of yellow from pale to greenish to deep. They bloom in spring on bare branches before the leaves emerge. 'Spectabilis' has bright yellow flowers. Zones 5-9.

Growing conditions. Plant forsythia in full sun and deep, fertile soil. It tolerates transplanting and urban conditions. Prune after flowering to thin out crowded older branches. Blooming occurs on the previous year's growth. Propagate by division and from hardwood or softwood cuttings.

Uses. Use the fresh, arching branches in low or tall arrangements to provide color and movement. Individual flowers can be used in pressed designs.

Harvesting and preparing. To force branches to bloom, cut in early January, hammer the stem ends and condition normally. Flowers should open five weeks later. Or, wait until plants blossom on their own and then cut and condition the branches in the same fashion.

—

Fountain grass see *Pennisetum*
Fountain plant see *Amaranthus*
Foxglove see *Digitalis*
Foxtail grass see *Hordeum*

—

Freesia (FREE-zha)

Tender perennials from bulblike corms with sword-shaped leaves that are usually narrow and basal. Flowers are fragrant, white or yellow, funnel-shaped or tubular and occur in terminal spikelike racemes, usually at right angles to the stem. Zones 9 and 10.

Selected species and varieties. *F. × hybrida* is a group of horticultural hybrids from 1½ to 2 feet tall. Flowers are 2 inches long, white or yellow, and veined with pink, purple, blue, orange or brown. Blooming time varies.

Growing conditions. Plant freesia in a sunny location in rich, well-drained soil. It may be planted in tubs. Freesia corms do not need a period of low temperature before starting to grow. Space plants 8 inches apart. Stake weak-stemmed plants. Blooms appear 10 to 12 weeks after planting. When leaves begin to die, shake out corms and store in a cool, slightly moist, dark place until the next growing season. Propagate from offsets and seeds.

Uses. Freesias make long-lasting cut flowers that may be grouped by themselves to form simple, striking bouquets. Individual flowers may be used in dried arrangements, pressed designs or in potpourris.

Harvesting and preparing. Cut the flowers but not the foliage to allow the corms to continue growing before lifting and storing them for the next year. Dry individual flower heads in silica gel or in a microwave oven, and glue them back onto the stems. Press flowers open or flat, or air-dry them for use in a potpourri by standing them upright.

—

French marigold see *Tagetes*

—

Gaillardia (gay-LAR-dee-a)
Blanketflower

Genus of leafy, erect annuals, biennials and perennials with basal leaves and alternate stem leaves. Flower heads are showy with purple disk flowers surrounded by ray flowers that are yellow, orange, orange-red or white and are fringed. Flowers bloom from June to the first frost. Zones 3-10.

Selected species and varieties. *G. × grandiflora* is a perennial that ranges from 6 to 36 inches tall. Flowers are 3 to 4 inches across and are red and yellow. A wide selection of colors is available. 'Baby Cole' grows 6 to 8 inches tall and has yellow ray flowers with red bands. 'Dazzler' is colored the same, but it grows to a height of 24 inches. 'Burgundy' grows to 24 inches tall and has wine red flowers. 'Goblin' grows to 1 foot tall and has red and yellow bicolored flowers. 'Golden Goblin' grows to 15 inches tall and has yellow ray flowers.

FREESIA × HYBRIDA

GAILLARDIA × GRANDIFLORA 'GOBLIN'

GALAX URCEOLATA

GERBERA JAMESONII

GLADIOLUS × HORTULANUS

Growing conditions. Blanketflower is drought-resistant and prefers full sun and well-drained soil. Propagate from seeds or from cuttings in August or September and by division in spring. Where winters are mild, sow seed outdoors in fall; elsewhere, start seed indoors six weeks before the last frost. Seedlings can be set out after danger of frost is past. *G. × grandiflora* will flower the first year from seeds.

Uses. Blanketflowers are long-lasting and colorful, and may be used as mass flowers in informal fresh arrangements. They may also be dried and used in wreaths or other mixed arrangements.

Harvesting and preparing. Dry blanketflowers in silica gel or in a microwave oven.

—

Galax (GAY-laks)

An evergreen perennial that grows from scaly rhizomes with a basal tuft of simple, long-stalked, round or broadly ovate leaves. Small white flowers bloom in a spikelike raceme from late spring through early summer. Zones 5-8.

Selected species and varieties. *G. urceolata,* galaxy, wandflower, wand plant, has scallop-toothed, glossy leaves that turn purple or bronze in the fall.

Growing conditions. Grow galax in full to partial shade in moist, slightly acid soil. Propagate by division in spring or fall or from seeds sown in fall or late winter. In areas with a cold climate, use a cold frame to start seeds.

Uses. Galax makes a long-lasting cut flower, and may be used to lend a woodsy accent to an informal arrangement. It can also be used as a focal point, at the base of an arrangement, or allowed to spill over the container rim. The leaves can be used in either fresh or dried arrangements, and they may be skeletonized.

Harvesting and preparing. Preserve leaves in a glycerine solution.

—

Galaxy see *Galax*

Garden sorrel see *Rumex*

Garden wolfsbane see *Aconitum*

Garlic see *Allium*

Gas plant see *Dictamnus*

Gay-feather see *Liatris*

—

Gerbera (jer-BEER-a)

A tender perennial having a basal rosette of divided leaves that are usually hairy underneath, and a solitary, daisylike flower that blooms from spring through autumn at the top of a stout leafless stalk. Zones 9 and 10.

Selected species and varieties. *G. jamesonii,* Transvaal daisy, gerbera daisy, grows 1½ feet tall and has 10-inch leaves and 4-inch orange-red flower heads. 'California Mix' reaches 2 feet tall and has ray flowers in yellow, orange, white, scarlet, crimson or pink with pale centers.

Growing conditions. Grow Transvaal daisies in full sun in porous, fertile and well-drained soil; give plants lots of space, and apply mulch. Propagate from seeds or from stem cuttings. In cold areas, sow seeds indoors in January and set the plants outside after frost danger is past.

Uses. Transvaal daisies make colorful, dramatic mass flowers, and may be used in fresh arrangements. When dried, they can be arranged in containers and in flower wreaths.

Harvesting and preparing. To use fresh, wire the stems to prevent the flower heads from drooping or from turning toward strong sunlight. To dry, wire the stems and place the flowers in silica gel or in a microwave oven.

—

Giant reed see *Arundo*

Gillyflower see *Matthiola*

—

Gladiolus (gla-dee-O-lus)
Gladiolus, sword lily, corn lily

Large genus of corm-grown plants with long, narrow leaves. Flowers are showy, stalkless, funnel-shaped and bloom from the base to the top on a terminal spike in summer and early fall. Zones 5-10.

Selected species and varieties. *G.* × *hortulanus,* garden gladiolus, grows to 3 feet or more with 12-inch sword-shaped leaves. The many varieties of this hybrid have 3- to 4-inch flowers in many colors. Zones 8-10.

Growing conditions. Grow gladioli in full sun in well-drained, neutral to slightly acid soil. Plant every two weeks from early May to mid-July for bloom over several months. Stake the plants. Propagate from cormlets found in the fall at the base of the old corm or from seeds. Store corms in a cool, dry room over winter. Plant corms 4 inches apart.

Uses. Gladiolus flowers are showy and long-lasting, and because of their long stems, they are especially appropriate in tall or vertical arrangements. Individual flowers can also be used in wreaths and other dried arrangements.

Harvesting and preparing. To use fresh, cut the flower spike between the third and fourth leaves once the first flower shows its color; the plant needs the lowest leaves to continue growing and producing flowers. Dry individual flowers in silica gel or in a microwave oven.

—

Globe amaranth see *Gomphrena*

Globe thistle see *Echinops*

Godetia see *Clarkia*

Golden buttons see *Tanacetum*

Golden marguerite see *Anthemis*

Golden rain tree see *Koelreuteria*

Goldenrod see *Solidago*

—

Gomphrena (gom-FREE-na)
Globe amaranth

Genus of annual or perennial, erect or prostrate, hairy everlasting plants. Leaves are opposite, oblong or elliptical. Flowers occur in dense, papery flower heads.

Selected species and varieties. *G. globosa* is an erect, branching and somewhat stiff annual that grows 8 to 20 inches tall. The flower heads are 1 inch across and red, pink, white or orange, without petals, and not as crispy as most everlastings.

Growing conditions. Globe amaranth thrives in hot weather, full sun and fertile soil that does not dry out excessively. Water during dry spells. The plant will tolerate early frost. Propagate from seeds sown indoors in March, or outdoors in full sun after danger of frost is past. Space plants 1 foot apart.

Uses. Globe amaranth makes a good filler in a fresh arrangement. When dried, it retains much of its color and can be used in a dried bouquet, nosegay or wreath.

Harvesting and preparing. Air-dry the entire plant by hanging, or cut individual flowers, wire their stems and stand them upright to dry.

—

Gramma see *Bouteloua*

Groundsel bush see *Baccharis*

Gumbo see *Abelmoschus*

Gum tree see *Eucalyptus*

—

Gypsophila (jip-SOF-i-la)

Genus of annuals, biennials and perennials with small, opposite, bluish leaves and slightly swollen stem joints. Profuse, small, white to pink flowers borne on many branches give the plant a light, frothy appearance. Zones 3-9.

Selected species and varieties. *G. pacifica,* baby's breath, is a 3-foot-tall perennial with fleshy, ovate to oblong leaves and double rose or purple flowers. *G. paniculata* has glaucous, glabrous and lanceolate leaves. Flowers are loose panicles in white or pink to red. 'Bristol Fairy' grows 4 feet tall. Pure white double flowers bloom in June and July.

Growing conditions. Baby's breath grows well in sun and slightly alkaline, well-drained soil. Transplanting is not advised because of the deep taproot. Stake plants when they reach 18 inches tall. Propagate from cuttings in midsummer. Space plants 3 to 4 feet apart.

Uses. Baby's breath flowers make dainty, mistlike filler in both fresh and dried arrangements. They can also be used in bouquets or nosegays, or in pressed flower designs.

GOMPHRENA GLOBOSA

GYPSOPHILA PANICULATA

HELIANTHUS × MULTIFLORUS

HELICHRYSUM BRACTEATUM

HELIOPSIS HELIANTHOIDES SCABRA

Harvesting and preparing. To use baby's breath flowers dried, pick at midday, when most of the flowers are open, and hang in bundles. For greater flexibility, preserve in a glycerine solution.

—

Hare's tail grass see *Lagurus*

Heartsease see *Viola*

Heather see *Calluna*

—

Helianthus (hel-ee-AN-thus)
Sunflower

Genus of coarse annuals and perennials with usually alternate or opposite leaves having mostly toothed margins. Flower heads range from 3 to 12 inches wide with ray flowers that are usually yellow, but may be orange, white or mahogany, and tubular disk flowers that are yellow, brown or purple. Zones 2-9.

Selected species and varieties. *H. × multiflorus* is a 4- to 6-foot-tall perennial with alternate, ovate 10-inch long leaves. Flower heads are 3½ to 5 inches across and may be single or double. Flowers bloom from July to September. Zones 4-9.

Growing conditions. Sunflower prefers sun and ordinary soil that is moist but well drained. It tolerates dry conditions but does best with regular watering. Stake plants. Cut off faded flower heads, except when you want seeds to form. Every second year, dig up, divide and replant in newly spaded and fertilized ground. Propagate by division in spring or from seeds. Perennials started from seed usually bloom the second year. Space plants 2 feet apart.

Uses. Because of their long stems, sunflowers make good mass flowers in tall fresh or dried arrangements. They can also be used dried in flower wreaths.

Harvesting and preparing. Dry the flower in silica gel or in a microwave oven.

—

Helichrysum (hel-i-KRY-sum)
Strawflower

Genus of everlasting annuals, perennials and shrubs with mostly alternate, entire, downy leaves. Flower heads may be solitary or clustered, have disk flowers surrounded by large, colorful bracts and bloom from midsummer through the first frost.

Selected species and varieties. *H. bracteatum* is an annual, 3 feet tall, stout-stemmed and branched with oblong to lanceolate 2- to 5-inch leaves. Flower heads are 1 to 2½ inches across; bracts are bright yellow, orange, crimson or white with green at their bases.

Growing conditions. Strawflower grows well in sun, warm weather and fertile, well-drained soil. Water during dry periods. Weed and fertilize every two weeks in summer to ensure consistent bloom quality. Propagate from seeds sown indoors in March or outdoors in May after frost.

Uses. The color and different-sized blossoms of strawflowers add interest to both fresh and dried arrangements. Use strawflowers as filler in large arrangements and as mass flowers in small arrangements. Tiny bud flowers can be used in nosegays and miniature dried arrangements.

Harvesting and preparing. To air-dry, cut the flowers before they are fully open or when the first row of colored bracts shows; wire the stems and stand them in a container. After the first light frost, cut entire plants, remove their foliage and hang to air-dry.

—

Heliopsis (hel-ee-OP-sis)

Genus of coarse perennials and annuals with long stems and opposite, simple, often three-veined leaves. Flower heads are showy; they appear on branches and consist of long yellow ray flowers and yellow, brown, purple or red disk flowers. Zones 3-9.

Selected species and varieties. *H. helianthoides,* false sunflower, is a 5-foot-tall perennial. Leaves are lanceolate to oblong. Flowers heads are 2½ inches across with 10 to 20 notched, yellow ray flowers and brown disk flowers. *H. helianthoides scabra,* rough heliopsis, has orange-yellow double or semidouble flowers, rough-textured leaves and grows up to 5 feet tall. 'Summer Sun' grows 4 feet tall with semidouble, golden yellow, 3-inch flowers that bloom from June to September.

Growing conditions. False sunflower requires full sun and fertile, well-drained soil for best growth and many blooms. The plant will tolerate shade and poor, dry soil, but grows best when watered during dry periods. Stake if necessary. Every three to four years, divide and replant in compost-enriched and newly spaded soil. Space 2 feet apart. Propagate by division in early summer. Plants raised from seed tend to revert to wild form.

Uses. False sunflower's color and long stem make it appropriate as a mass flower in a tall fresh or dried arrangement. False sunflower can also be used in a wreath.

Harvesting and preparing. Dry false sunflower in silica gel or in a microwave oven.

Heliotrope see *Heliotropium*

Heliotropium
(hel-ee-o-TRO-pee-um)
Heliotrope

Genus of hairy perennials and shrubs with simple, alternate leaves. Flowers occur in terminal umbels of blue, purple, pink or white, and bloom from May to September.

Selected species and varieties. *H. arborescens* is a 4-foot-tall tender perennial with 1- to 3-inch leaves that is treated as an annual. Flowers are vanilla-scented, ¼ inch long, violet, purple or white, and bloom in flat clusters.

Growing conditions. Grow heliotrope in morning sun and afternoon shade in a rich, moist soil. Propagate from seeds, from cuttings or by layering. Sow seeds indoors and transplant seedlings outdoors when danger of frost is over. Take cuttings in the fall, grow indoors over the winter, transplant outdoors after danger of frost is past. Space plants 1 to 2½ feet apart.

Uses. Heliotropes last well, and make good filler in a variety of fresh or dried arrangements. They can be used young, when the leaves are light green, or when they are mature and gray. The leaves, and parts of the flower clusters, can be used in pressed designs.

Harvesting and preparing. Dry the flower clusters in silica gel or in a microwave oven. Press parts of the flower cluster.

Helmet flower see *Aconitum*

Heuchera (HEW-ker-a)
Alumroot

A perennial with long-stalked rounded or lobed leaves that are usually basal. Flowers are bell- or saucer-shaped in a narrow panicle on a stalk, often leafy, that originates in the rootstock. Each flower has a five-lobed calyx that provides most of the color. Blooms occur through most of the summer. Zones 3-9.

Selected species and varieties. *H. sanguinea,* coral bells, grows 2 feet tall with ½-inch bright red flowers. The petals are shorter than the calyx lobes. Blooming starts in late May and continues through the summer. 'Alba' is similar, but has white flowers. 'Splendens' is also similar, but has dark crimson flowers.

Growing conditions. Coral bells thrive in an open, sunny location and rich, moist, well-drained soil. They tolerate some shade. Water during dry spells. In the north, a light winter mulch will help these shallow-rooted plants from being forced from the ground. Divide every three years for good growth and bloom. Propagate by dividing clumps in spring or fall, or by sowing seeds in spring. Plants bloom the following spring. Young plants and newly divided plants should be set out with their crowns about 1 inch deep and spaced 10 inches to 12 inches apart.

Uses. Coral bells last well and add a graceful touch to small fresh arrangements. They can be grouped and used as filler in centerpieces. Coral bells can also be used dried, and though the bell-shaped blooms are flattened when pressed, they will add an interesting shape to pressed designs.

Harvesting and preparing. Preserve coral bells with a drying agent, or press them.

HELIOTROPIUM ARBORESCENS

HEUCHERA SANGUINEA

HORDEUM JUBATUM

HOSTA UNDULATA

HUMULUS LUPULUS

Higan cherry see *Prunus*

Holly fern see *Polystichum*

Hollyhock see *Alcea*

Honesty see *Lunaria*

Hop see *Humulus*

Hordeum (HOR-dee-um)
Barley

Genus of annual, biennial and perennial grasses with flat leaf blades and dense, bristly spikes. Spikelets occur in threes, only one of which generally flowers. Often only the central spikelet is fertile.

Selected species and varieties. *H. jubatum,* foxtail grass, squirreltail grass, grows 1½ to 2 feet tall. It is a tufted biennial or perennial usually grown as an annual. Leaves are narrow and rough. Flower spikes are graceful, green or brown, and 2 to 4 inches long with bristles spreading 1 to 3 inches long.

Growing conditions. Foxtail grass grows well in coastal areas in full sun and ordinary, well-drained soil. Propagate foxtail grass in early spring from seeds sown where plants are to grow. Thin seedlings to 1 foot apart.

Uses. Foxtail grass spikes add texture and motion to tall fresh or dried arrangements. They may be used as filler in mixed bouquets.

Harvesting and preparing. To air-dry, cut the stalks before the buds mature and hang them upside down, or stand them upright in an empty container.

Horehound see *Marrubium*

Horsemint see *Monarda*

Hosta (HOS-ta)
Plantain lily

A clumping perennial with basal leaves that grow 1 foot or more in length. Some leaves are as wide as 1 foot; others are smaller, delicately twisted or variegated. White or blue to purple, lilylike flowers rise on several terminal spikes; they usually grow taller than the foliage and are followed by seed heads. Zones 3-10.

Selected species and varieties. *H. plantaginea,* fragrant plantain lily, has leaves 6 to 10 inches long and 4 to 6 inches wide. The flowers are pure white and scented, tilted upward and 4 to 5 inches long on 1½- to 2½-foot leafless stalks. Flowering occurs in late summer and early fall. *H. undulata,* wavyleaf plantain lily, is 3 feet tall with variegated leaves that are 6 inches long and elliptical to egg-shaped. Flowers are lavender-colored, 2 inches long and bloom in midsummer. Zones 4-10. *H. ventricosa,* blue plantain lily, reaches 3 feet tall. Leaves are 9 inches long and 5 inches wide. Flowers are lilac-colored or blue striped with purple, and 2 inches long. They widen abruptly into a bell-like shape in the upper half of the flower.

Growing conditions. Plantain lily grows best in full or partial shade, but will tolerate sun. Soil should be fertile and moist in summer. Water during dry spells. At planting add peat moss and compost. Space plants 1 to 2 feet apart, or closer to mass the plants. Propagate by dividing clumps in spring or fall or from seeds. Plantain lily often self-sows.

Uses. The cut flowers can be used in tall fresh arrangements, and the leaves can be used to add texture to centerpieces. Seed heads, with their clusters of jet black seeds, can be used alone or in mixed dried fall arrangements.

Harvesting and preparing. To use fresh young leaves, sear the stem ends and then submerge the leaves in cold water overnight. To use the seed heads, pick them when they are well formed but unopened, and stand upright in a small amount of warm water, preferably in a warm room. The seed heads will burst and display their seeds.

Humulus (HEW-mew-lus)
Hop

Rough-stemmed, tall-twining annual or perennial with opposite, more or less lobed leaves, and green male and female flowers on separate plants. Female flowers occur in pairs beneath a large bract and form the ¼- to 2½-inch-long conelike hop. Male flowers occur in loose panicles. Zones 3-9.

Selected species and varieties. *H. lupulus,* common hop, is a 25-foot-long perennial vine with bristly stems and heart-shaped, three-lobed leaves.

Growing conditions. Grow hop in full sun and moist soil. Propagate plants from cuttings of underground stems.

Uses. The flowers provide a graceful, curving line in large fresh arrangements. Dried green and gold sprays of seed heads add movement to dried arrangements. The cones may be used in wreaths or garlands.

Harvesting and preparing. Use gloves when handling the prickly stems and leaves. Air-dry both the flowers and the seed heads; cluster and then wire the cones.

—

Hydrangea (hy-DRAN-jee-a)

Genus of erect or climbing, deciduous or evergreen shrubs and woody vines. Leaves are opposite, stalked and usually toothed. The small individual flowers are white, blue, pink or lavender and occur in dense clusters that may be flat-topped, globular or pyramidal. Flowers bloom in summer. Zones 4-10.

Selected species and varieties. *H. macrophylla,* bigleaf hydrangea, is a 6-foot shrub. Leaves are 3 to 9 inches long, broadly oval, shortly tapering at the tip, coarsely toothed, shiny green above and lighter underneath. Six- to 10-inch globular clusters of blue or pink flowers bloom in July or August. Zones 7-10. *H. paniculata* is an 8- to 30-foot treelike shrub. Leaves are elliptical, rounded or wedge-shaped at the base, and 3 to 6 inches long. Flower clusters are 8 to 12 inches long and white, later changing to pink, green, purple and finally brown. Blooming occurs in late summer. 'Grandiflora', peegee hydrangea, has showy pyramidal clusters of mostly sterile white flowers. Flowers bloom in late summer and remain on the plant for many months.

Growing conditions. Grow hydrangea in full sun or partial shade in rich, moist, well-drained soil. Water during dry periods. Mulch with compost, wood chips or peat moss to retain moisture. Bigleaf hydrangea produces blue flowers in an acid soil and pink flowers in an alkaline soil. Prune in late winter or spring to remove weak, crowded shoots and cut the plant 1 to 3 inches above the base. Propagate from softwood cuttings in summer.

Uses. Hydrangeas can be used as mass flowers in large fresh arrangements. Dried, the flowers may be used whole, or separated and wired for use in wreaths and other dried arrangements. Individual florets may be used in pressed designs.

Harvesting and preparing. To use fresh, allow the fully opened blossoms to remain on the plant for one week before cutting. Once cut, sear the stem ends and then condition normally. To retain some color in drying the flowers, cut blossoms as the petals start to feel papery, and place the stems in a small amount of water. For satiny brown flower heads, cut the stems with some leaves intact and place in a glycerine solution. For cream- or golden-brown-colored blossoms, allow flower heads to dry naturally on the plant. For flat designs, press individual florets at different stages of color.

—

Iceland poppy see *Papaver*
Immortelle see *Xeranthemum*
Indian pink see *Lobelia*

—

Iris (I-ris)
Iris, flag, fleur-de-lis

Genus of rhizomatous or bulbous perennials with leaves that are mostly basal. They are linear to sword-shaped. Flowers are many-colored, showy, branched or unbranched, and occur in six segments: three outer ones called falls, which are reflexed, and three inner ones called standards, which are usually smaller and erect. Blooms appear in spring and early summer and are followed by large, three-celled seedpods. Zones 3-10.

Selected species and varieties. *I. × germanica,* German iris, grows 2½ feet tall with sword-shaped leaves. It is a natural hybrid. Flower falls are purple with brown veins, white bases and yellow beards.

HYDRANGEA MACROPHYLLA

IRIS SIBIRICA

ISATIS TINCTORIA

KALMIA LATIFOLIA

Variation in flower color is common. Flowers are fragrant and bloom in May and June. One variety of this species, *I.* × *germanica florentina,* is the source of orris, the rhizome that is dried, powdered, and used in perfume and potpourri. Zones 4-10. *I. sibirica,* Siberian iris, grows 2 feet tall and has hollow stems with linear leaves. Flowers are beardless, blue-purple, lavender and, rarely, white in terminal heads of two to five blossoms. Blooming occurs in June. Zones 3-10. 'Alba' has white flowers. *I. xiphium* hybrids, Dutch irises, grow 2 feet tall and have almost cylindrical 2-foot-long leaves. Flowers are 4 inches long with fiddle-shaped falls and large, erect standards, and are white, blue, purple, plum, orange, yellow-brown or bicolored. Blooming occurs in late spring. Zones 7-10.

Growing conditions. Bearded iris grows in full sun to light shade. It adapts to almost any soil, so long as it is well drained, but does best in neutral soil. When planting, add well-rotted manure, humus, leaf mold or peat moss. Dig up, divide and replant every three or four years. In northern regions, divide a few weeks after plants have bloomed and cut the foliage by one-half to two-thirds; in southern regions, wait until late August or early September. Set in a group 8 to 9 inches apart. Propagate from divided rhizomes. Siberian iris grows in full sun and in moderately moist, neutral to slightly acid soil. Water during dry periods. Propagate Siberian iris by division in early spring or fall. Space 2 feet apart. Dutch irises grow in full sun to partial shade, and in cool, moist, acid soil. Propagate by separating offsets —the small bulbs that form at the base of the mother bulb—and when planting, space 3 to 6 inches apart.

Uses. The elegant form of iris makes it appropriate as a focal or line flower in a fresh spring arrangement. The seed head provides a warm brown color to a mixed dried arrangement or a cone wreath.

Harvesting and preparing. Submerge iris leaves in water before using them to make them last longer. To use the seed heads, allow some blossoms to remain on the plant; pick the seed heads as they start to shed and air-dry by laying the stalks on their sides.

Isatis (I-sa-tis)
Woad

Genus of erect, branching, hairy to hairless annuals, biennials and perennials with simple leaves. Flowers are yellow, ¼ inch across and bractless, and bloom in loose, branching clusters. The fruit is a flat, black, drooping, paddle-shaped, one-sided pod that is ½ inch to 1 inch long. Flowers bloom in late spring or early summer. Zones 7-9.

Selected species and varieties. *I. glauca* is a 3-foot perennial with oblong, grayish 10-inch leaves and mustard yellow flowers. *I. tinctoria,* dyer's woad, asp of Jerusalem, is a 3-foot biennial with leaves that are oblong to lanceolate, entire or toothed, and 4 inches long. Before synthetic dyes were developed, blue dye was extracted from the leaves.

Growing conditions. Woad grows in a sunny site with reasonably fertile, well-drained soil. Propagate the biennial from seeds sown in summer for bloom the following year. Propagate the perennial by division.

Uses. Dyer's woad flowers provide a mustard yellow color to fresh arrangements; they can be used as accents in small arrangements, and as filler in larger arrangements. Sprays of black seed heads can provide accent and contrast in dried arrangements.

Harvesting and preparing. Air-dry the seed heads by standing them upright in a container.

—

Japanese fleece-flower
see *Polygonum*

Japanese lantern see *Physalis*

Japanese rose see *Rosa*

Japanese yew see *Podocarpus*

Joe-Pye weed see *Eupatorium*

Johnny-jump-up see *Viola*

Joseph's coat see *Amaranthus*

—

Kalmia (KAL-mee-a)
Laurel

An evergreen or rarely deciduous shrub with entire, opposite, alternate or whorled leaves. Flowers are purple, pink or white, cup- or saucer-shaped, five-lobed and have 10 bowlike, slender stamens that spring up and release pollen when touched or disturbed. Zones 4-9.

Selected species and varieties. *K. latifolia,* mountain laurel, calico bush, is a 7- to 15-foot-tall, round-topped shrub. Leaves are shiny, leathery and 2 to 4 inches long. Flowers are rose to white, ¾ inch across and bloom in 4- to 6-inch-wide terminal clusters in late spring to early summer.

Growing conditions. Mountain laurel likes a shady location in a moist, peaty or sandy, acid soil. It will tolerate a dry, exposed area if given a permanent mulch of oak or beech leaves. Water during dry periods. Transplant in early spring, late summer or early fall. A straggly plant can be pruned back to 1 to 2 feet from the ground.

Uses. Mountain laurel makes a long-lasting mass flower in a fresh arrangement. When preserved, the leaves turn gold and then brown, and can be used in dried arrangements such as wreaths and garlands.

Harvesting and preparing. Pick branches of shiny leaves and place them in a glycerine solution; remove when leaves reach the desired color.

Kangaroo thorn see *Acacia*

Koelreuteria
(kol-roo-TEER-ee-a)
Golden rain tree

A deciduous, deep-rooted, round-headed tree with alternate, compound leaves and feathery leaflets with an odd leaflet at the end. Flowers are small, five-lobed, fragrant and yellow, and bloom in large, pyramidal terminal panicles. Fruit is a bladderlike, three-valved capsule. Zones 5-10.

Selected species and varieties. *K. paniculata* reaches 40 feet tall with 9- to 18-inch leaves, seven to 15 oval to oblong, coarsely toothed leaflets that are sometimes deeply cut at the base. Flowers are ½ inch wide and bloom in 12- to 15-inch-long clusters in June and July. Fruit is a papery, nodding, pale green pod that turns pinkish tan, then light brown in fall and winter.

Growing conditions. Mature golden rain trees will withstand drought. They grow well in open sunshine and an ordinary soil that is acid to slightly alkaline. Stake and prune young trees. Older trees will self-sow.

Uses. Golden rain tree branches with flowers provide color and line in fresh arrangements. The papery seedpods may be used in wreaths and in other dried arrangements.

Harvesting and preparing. Air-dry seedpods at different stages of development for a variety of colors.

Ladder fern see *Nephrolepis*
Ladies' cushion see *Armeria*
Lady's-finger see *Abelmoschus*
Lady's mantle see *Alchemilla*

Lagurus (la-GEW-rus)

Hardy annual grass reaching 1 foot tall with soft-haired leaves. Flower spikelets are 2 inches long, oblong-shaped, dense and woolly.

Selected species and varieties. *L. ovatus,* hare's tail grass, is the only species. Flower spikelets are egg-shaped and off-white.

Growing conditions. Grow hare's tail grass in full sun. It grows best in warm weather. Propagate from seed sown indoors (three to five seeds per pot) eight weeks before the last frost date, or sow seeds outdoors in the spring where they are to bloom about three weeks before the last frost date. In mild climates, sow seed in late summer or fall. Thin seedlings to 1 foot apart.

Uses. Hare's tail grass can be used in a fresh or dried arrangement to add texture, form and motion. Both flowers and seed heads can be used dried in wreaths or in bouquets.

Harvesting and preparing. Allow flowers and seed heads to dry naturally on the plant, and then cut and hang them to allow them to finish drying inside. They can also be harvested when fully mature and placed in a glycerine solution.

KOELREUTERIA PANICULATA

LAGURUS OVATUS

LATHYRUS ODORATUS

LAVANDULA ANGUSTIFOLIA

LEONTOPODIUM ALPINUM

Lamb's-ears see *Stachys*

Larkspur see *Consolida*

—

Lathyrus (LATH-i-rus)

A large genus of annuals and perennials with alternate compound leaves, winged stems and tendrils. Flowers bloom three to 10 in terminal clusters. Fruit is borne in pods. Zones 3-8.

Selected species and varieties. *L. latifolius,* perennial sweet pea, climbs by tendrils to 9 feet or more and is hardy. Flowers are 1 to 1½ inches wide and rose-pink, red or white. Seedpods are flattish and 3 to 5 inches long. Zones 4-8. *L. odoratus,* sweet pea, is a 6-foot annual vine with oval leaflets. Flowers are fragrant, one to four on a stem and usually purple with pale wing petals. Seedpods are 2 inches long. Hundreds of varieties are available in myriad colors.

Growing conditions. Perennial sweet pea will grow in sun in any soil. Prune old stems and foliage of perennial sweet pea in the fall. Propagate the perennial sweet pea from seeds and from cuttings. Annual sweet pea thrives in sun and deep, moist soil. Support the vines. Do not transplant vines. Propagate annuals from seeds.

Uses. Sweet peas can be used fresh in mixed arrangements or bouquets; they make an especially attractive small arrangement when grouped with miniature roses and violets. The dried flowers can be used in wreaths or other arrangements.

Harvesting and preparing. Preserve flowers in silica gel or dry in a microwave oven.

—

Laurel see *Kalmia*

—

Lavandula (la-VAN-dew-la)
Lavender

Genus of aromatic perennials and shrubs, some of which are evergreen in mild climates, with narrow, opposite leaves. Flowers are blue, lavender, dark purple or dingy white, and form dense clusters in the leaf axil. Zones 5-9.

Selected species and varieties. *L. angustifolia,* English lavender, grows 1 to 3 feet tall. Leaves are white, felty and sometimes lance-shaped. Flowers are purple and ⅓ inch long, and bloom in late June. 'Hidcote' is a compact, 20-inch-tall plant. It is slow-growing and has deep purple flowers. 'Munstead' grows to 12 inches tall and blooms early with lavender-blue flowers.

Growing conditions. Lavender grows well in sun and well-drained, sandy soil. It will not be as hardy if grown in a rich, fertile soil. Older plants do not transplant well. Mulch plants over the winter with evergreen boughs or salt hay. Applying a complete fertilizer in spring will help nonvigorous plants. Prune back deadwood in April. After plants have finished flowering, prune only to shape. Propagate from seeds, by division of clumps in spring, or from cuttings taken in spring or fall. Space plants 9 inches to 3 feet apart.

Uses. Lavender blossoms can be used in small, fresh arrangements for line and scent. Dried, they can be used in dainty nosegays, sachets and potpourris.

Harvesting and preparing. To air-dry, pick as the flower spikes start to bloom and hang in small, loose bundles.

—

Lavender see *Lavandula*

—

Leontopodium
(lee-on-toh-PO-dee-um)

Hardy, tufted, woolly perennial from 1 inch to 1 foot tall. Leaves are basal, alternate and entire. Clustered heads of small flowers are encircled by a collar of grayish white felted bracts. Zones 4-8.

Selected species and varieties. *L. alpinum,* edelweiss, grows to 9 inches tall. Flowers are starfishlike, 1½ inches across and yellow in the center of the bracts. They bloom from June to August.

Growing conditions. Edelweiss is drought-resistant. It grows well in full sun and well-drained, gritty or sandy, alkaline soil. Seeds ripen well during a dry summer. Propagate by division or from seeds sown indoors in a cool place eight to 10 weeks before the last frost. Plants can be set in a permanent location by late spring. Space plants 8 to 12 inches apart.

Uses. Edelweiss can be used as a focal point in a miniature fresh or dried arrangement.

Harvesting and preparing. To dry, pick young, open flower heads; then, either spread them face up on wire mesh to air-dry, or dry them in silica gel or in a microwave oven.

—

Liatris (ly-AY-tris)
Gay-feather, blazing star

A perennial having a clump of basal leaves that are simple, alternate and mostly linear to lanceolate. Flower heads are rose-purple or white balloonlike disk florets surrounded by many close, green bracts and borne on spikes. Flowers bloom in summer and early fall, starting at the top of the plant and moving downward. Zones 3-8.

Selected species and varieties. *L. pycnostachya*, Kansas gay-feather, has spikes that are 4 feet long. Lower leaves grow up to 1 foot in length. Stalk leaves are smaller and may be either smooth or hairy. Spikes bloom in July and August. 'Alba' has white flower spikes. *L. spicata* grows 4 to 6 feet tall with a leafy stem and 6- to 12-inch, dense, purple or white flower spikes. Zones 4-8. 'Kobold' is a compact, 18- to 24-inch-tall plant with dark purple flowers.

Growing conditions. Gay-feathers grow in sun or light shade and fertile, moist, well-drained soil. Most need to be watered during dry spells, but *L. spicata* is fairly drought-resistant. Mulch in fall in colder areas with compost or peat moss. When plants deteriorate after several years, divide and re-plant. Propagate by division in early spring or early fall and from seed. Gay-feather blooms the second year when grown from seed.

Uses. Gay-feather can be used as a line flower in a large, fresh or dried vertical arrangement.

Harvesting and preparing. To use dried, pick the flower spikes before the top flower begins to fade; air-dry by hanging, or preserve the flowers in silica gel.

Lilac see *Syringa*

—

Lilium (LIL-ee-um)
Lily

Large genus of showy, bulbous, erect perennials with usually narrow, smooth-margined leaves that are scattered or that occur in whorls. Flowers are funnel-shaped, erect, horizontal or nodding, solitary or in racemes, sometimes densely flowered. Fruit is a many-seeded capsule. Zones 4-8.

Selected species and varieties. *L.* hybrids, hybrid garden lilies, are divided into classes based on geographical or horticultural origin and on shape. Hybrid garden lilies bloom in summer. American hybrids grow 4 to 8 feet tall with whorled leaves and nodding, spotted 4- to 6-inch-wide flowers. Colors are red, pink, orange and yellow. Asiatic hybrids grow 2 to 5 feet tall with flowers that may be upright, outward-facing or pendant. Color ranges from white through yellow, orange, pink, lavender and red, alone or in combination, with or without spotting. 'Connecticut King' is an upward-facing yellow lily without spots that grows 30 to 36 inches tall and blooms in early to middle summer. Zones 4-7.

Aurelian hybrids grow 3 to 8 feet tall. Flowers are 6 to 8 inches long, up to 8 inches wide and usually fragrant. Flowers can be trumpet-shaped, bowl-shaped, pendant or sunburst. Colors are white through greenish white, yellow, orange, pink and gold, alone or in combination, some with yellow throats or maroon stripes. Zones 4-7. Candidum hybrids grow 3 to 4 feet tall and have lance-shaped leaves. Flowers are pure white, 4 to 5 inches wide and fragrant. Zones 5-7. Oriental hybrids grow 2½ to 7 feet tall. Flowers are 3 to 10 inches wide and fragrant, and may be bowl-shaped or flat-faced, or have backswept petals. Colors are white, white with yellow, pink or crimson stripes, or pink to crimson edged with white, generally spotted. Zones 5-7.

Growing conditions. Grow hybrid garden lilies in full sun and well-drained, slightly acid soil with plenty of humus. Shelter from strong winds. Water in hot, dry weather. In spring, apply a slow-

LIATRIS SPICATA 'KOBOLD'

LILIUM 'CONNECTICUT KING'

LIMONIUM SINUATUM

LINUM PERENNE

release synthetic fertilizer, and mulch with 2 to 5 inches of leaf mold in late spring. Stake tall plants. Divide thick clumps. Propagate from bulbs or bulb scales in autumn or early spring. Plant bulbs three times as deep as bulb height and space 8 inches to 1 foot apart. Plant candidum hybrids 1 inch below ground level.

Uses. Lilies can be used in tall or horizontal fresh arrangements as focal or accent flowers; they are also stately enough to be used alone with greens. Dried flower and seed heads can be used in wreaths or in other dried arrangements.

Harvesting and preparing. After cutting fresh flowers, remove the anthers; lily pollen can stain clothing and tablecloths. To use dried, preserve the flowers in silica gel or dry in a microwave oven; keep in a dry area so that the flowers cannot reabsorb moisture. To use the seed heads, pick them before they split and then air-dry by standing them upright in an empty container.

▬

Lily see *Lilium*
Lily-of-the-Incas
see *Alstroemeria*
Lily-of-the-Nile see *Agapanthus*
Lily-of-the-valley
see *Convallaria*

▬

Limonium (ly-MO-nee-um)
Statice, sea lavender

Genus of annuals, biennials and perennials with leaves forming a basal rosette. The flower stem is multibranched with numerous small flowers in open, loose panicles. Flowers are lavender, rose-pink, blue, yellow or white, and bloom in summer or early fall. Zones 3-9.

Selected species and varieties. *L. latifolium,* German statice, is a perennial that grows 2½ feet tall. Flowers are ⅛ inch wide and lavender-blue, blooming in large, feathery panicles. *L. sinuatum* is a biennial grown as an annual. It is a 2-foot-tall, rough, hairy plant with lyre-shaped, 6-inch leaves. It has a winged or flat stem. Flower colors are rose, lavender, blue, yellow and salmon.

Growing conditions. German statice is resistant to salt spray. Plant it and annual statice in full sun and sandy, moist soil. Statice likes warm weather. Staking may be needed in fertile soil. Propagate annuals from seeds sown indoors in March and transplanted outside when danger of frost is over. Propagate perennial statice by division in spring.

Uses. Use statice in a mixed, fresh or dried bouquet or an arrangement. German statice makes a light, airy filler; annual statice provides bright color and a strong shape. Either type of statice can be used in a wreath.

Harvesting and preparing. Pick flower heads before blossoms are fully open and hang in bunches to air-dry. To extend the height of the flowers, separate small flower clusters from the stem and wire them. To make a wreath, shape fresh flowers into a wreath form and allow them to air-dry.

▬

Linum (LY-num)
Flax

Genus of annuals, perennials and small shrubs with simple, narrow, entire and usually alternate leaves, and delicate blue or yellow flowers, usually occurring in terminal racemes or cymes, followed by seed heads. Zones 5-9.

Selected species and varieties. *L. perenne,* perennial flax, is a graceful, arching, short-lived perennial that lasts three to four years. It grows 2 feet tall with 1-inch leaves that are linear to lanceolate. Flowers are deep blue, 1 inch wide and bloom in multibranched panicles from early summer to mid-summer.

Growing conditions. Grow flax in full sun and well-drained soil. Add a light leaf mulch in winter. Propagate from seeds, by division or from cuttings. Sow seeds in May or June in a cold frame or an outside seedbed. In the fall, transplant to a permanent location. Thin seedlings to 4 inches apart.

Uses. With its delicate color and texture, flax can be used as a filler or an accent flower in a fresh arrangement. The seed head can be used as airy filler in a small dried arrangement.

Harvesting and preparing. To use the seed heads, allow some flowers to mature on the plant. The seed heads will air-dry naturally on the plant.

—

Liquidambar (lik-wid-AM-ber)

A deciduous tree with leaves that are alternate, star-shaped, five- to seven-lobed and 4 to 7 inches across. Male flowers occur in racemes or branching clusters. Female flowers occur in globular heads hanging below male flowers. Fruit is a pendant, spiny dense ball. Zones 5-9.

Selected species and varieties. *L. styraciflua,* sweetgum, grows 75 feet tall. Leaves are 7 inches across with finely serrated lobes. Fall foliage is brilliant yellow, scarlet or purple. Fruit remains on the tree from fall to winter.

Growing conditions. Choose the site for sweetgum carefully; dropping fruit can be a nuisance. It needs moist, fertile, acid soil. It will tolerate poor drainage, but not dryness. Mulch young trees and water during dry periods.

Uses. Preserved branches of green leaves can be used in large dried arrangements; red autumn leaves or skeletonized leaves can be used in fall arrangements. The seed head can be used in wreaths.

Harvesting and preparing. Harvest branches of green leaves in July or August, and preserve them in a glycerine solution. Dry red autumn leaves by standing them upright in a container with or without water. To use the seed heads, wire them and then stand them upright to air-dry.

—

Lisianthus see *Eustoma*

—

Lobelia (lo-BEE-lee-a)

Genus of annuals and perennials with alternate, simple leaves. Flowers occur in terminal clusters forming spikes or racemes that are often leafy and bracted. Blooming occurs from early summer to killing frost. Zones 3-8.

Selected species and varieties. *L. cardinalis,* cardinal flower, In-dian pink, is a 3- to 6-foot-tall hairless perennial that is erect and mostly branchless. Stems are leafy. The spikes have 1½-inch scarlet flowers that bloom from July to September.

Growing conditions. Plant cardinal flower in full sun or partial shade in an evenly moist, ordinary soil. Water during dry periods. In Zones 3 to 5, apply a 1-foot-deep mulch of straw or leaves when cold weather sets in. Every third year, renew plants by dividing clumps in spring or fall. Propagate by division in spring. Cardinal flower self-sows and can become weedy.

Uses. Cardinal flower makes a long-lasting line flower in a tall or Oriental fresh arrangement. It can also be used dried in a mixed bouquet.

Harvesting and preparing. To use fresh, sear the stem ends before normal conditioning. Dry cardinal flowers in silica gel or in a microwave oven to preserve their color and shape. The stems can be wired to extend their length.

—

Loosestrife see *Lythrum*
Lotus see *Nelumbo*
Love-in-a-mist see *Nigella*
Love-lies-bleeding
see *Amaranthus*

—

Lunaria (loo-NAR-ee-a)
Honesty, money plant

An erect, branching biennial or perennial with simple, broad, toothed leaves. White to purple flowers occur in terminal racemes. Seedpod is showy, flat, oblong to elliptical to nearly round with a satiny, papery white septum.

Selected species and varieties. *L. annua,* silver dollar, is a biennial that reaches a height of 3 feet. Flowers are fragrant, purple and white, and grow to 1 inch across. 'Alba' has white flowers.

Growing conditions. Grow honesty in partial shade in light, dryish soil. It prefers cool weather and good air circulation. Plants die after blooming. Propagate by sowing seeds outdoors in fall or in April. Plants are winter-hardy and will live

LIQUIDAMBAR STYRACIFLUA

LOBELIA CARDINALIS

LUNARIA ANNUA

LYTHRUM VIRGATUM 'MORDEN'S PINK'

MAGNOLIA GRANDIFLORA

MALUS FLORIBUNDA

over winter to bloom in midspring. Honesty is a self-sower. Thin to allow air to circulate between plants.

Uses. The delicate-looking flowers of honesty can be used in small, fresh spring arrangements, or they can be used in pressed designs. The dried seedpods can be used in mixed bouquets or grouped alone.

Harvesting and preparing. To use the seedpods, pick them once they are fully developed, but before the seeds become too dark and stain the inner membrane. Remove the outer coverings by hand.

Lythrum (LITH-rum)
Loosestrife

Genus of annuals, perennials and shrubs having short-stalked or stalkless leaves that are opposite and alternate, and may be ovate or linear. Flowers are pink, rose-purple or, rarely, white on terminal spikes, solitary or in pairs in the leaf axil; they bloom in summer. Fruit is a capsule. Zones 3-9.

Selected species and varieties. *L. virgatum,* purple loosestrife, is a 1½- to 2-foot perennial with stalkless leaves that are opposite or whorled, lance-shaped and 4 inches long. Flowers are ¾ inch, magenta-pink and clustered on narrow 6- to 12-inch spikes. The plants bloom from June to September and are extremely invasive. Grow only cultivars. 'Morden's Pink', often designated *L. salicaria,* is dense and bushy and grows to 4 feet tall. It has pale to rosy pink flowers that bloom abundantly from July to September.

Growing conditions. Loosestrife prefers sun, but grows in partial shade and rich, moist soil. Transplanting slows the growth of the plant considerably. 'Morden's Pink' is not invasive since it is sterile. Propagate by division in the spring or from cuttings in early fall. Space plants 2 to 3 feet apart.

Uses. Loosestrife mixes well with red or other pink flowers, and provides line in a tall fresh arrangement. It turns a darker color when dried, and can be used in a mixed dried bouquet.

Harvesting and preparing. To use dried, pick the spike when it is two-thirds developed; air-dry by hanging.

Magnolia (mag-NO-lee-a)

Genus of evergreen and deciduous flowering trees and shrubs with alternate and entire leaves. Flowers are large, showy, solitary and terminal; white, pink, purple or yellow; and bloom in early spring or midsummer, depending on species. Fruit is bright red. Zones 7-9.

Selected species and varieties. *M. grandiflora,* southern magnolia, bull bay, is an evergreen and grows to 80 feet tall. Leaves are 5 to 8 inches long, oblong, leathery, shiny on the upper surfaces, woolly and rusty underneath. Flowers are fragrant, waxy, cream-white and 8 to 10 inches wide. Blooms appear in June and July. Fruit is conelike, 4 inches long, woolly and rusty, and opens to disclose red seeds when ripe in the fall.

Growing conditions. Southern magnolia grows best in sun in fertile, well-drained but moist, loamy soil. It tolerates shade. Soil should be acid to nearly neutral. Mulch to keep root zone moist. Water during drought.

Uses. Fresh magnolia blossoms can be floated in water singly or in a group. The dried flowers can be used as focal points in wreaths and other dried arrangements. The glossy brown preserved leaves or skeletonized leaves can also be used in dried arrangements.

Harvesting and preparing. To use the flowers fresh, cut as the petals of buds begin to loosen; then cut a cross on the bottom of the stem to help it take up water. Briefly submerge the buds in cool water. To dry, place the flowers in silica gel or in a microwave oven. Preserve the foliage by placing it in a glycerine solution.

Malus (MAY-lus)
Crabapple

Genus of deciduous shrubs and trees having leaves that are alternate, elliptical and sometimes three-lobed. Flowers have five petals that occur in umbel-like terminal racemes. They are white to pink or carmine. Blooming occurs in early spring, usually before the foliage appears. Fruit may be as small as a pea or as big as a tennis ball and is purple, red, orange or yellow.

Some varieties retain fruit through most of the winter. Some are sour or bitter and inedible. Fruit begins to color in August and peaks in October. Zones 2-8.

Selected species and varieties. *M. floribunda,* Japanese flowering crabapple, is round in form, densely branched with mostly arching branchlets and grows from 25 to 30 feet tall. Leaves are ovate to oblong, toothed and 2 to 3 inches long. Flowers are fragrant, deep carmine in bud, rose in early bloom and paler later. They are 1 to 1½ inches across. Fruit is ⅜ inch in diameter and yellow or red. Flowers bloom in early May. Zones 4-8.

Growing conditions. Plant crabapple in full sun in any well-drained soil. Established trees tolerate drought. Prune to remove crowded or crossed branches, suckers or water sprouts in late winter or early spring before growth. Plant in early spring or fall. Crabapple transplants easily. Mulch during the first summer. Japanese flowering crabapple is resistant to apple scab and powdery mildew.

Uses. Crabapple branches can be used with or without flowers to give an arching line to fresh arrangements. Branches may be cut in January for forcing indoors. Individual flowers can be used in pressed designs.

Harvesting and preparing. To use the branches fresh, hammer the ends of the stems before conditioning normally.

▬

Maple see *Acer*

Marigold see *Tagetes*

▬

Marrubium (ma-ROO-bee-um)

Whitish, woolly aromatic perennial with square stems and leaves that are opposite, scalloped, or dissected and wrinkled. Flowers are numerous and bloom in globular clusters. Fruit is a small nutlet. Zones 3-8.

Selected species and varieties. *M. vulgare,* horehound, grows to 18 inches tall with 2-inch-long leaves. The plant has a musky odor. Flowers are white, ¼ inch long and densely crowded in axils of rather widely spaced upper leaves; they bloom from mid-June to September.

Growing conditions. Grow horehound in full sun and well-drained, sandy soil. It tolerates dry periods. Propagate from seeds sown 1 inch apart in spring after danger of frost is past. Thin the seedlings to 9 inches apart. Horehound can also be propagated from cuttings in summer.

Uses. The wrinkled, silver-white leaves on curving stems add texture and movement to fresh arrangements, and they may also be used to form the base of dried wreaths.

Harvesting and preparing. To make a wreath, work branches into shape and let them air-dry in place.

▬

Matthiola (ma-tee-O-la)

Genus of annuals, biennials, perennials and small shrubs with 4-inch, oblong, alternate leaves that may be wavy or cut into segments. Flowers are single or double, 1 inch wide, fragrant, white, red, rose, bluish, purple or yellow, and bloom on rigid upright spikes in terminal racemes.

Selected species and varieties. *M. incana,* stock, gillyflower, is a 2½-foot-tall biennial grown as a hardy annual. Flowers are purple, red, yellow or white, and the racemes elongate as the blooms open in succession from the bottom upward. 'Annua', ten weeks stock, is an early-flowering annual; it blooms 10 weeks after germination—hence the common name.

Growing conditions. Grow stock in a sunny location in any soil that is fertile and well drained. It thrives in cool weather. Propagate from seeds sown indoors in early March and transplant outdoors when plants are in bud and there is no danger of frost. It may also be sown outdoors in full sun in early spring. Where winters are mild, sow seeds in late summer for winter or spring bloom. Sow the seeds thickly; crowding will force the plants to bloom early. Start ten weeks stock from seed indoors eight weeks before plants are to be set outdoors. Space plants 1 foot apart.

Uses. Stock flowers are spicy-fragrant, long-lasting, and may be used to give line to fresh arrange-

MARRUBIUM VULGARE

MATTHIOLA INCANA

MOLUCCELLA LAEVIS

MONARDA DIDYMA 'CROFTWAY PINK'

ments and bouquets. Dried flowers may be used in mixed dried arrangements, wreaths and in potpourris.

Harvesting and preparing. Air-dry the flowers for use in potpourris by laying the stalks on their sides. To preserve their shape and color, dry flowers in silica gel or in a microwave oven.

—

Meadow rue see *Thalictrum*

Mexican bamboo
see *Polygonum*

Mexican sunflower see *Tithonia*

Milfoil see *Achillea*

Milkweed see *Asclepias*

Mimosa see *Acacia;*
Albizia

—

Moluccella (mol-u-SEL-a)

A genus of annuals with opposite, stalked, toothed leaves. The flower has a small, irregular corolla that is white or pinkish, and is surrounded by a larger, bristly, bell-shaped calyx. The fruit is a four-seeded nutlet.

Selected species and varieties. *M. laevis,* bells-of-Ireland, shell-flower, grows 2 feet tall. Leaves are round or heart-shaped and 1¾ inches across. Flowers are fragrant, white and very small; green shell-like calyxes are whorled in tiers on the stems.

Growing conditions. Bells-of-Ireland prefers full sun, well-drained sandy soil and cool weather. It may need staking. Propagate from seeds sown in April where winters are cold, or in late summer where winters are mild. Space plants 1 foot apart. Bells-of-Ireland usually reseeds itself.

Uses. Bells-of-Ireland can be used in fresh or dried arrangements for their line, both vertical and curvilinear. The flowers are attractive when grouped by themselves or with flowers of other colors.

Harvesting and preparing. To use either fresh or dried, remove the leaves. Dry by hanging stalks separately, or by standing the flowers in a glycerine solution or upright in a small amount of water.

Monarda (mo-NAR-da)
Wild bergamot, horsemint

Genus of aromatic annuals and perennials, somewhat coarse, with opposite, entire or toothed leaves. Flowers are irregular, showy, white, red, purplish, yellow or mottled, often with bright-colored bracts. Flowers bloom in summer and fall and are followed by 1-inch, roundish seed heads. Zones 3-9.

Selected species and varieties. *M. didyma,* bee balm, oswego tea, is a 3-foot-tall perennial with leaves that are ovate to nearly lanceolate, downy on their undersides and 3 to 6 inches long. Flowers are 2 inches long, scarlet, surrounded by red-winged bracts and bloom from June to August. Tubular flowers may be borne in single or double whorls on the flower heads. Zones 4-9. 'Cambridge Scarlet' grows 2 to 3 feet tall with crimson flowers that bloom from late June to September. 'Croftway Pink' has rose-pink flowers. 'Snow Queen' has large white flowers. 'Violet Queen' has violet flowers.

Growing conditions. Grow bee balm in full sun or partial shade and in moist, ordinary soil. Good air circulation is important. It spreads quickly and needs to be controlled. Propagate by division in spring, and from seeds sown in spring.

Uses. Bee balm flowers can be used to create brightly colored focal points in fresh arrangements. The dried flowers and seed heads can be used in mixed dried arrangements.

Harvesting and preparing. Hang the flowers upside down to dry. To use the seed heads, allow the flowers to finish blooming on the plant; then harvest the seed heads and hang to air-dry.

—

Money plant see *Lunaria*

Monkshood see *Aconitum*

Monk's pepper tree see *Vitex*

Mountain laurel see *Kalmia*

Mullein see *Verbascum*

—

Myrica (mi-RY-ka)

Genus of deciduous and evergreen shrubs and small trees with leaves that are short-stalked, alternate and usually dotted with resin glands. When crushed, the foliage gives off a pleasant fragrance. Flowers are greenish and nonshowy, without sepals or petals. Fruit is gray or purple. Zones 1-9.

Selected species and varieties. *M. cerifera*, wax myrtle, bayberry, can reach 36 feet tall. Leaves are evergreen, leathery, 3 inches long and more or less lance-shaped. Fruit is ⅛ inch thick, covered with a gray, waxy coating and appears in dense clusters along the stem. Branches, leaves and fruit are aromatic. Zones 6-9.

Growing conditions. Wax myrtle grows in full sun to partial shade and in moist, peaty, acid soil. It tolerates salt and dry, sterile soils. Prune back severely only when planting. Prune lightly to renew leggy plants. Male and female plants are separate; female plants produce the gray fruit.

Uses. Branches with or without berries can be used in fresh or dried arrangements. The leathery leaves make a good filler in both fresh and mixed dried arrangements.

Harvesting and preparing. Air-dry branches with berries by hanging them upside down; preserve the leaves in a glycerine solution.

—

Narcissus (nar-SIS-us)

Genus of bulbs having basal leaves that are flat, linear, or cylindrical and rushlike, and flowers that bloom on top of branchless stalks. The flower head consists of a perianth of six spreading petals surrounding a crown that may be trumpet-shaped, cup-shaped or a shallow ring. Zones 4-8.

Selected species and varieties. *N.* hybrids, daffodils, are so numerous (they exist in the hundreds) that they are classified in divisions and subdivisions according to flower size, coloration and derivation. All cultivated daffodils bloom in spring: some early, some late. Some bloom one per stem; some bloom in clusters. Most are yellow, yellow and orange, white and yellow, or white and orange. Some are fragrant.

Growing conditions. Grow daffodils in full sun and in fertile soil that has enough clay to give it body and ensure reasonable water retention. Propagate from offsets—small bulbs that develop at the base of a mother bulb. Plant in September or October. Space large bulbs 6 to 8 inches apart, medium bulbs 4 to 5 inches apart and small bulbs 1½ to 3 inches apart.

Uses. Fresh daffodils can be grouped by themselves or used as mass flowers in a mixed spring-flower centerpiece. They can also be used dried in mixed arrangements. Use a single dried blossom to decorate the top of a bowl of potpourri.

Harvesting and preparing. Dry daffodils in silica gel or in a microwave oven.

—

Needle palm see *Yucca*

—

Nelumbo (ne-LUM-bo)
Water lily

Genus of large aquatic plants with wide-spreading, horizontal rhizomes that root in mud. Leaves are round, peltate (having the stem attached to the lower surface instead of at the margin) and grow several feet out of the water. Flowers are large, solitary, terminal and occur on long stems. The seedpod is funnel-shaped and flat-topped with many small holes containing seed-like nuts.

Selected species and varieties. *N. nucifera*, East Indian lotus, has rough, somewhat prickly stalks that rise 3 to 6 feet above the water, and 1- to 3-foot-wide leaves. Flowers are fragrant, 4 to 10 inches across, pink, rose or sometimes white, and they rise above the foliage and bloom for three successive days.

Growing conditions. Grow lotus in the sun in a pool or a very large and deep container that is at least 2 feet in diameter. Roots are buried beneath 2 inches of rich soil with 6 to 12 inches of water over them. Propagate by dividing the rhizomes in late spring or from seeds that have been scarred and chilled before sowing. Roots should not be allowed to freeze. If soil in your area is subject to deep freezing, drain the pool and protect the plant roots with a 3-foot covering of salt hay, straw or leaves, or lift the rhizomes and

MYRICA CERIFERA

NARCISSUS 'ACTEA'

NELUMBO NUCIFERA

NEPHROLEPIS EXALTATA

NIGELLA DAMASCENA

OSMUNDA REGALIS

store them in damp moss and moist compost over winter, replanting outdoors in late April.

Uses. Lotuses can be floated in a bowl of water or used as focal flowers in mixed centerpieces. They can be dried and used in mixed arrangements or used as focal points in wreaths. The seedpods, too, can be used in garlands or in wreaths.

Harvesting and preparing. Dry lotuses in silica gel or in a microwave oven. To use the seedpods, pick them while they are still green, and then air-dry by supporting the heads on a wire mesh.

Nephrolepis (ne-FROL-e-pis)
Ladder fern

Genus of tropical and subtropical terrestrial ferns, usually stoloniferous, having short, erect rhizomes that send out runners from which new plants emerge. Leaves are scaly, often drooping, usually long, narrow, pinnate to decompound and form dense, attractive crowns. Zone 10.

Selected species and varieties. *N. exaltata,* sword fern, has erect, stiff fronds 2 to 5 feet long and 3 to 6 inches wide. Leaflets are 3 inches long, entire or slightly toothed, and close together on the frond. Round spore cases lie midway between the midribs and margins of the leaflets.

Growing conditions. Sword fern thrives in light shade in warm, moderately dry regions where frost seldom occurs. Soil should be fertile but coarse and evenly moist. Propagate by dividing the runners or the crowns.

Uses. Sword fern can be used to give line to a tall arrangement. It can also be used in a pressed design.

Harvesting and preparing. Press sword fern to retain the plant's color and shape.

Nigella (ni-JEL-a)
Fennel flower

Annual that is erect and branching with alternate, finely cut leaves, often divided into lacy segments. Flowers are blue, purple, yellow or white, and grow at the ends of branches and branchlets. Fruit is globelike and conspicuous.

Selected species and varieties. *N. damascena,* love-in-a-mist, devil-in-a-bush, grows 18 to 24 inches tall. The foliage is lacy and bright green. Flowers are white, blue, pink, rose, mauve or purple, 1½ inches across and surrounded by threadlike bracts that give them the appearance of mist, hence the common name. Fruit is a lobed pink pod that darkens to burgundy as it ripens.

Growing conditions. Love-in-a-mist prefers cool weather, a sunny location and fertile, well-drained soil. Staking may be necessary. Propagate from seeds sown outdoors as soon as the ground can be worked in the spring. Where winters are mild, sow outdoors in autumn. Seedlings do not tolerate transplanting. Thin plants 6 to 8 inches apart.

Uses. Dainty love-in-a-mist can be used as a mass flower in a small fresh arrangement. Both flowers and pods can be used in dried bouquets or wreaths.

Harvesting and preparing. Dry the flowers in silica gel. Pick pods when the area between the lobes turns a burgundy color, and air-dry by hanging them upside down.

Oak see *Quercus*

Okra see *Abelmoschus*

Onion see *Allium*

Orange coneflower
see *Rudbeckia*

Oriental bittersweet
see *Celastrus*

Oriental cherry see *Prunus*

Oriental poppy see *Papaver*

Ornamental pepper
see *Capsicum*

Osmunda (os-MUN-da)

Deciduous, coarse, deep-rooted fern with stout rhizomes. Fronds grow from 18 inches to 8 feet long and are long-stalked, erect, and pinnately divided or lobed. Spore cases are large and more or less globular. Zones 2-8.

Selected species and varieties. *O. regalis,* royal fern, has twice-compound fronds up to 6 feet long with leaflets 2 to 3 inches long. Leaves are wine red when young and mature to a rich green, then change in fall to a soft golden yellow. Fertile flowerlike spikes grow at the tips of the fronds.

Growing conditions. Plant royal fern in sun or partial shade near a stream or a pond. It prefers highly acid, constantly moist soil. Mulch with rotted leaves in the fall. As added protection, leave dead fronds on plants until spring. Propagate by division.

Uses. Royal fern can be used fresh —both when it is green, and when it is mature and a golden color—to create line in arrangements. It can also be used dried in wreaths and pressed designs.

Harvesting and preparing. For preserved yet flexible foliage, place the side shoots of each frond in a glycerine solution. Press fronds at different stages of maturity to obtain a variety of colors.

—

Oswego tea see *Monarda*

—

Paeonia (pee-O-nee-a)

Genus of mostly clump-forming perennials and shrubs with tuberous roots and large, compound and alternate leaves. Flowers are terminal and may be solitary or clustered, single or double, and purple, red, pink, yellow or white. Zones 3-10.

Selected species and varieties. *P. lactiflora,* garden peony, Chinese peony, grows 1½ to 3 feet tall. Leaves are 4 to 12 inches long, deep green, long-stalked and have leaflets that are elliptical to lanceolate. Flowers are 2¾ to 4 inches across, fragrant, usually white but sometimes pink and red, and can be single or double. Seedpods are winglike and erect, occurring in the center of a calyx that is shaped like an upside-down saucer. 'Dixie' has double, magenta-colored flowers; petals have scalloped edges. *P. officinalis,* common peony, is a 2- to 4-foot-high plant with 3- to 6-inch-wide blooms of red, pink, light yellow or white. The many hybrids have blossoms of various forms,

such as single, semidouble and double, and with different blooming times, from spring to early summer. Zones 3-10.

Growing conditions. Grow peony in full sun to partial shade in well-drained, slightly acid soil. Space plants 1½ feet apart and stake early. Mulch the first winter with a thick covering of straw, evergreen boughs or oak leaves. Propagate by dividing crowns in fall or from cuttings. When propagating from crowns, plant them only 1 to 2 inches below the soil surface; planting them deeper may prevent the plants from flowering. Make sure each crown contains at least one growth bud.

Uses. Single, fresh-cut peonies with their own foliage may be floated in bowls of water, or they may be grouped so that they form a centerpiece. Dried peonies can be used in mixed arrangements, and the seedpods can be used in cone wreaths.

Harvesting and preparing. To use peonies fresh, cut them when the buds start to open. To use dried, preserve the flowers in silica gel or dry them in a microwave oven; once dried, the flowers should be kept in a dry location. When the seedpods appear on the plant, harvest and air-dry them by laying them on their sides.

—

Painted daisy
see *Chrysanthemum*

Painter's palette see *Anthurium*

Pampas grass see *Cortaderia*

Pansy see *Viola*

—

Papaver (pa-PAY-ver)
Poppy

Genus of annuals and perennials from 6 to 48 inches tall with basal, usually hairy, leaves. Cut stems exude a milky juice. Flower stalks nod when in bud and become erect as the flower opens. Flowers are solitary, terminal and five-petaled. Fruit is a four- to 20-celled dry capsule containing hundreds of minute seeds. Zones 2-7.

Selected species and varieties. *P. nudicaule,* Iceland poppy, is a

PAEONIA LACTIFLORA 'DIXIE'

PAPAVER ORIENTALE

PENNISETUM SETACEUM

PHLOX PANICULATA 'BRIGHT EYES'

1- to 2-foot perennial grown as a half-hardy annual. Leaves are petioled, pinnately lobed or cleft. Flowers are fragrant, 1 to 3 inches across, single or double, and white with yellow, orange or red at their bases. *P. orientale*, Oriental poppy, is a bristly-haired perennial that grows 4 feet tall. Many cultivars exist. Flowers have four to six petals, are up to 6 inches across, and are red, pale pink, or orange with a dark basal spot. Flowers are sometimes double. Blooming occurs in late May and June. 'Glowing Embers' has bright orange-red blossoms with ruffled petals.

Growing conditions. Grow poppy in full sun and in fertile, well-drained soil. It thrives in cool weather. Do not transplant Iceland poppy. In areas where winters are mild, propagate Iceland poppy from seeds sown the previous fall; elsewhere, start indoors in peat pots in midwinter and transplant oudoors when seedlings are a good size. Space 12 inches apart. Propagate Oriental poppy from seed, by division in late summer or from root cuttings in late summer. Space 1½ feet apart.

Uses. Poppies can be used fresh in arrangements; they make especially good mass flowers in centerpieces. They do not last long. The dried pods can be used in garlands, wreaths and other dried arrangements.

Harvesting and preparing. To use fresh, sear the stems of poppies as soon as they are cut, before conditioning normally. To use the pods, pick when they reach maturity, but before they turn brown.

—

Paper moon see *Scabiosa*
Pearl grass see *Briza*
Pearly everlasting
see *Anaphalis*

—

Pennisetum (pen-i-SEE-tum)

Genus of annual and perennial, mainly tropical, tufted grasses having erect, slender to stout stems. Leaf blades are flat, narrow, and sometimes tinted purple, red or rose. Flowers occur in spikelike panicles with spikelets having bris-

tles beneath them that are sometimes plumed. Zones 5-10.

Selected species and varieties. *P. setaceum*, fountain grass, reaches 2 to 3 feet tall in a mounded form, and has fine-textured green leaf blades. Flower panicles are pink or purple, 9 to 12 inches long and nodding, and they bloom from late June to October. The plant is perennial in Zones 8 and 9, and is grown as an annual elsewhere. *P. villosum*, dwarf feather top, is a 1½- to 2½-foot-tall perennial. Flower spikes are 3 to 5 inches long, and light green or white, tinged with purple, changing to tawny as they age. They bloom from August to late September. Zones 8 and 9.

Growing conditions. Grow pennisetum in full sun to partial shade in ordinary garden soil. Feather top prefers moist, fertile soil. Both grasses can be grown as annuals in the north. Propagate from seed and by division in spring. Fountain grass often reseeds itself. In colder climates, sow seeds outdoors in early spring where the plants are to grow.

Uses. Fountain grass and dwarf feather top may be used in a fresh or dried arrangement to provide line and movement.

Harvesting and preparing. To use either species dried, gather the plumes before they are fully mature; this will prevent the spikelets from shedding and will help them to retain their color. Hang to air-dry.

—

Peony see *Paeonia*
Pepper see *Capsicum*
Peruvian lily see *Alstroemeria*

—

Phlox (FLOKS)

Genus of annuals and perennials having stiff, woody stems that may be trailing or erect. Leaves are opposite or alternate and lance-shaped. The individual flower bud is a short tube that opens to reveal a corolla with five petals. The flowers are white, deep pink, pale lavender or purple, usually with an eye of a different color in the base of the flower lobe; they bloom in loose terminal clusters. Zones 4-9.

Selected species and varieties.
P. paniculata, summer phlox, is a 2- to 4-foot-tall perennial. Flowers are 1 inch across, fragrant and bloom for many weeks, beginning in July. 'Bright Eyes' has light pink blooms with contrasting deep pink centers.

Growing conditions. Grow phlox in full sun and in moist, rich garden soil. The foliage needs to be kept dry. Phlox tolerates light shade. Prune old plants heavily in spring, leaving three to four stalks. Divide every three years for vigorous growth. Propagate from seeds, from stem cuttings and by division. Space 2 feet apart.

Uses. A few stems of fresh white phlox can be used in a mixed summer arrangement in a white vase; fresh colored phlox can be grouped alone. Phlox makes an excellent filler in a tall fresh arrangement. The individual florets may be used in pressed flower designs.

Harvesting and preparing. To press, separate the individual florets from the flower head.

—

Physalis (FIS-a-lis)

Genus of annuals and perennials having alternate, ovate or heart-shaped leaves. Inconspicuous flowers grow in the axils of leaves. Fruit is a yellow or green, sometimes sticky, berry that is enclosed by an inflated, round green calyx. In late summer, the calyx turns pale yellow to deep orange or red. Zones 2-8.

Selected species and varieties.
P. alkekengi, Chinese lantern, Japanese lantern, grows to 2 feet tall and spreads rapidly on underground stems. Leaves are 3 inches long. Flowers are white, ½ inch wide and bloom in summer. The calyx inflates to 2 inches wide. Zones 4-8.

Growing conditions. Plant Chinese lantern in sun or partial shade and in rich soil. Because it spreads so quickly, it should be confined; plant in bottomless containers that are then buried. Propagate Chinese lantern by division in early spring and from seeds. Plants grown from seeds will bloom the second year.

Uses. Use the ornamental calyx of Chinese lantern while it is still green in fresh arrangements, or dry it and use in wreaths and other dried arrangements. The calyx may be used whole, or split at the seams to form a star shape, revealing the berrylike fruit inside.

Harvesting and preparing. To use fresh, pick the calyxes while still green and place in water; they will last for weeks. To use dried, pick at various stages of coloration; then stand the stems with whole calyxes upright in a container, or split the calyxes at the seams before standing them upright to dry.

—

Pincushion flower see *Scabiosa*

Pinkhead knotweed
see *Polygonum*

Pinks see *Dianthus*

Plantain lily see *Hosta*

Plume thistle see *Cirsium*

—

Podocarpus (po-doh-KAR-pus)

Genus of evergreen trees and shrubs with alternate, mostly narrow or ovate leaves. Male flowers are naked, catkinlike masses of anthers. The female flower is a solitary, naked ovule between one or two small bracts. Fruit is stonelike, often fleshy-stalked, and red or reddish purple. Zones 7-10.

Selected species and varieties.
P. macrophyllus, southern yew, Japanese yew, grows to 60 feet tall. Branches and branchlets are slightly pendulous. Leaves are 3 to 4 inches long, leathery and arranged spirally. Fruit is purplish, fleshy and about ½ inch long. Zones 8-10.

Growing conditions. Southern yew grows in sun or partial shade and in good garden soil that is kept relatively moist and well mulched. Plant in spring or fall and allow adequate space for growth. Propagate from seeds or from stem cuttings taken in the summer. In cold climates, young plants can be grown in pots or tubs and brought indoors over the winter.

Uses. Fresh foliage with or without berries can be used as filler, or it can be used to add line to a centerpiece, a bouquet or a tall arrangement. The preserved branches can be used in wreaths, garlands and other dried arrangements.

PHYSALIS ALKEKENGI

PODOCARPUS MACROPHYLLUS

POLYGONUM CUSPIDATUM

POLYSTICHUM ACROSTICHOIDES

PROTEA COMPACTA

Harvesting and preparing. To preserve the branches with leaves, place them in a glycerine solution.

Polygonum (po-LIG-o-num)

Large genus of fast-growing annuals and perennials, sometimes vining, that have angled stems that are swollen where the leaf base clasps the stem. Leaves are alternate, simple, entire, variously shaped, and sometimes spotted or streaked with brown. Flowers bloom in terminal spikes or in loose racemes, and are sometimes showy. Zones 3-9.

Selected species and varieties. *P. aubertii,* silver lace vine, is a perennial vine that grows 20 feet long. Leaves are 2½ inches long and ovate to lanceolate. Fragrant white flowers bloom on erect, dense panicles in August. Zones 5-9. *P. capitatum,* pinkhead knotweed, is a perennial that grows about 3 inches tall with 10-inch-long trailing branches. Leaves are elliptical and 1½ inches long. Flower heads are pink, ¾ inch across and dense. Zones 6-9. *P. cuspidatum,* Mexican bamboo, Japanese fleece-flower, is an 8-foot-tall perennial that grows from a vigorous rhizome and has hollow stems. Leaves are 5 inches long, elliptical to nearly orbicular and sharply pointed. Flowers are small, greenish white in axillary, panicled racemes, and bloom in August and September. *P. cuspidatum compactum* is a smaller form; its flowers have red sepals. Zones 4-9.

Growing conditions. Grow polygonum in full sun or partial shade in moist but well-drained soil. Prune silver lace vine in late winter or in spring to keep it from being invasive. Propagate from seeds sown indoors or in a cold frame and set outdoors after danger of frost is past. Polygonum may also be propagated by division in early spring.

Uses. Silver lace vine can be used fresh as filler; its spray of white flowers can be dried and placed in a mixed dried arrangement. Pinkhead knotweed, with its small, cloverlike flower, makes a useful filler in a fresh or dried arrangement. Mexican bamboo, with its delicate, vertical airy spray, also makes a good filler in a fresh or dried arrangement. Its dried, hollow stem can be used for line in a vertical or Oriental arrangement.

Harvesting and preparing. Air-dry silver lace vine flower sprays by standing them upright in a small amount of water. Air-dry both pinkhead knotweed and Mexican bamboo by hanging them upside down.

Polystichum (po-LIS-ti-kum)
Shield fern, holly fern

Genus of mostly evergreen ferns having erect rhizomes and elongated, clustered fronds (leaves) with blades that are divided one or more times and with pinnately lobed leaflets. Zones 4-7.

Selected species and varieties. *P. acrostichoides,* Christmas fern, dagger fern, has evergreen, leathery leaves that are 2 feet long and 5 inches wide. Small upper pairs of leaflets have spores.

Growing conditions. Christmas fern likes shade and moist woodland soil. It will tolerate a sunny location if kept extra moist. Propagate by division in spring.

Uses. Christmas fern can be used fresh to add texture to, and establish line in, a fresh arrangement. Cut short, it can be used as a filler. It can be pressed and used in a dried arrangement or a pressed flower and foliage design.

Harvesting and preparing. Press Christmas fern to preserve it.

Pot marigold see *Calendula*
Prairie gentian see *Eustoma*
Prince's feather
see *Amaranthus*

Protea (PRO-tee-a)

Large genus of evergreen shrubs having alternate, entire, leathery leaves. Flowers are tightly clustered, usually stalkless, in generally solitary, cup- or goblet-shaped heads with collars of overlapping, colored, showy bracts. Zone 10.

Selected species and varieties. *P. compacta* is a branched shrub that grows up to 10 feet tall. Leaves are ovate and 4½ inches long. Flower heads are 4 inches long with hairy bracts. Innermost bracts are colored pink to carmine. *P. neriifolia*, pink mink protea, oleander-leaved protea, grows 5 feet tall with downy branches and narrowly oblong, 6-inch leaves that are woolly at the bases. Flower heads are 5 inches long and have salmon-pink to deep rose-pink bracts with black fur-like tips.

Growing conditions. Protea grows well in areas with warm, dry summers and mild, moist winters. It needs partial shade in its first year, full sun thereafter and well-drained, sandy soil.

Uses. Used fresh, protea makes a long-lasting flower, which can be used to create a focal point in a fresh arrangement. Dried protea can be used in a wreath. Pink mink protea's outermost bracts recurve when dried, making the heads saucer-shaped; the dried heads can be used in wreaths.

Harvesting and preparing. Air-dry protea at various stages by hanging it upside down or by placing it face up on a mesh screen. Allow pink mink protea to dry naturally on the plant.

—

Prunus (PROO-nus)

Large genus of deciduous and broadleaf evergreen shrubs and trees having alternate, simple and mostly serrate leaves. Flowers are white, pink or red, and have five sepals and petals in corymbs or racemes. Fruits are fleshy with a single stone; they include almonds, apricots, cherries, peaches and Japanese flowering cherries. Flowers bloom in spring before, along with or after leaves. Zones 3-8.

Selected species and varieties. *P. serrulata*, Oriental cherry, grows to 25 feet tall with 2¾- to 5½-inch-long leaves. Nonfragrant flowers are single or double, white or pink, 1½ inches across and occur in clusters of three to five. They bloom in early to mid-May before the leaves appear. Fruit is black and the size of a pea. Zones 5-8. *P. subhirtella*, Higan cherry, grows from 25 to 30 feet tall with slender branches. Leaves are 1 to 3 inches long and are ovate to lanceolate, short-pointed, double serrate and hairy on the undersides. Flowers

are pink to nearly white and ¾ inch across, with notched petals and clusters of two to five flowers. Fruit is black, egg-shaped and ⁵⁄₁₆ inch long. Flowers bloom in late April before the leaves appear. Zones 6-8. 'Pendula', weeping Higan cherry, grows 20 to 30 feet tall with slender, drooping branches. Flowers are 1 inch wide and light pink.

Growing conditions. Plant the ornamental cherries in full sun and in reasonably moist, well-drained soil. Water deeply and regularly during a drought. Prune weak or crossing branches in early spring. Watch for insect or disease problems; diagnose and treat early.

Uses. Fresh branches of flowers can be used in tall fresh arrangements; cherry branches are especially appropriate in Oriental arrangements. Branches with buds can be cut in January and taken indoors for forcing. Branches of green leaves can be used to create line in summer arrangements. Individual blossoms can be used in pressed flower designs.

Harvesting and preparing. Hammer the ends of freshly cut branches before conditioning normally. Separate individual flowers from the branches and press them.

—

Purple coneflower
see *Echinacea*

Pussyfoot see *Ageratum*

Pussy willow see *Salix*

Pyrethum see *Chrysanthemum*

Quaking grass see *Briza*

Queen Anne's lace see *Daucus*

—

Quercus (KWER-kus)
Oak

Large genus of deciduous and evergreen trees having leaves that are alternate, pinnately nerved, dentate, serrate or pinnately lobed, and rarely entire. Many male flowers occur in slender, drooping catkins. One or more female flowers occur on spikes. Fruit is an acorn—a nut surrounded at its base by a cuplike bract. Zones 2-10.

Selected species and varieties. *Q. coccinea*, scarlet oak, is a decidu-

PRUNUS SERRULATA

QUERCUS COCCINEA

RHUS TYPHINA

ROSA RUGOSA

ous tree that can reach 80 feet tall. Leaves are oblong to elliptical, 6 inches long, with seven to nine very deep lobes. Leaves turn brilliant red in fall. Zones 4-9.

Growing conditions. Oak grows well in full sun and fertile, moist, light, sandy, loamy soil. It will tolerate partial shade and transplanting when young.

Uses. Branches with male flowers and young leaves may be used in fresh spring arrangements. Branches of fall leaves can be used either fresh or dried. Individual leaves maintain good shape and color when pressed; they can also be skeletonized.

Harvesting and preparing. Air-dry branches of fall leaves by standing them upright in a container. Branches can also be preserved in a glycerine solution. Press or skeletonize individual leaves.

—

Redbox see *Eucalyptus*
Reedmace see *Typha*

—

Rhus (ROOS)
Sumac

Large genus of shrubs and trees with compound leaves and pinnately arranged leaflets. Flowers are small, greenish, usually unisexual and occur in panicles. Fruit is small, berrylike, hairy, red and occurs in clusters in all the cultivated sumacs. Zones 2-9.

Selected species and varieties. *R. typhina,* staghorn sumac, is a shrub that grows from 10 to 30 feet tall and has densely brown, hairy branches and bright green pinnate leaves up to 1¼ feet long. Leaflets are lanceolate-oblong, toothed and 2 to 4½ inches long. Flower panicles bloom in summer and are followed in fall by cones of crowded red fruit. Fall foliage turns orange and scarlet. Zones 4-9.

Growing conditions. Staghorn sumac grows in full sun and in poor, sandy, dry soil. It transplants easily. Prune to keep within bounds.

Uses. Fresh branches of summer or fall foliage can be used with or without fruit clusters to provide sweeping lines and bright color in fresh arrangements. The fruit clusters may be used fresh, or used dried in wreaths and garlands.

Harvesting and preparing. Air-dry the seed clusters and branches by laying them flat.

—

Rosa (RO-za)

Large genus of deciduous or, less often, evergreen shrubs, usually prickly, with erect, trailing or clambering stems. Leaves are alternate and generally pinnate. Flowers may be single, semidouble or double, and solitary or occurring in clusters. Fruit is called a hip. Zones 2-10.

Selected species and varieties. *R. multiflora,* Japanese rose, grows to 10 feet tall in a dense arching habit. It is used as understock to graft other roses. Flowers are white, ¾ inch across and bloom in mid-June. Hips are red and ¼ inch across. Zones 5-10. *R. rugosa* is a 6-foot-tall, sturdy, very prickly bush having leaves of five to nine leaflets that are wrinkled and downy on the undersides. They turn bright orange and red in the fall. Flowers are rose to white, 3½ inches across, single or double, and fragrant; they bloom from spring through fall. Hips are bright red and 1 inch across. *R.* hybrids exist in thousands of varieties. They are classified by growth habit, manner of flowering and type of bloom. Some are shrubby; others climb. Some are highly fragrant. They are available in many colors and combinations of colors.

Growing conditions. Grow roses in areas receiving five hours of sun per day and in well-prepared, well-drained, slightly acid soil. *R. rugosa* tolerates saltwater spray and exposed sites. Propagate roses by division, from cuttings, from suckers and from seeds. In cold climates, space plants 2 feet apart; in milder climates, where they grow vigorously and need more space, plant them 3 feet apart.

Uses. Fresh roses may be displayed as single blossoms, or grouped in loose vase arrangements or centerpieces. They may also be dried for use in bouquets, wreaths and other dried arrangements. The dried rose hips add color and accent to wreaths and garlands.

Harvesting and preparing. To use fresh, cut the flower back to the first bud eye below the topmost five-leaflet leaf; this will allow the stalk to produce more blossoms. To use dried, cut when the rose is in bud or has opened only slightly. Dry the bud in silica gel or in a microwave oven, or tie in bunches and hang upside down. To use the hips, let them dry naturally on the plant.

—

Rose see *Rosa*

Royal fern see *Osmunda*

—

Rudbeckia (rud-BEK-ee-a)
Coneflower

Genus of annuals, biennials and perennials having alternate, simple or compound, sometimes deeply lobed leaves. Flower heads are showy, usually radiate, terminal or axillary. Ray flowers are generally yellow, and the disk flowers are sometimes brown or black. Fruit is dry, one-celled and one-seeded. Zones 3-9.

Selected species and varieties. *R. fulgida,* orange coneflower, is a 10- to 12-foot-tall perennial. Lower leaves are simple and long-stalked; upper leaves are stalkless. Flower head is 3 inches wide with orange-yellow ray flowers and a black disk flower. Flowers bloom in late summer. *R. hirta,* black-eyed Susan, is annual or biennial and grows 3 feet tall. It has rough, hairy stems and leaves. Basal leaves are ovate and twice as long as broad. Upper leaves are narrow. Flower heads are deep yellow, 2 to 3 inches wide, and occur on terminal or axillary stalks. The disk flower is cone-shaped and dark brown. Flowers bloom from June to August. *R. triloba,* brown-eyed Susan, is a biennial that grows up to 5 feet tall. Basal leaves are ovate to heart-shaped and long-stalked. The stem leaves are narrow, short-stalked and sometimes deeply lobed. Flower heads are 2½ inches across; ray flowers are deep yellow or almost orange, and disk flowers are brown or dark purple.

Growing conditions. Coneflower prefers warm weather. It thrives in full sun and well-drained but moist

soil. Propagate orange coneflower by division in early spring and from cuttings. Black-eyed Susan and brown-eyed Susan can be propagated from seeds sown in a cold frame in early spring and transplanted when seedlings are large enough to handle. Seeds can be sown outdoors in warm soil. Plant 18 inches apart.

Uses. Brilliantly colored coneflowers make long-lasting focal flowers in fresh, mixed summer centerpieces or in taller arrangements. Dried flowers and seed heads can also be used in wreaths or other dried arrangements.

Harvesting and preparing. To use the flowers dried, preserve them in silica gel or in a microwave oven. To use the seed heads, pick after the petals fall and air-dry.

—

Rumex (ROO-meks)
Dock

Large genus of annuals and perennials. Some develop woody stems and become shrubs. Stems are grooved with conspicuously large basal leaves; upper leaves become progressively smaller. Flowers are small, greenish or reddish, unisexual or bisexual, and occur in close or spreading panicles. Zones 3-9.

Selected species and varieties. *R. acetosa,* garden sorrel, is a perennial that grows 3 feet tall and has arrow-shaped leaves that are alternate, simple, entire and 5 inches long. Leaves are edible and are often used in salads. Flowers are unisexual and they occur in terminal panicles that turn red-brown when the seeds form. Flowers bloom from March to August.

Growing conditions. Grow sorrel in full sun and fertile soil. Propagate from seeds and by division.

Uses. Use the flower panicles fresh to establish line in vertical arrangements; cut short and use as filler in centerpieces. Use the dried flowers in mixed arrangements.

Harvesting and preparing. To use the flowers dried, pick at various stages of coloration and air-dry by standing the stalks upright, or preserve in a glycerine solution to maintain their flexibility.

RUDBECKIA FULGIDA

RUMEX ACETOSA

SALIX DISCOLOR

SALVIA FARINACEA

Safflower see *Carthamus*
Sage see *Salvia*
Sagebrush see *Artemisia*

Salix (SAY-liks)
Willow

Large genus of deciduous, often brittle-wooded, shrubs and trees having mostly lanceolate leaves that are alternate and usually narrow. Small flowers are borne in an axil of a bract and occur in dense catkins that bloom before or after the leaves. Fruit is a small capsule of seeds covered with hair or down. Zones 2-9.

Selected species and varieties. *S. discolor,* pussy willow, large pussy willow, is a 20-foot shrub or small tree. Leaves are 4 inches long and oblong, wavy-toothed or nearly entire. Catkins are silvery, 1 inch long and bloom in early spring before the leaves. Zones 3-9.

Growing conditions. Plant pussy willow in full sun in a moist location. Prune any time of the year.

Uses. Fresh branches with catkins can be used to establish line in triangular and vertical arrangements, or they can be used in fresh bouquets of spring flowers. When dried, the silver-colored catkins hold their color and shape; branches of catkins can lend line to medium or large dried arrangements, or they can be shaped to make a good base for wreaths.

Harvesting and preparing. To use dried, cut the branches before the catkins fluff out with seeds, and stand them upright in a vase to dry.

Salvia (SAL-vee-a)

Large genus of annuals, perennials and shrubs, usually having square stems. Leaves occur in pairs and are opposite, simple, ovate or lance-shaped; they sometimes have hairy margins, are toothed or deeply cut into segments, and are smaller toward the top of the plant. Flowers come in a variety of colors and emerge from the axils of small, leafy bracts. They occur in terminal spikes or racemes. Zones 3-9.

Selected species and varieties. *S. farinacea,* mealy-cup sage, is a 2- to 3-foot annual north of Zone 8, and a perennial in the South. It has shrubby stems and lanceolate leaves. Flowers are violet-blue, tubular, ½ inch long and bloom in racemes from July until frost. Zones 8 and 9. 'Blue Bedder' has leaves up to 8 inches long and deep blue flowers with a white spot. They occur in 8-inch racemes. 'Victoria' is a compact 18-inch-tall annual in northern zones, and a perennial in frost-free areas. Flowers are rich violet-blue and bloom in spikes.

S. officinalis, garden sage, is a 2-foot-tall shrub with 2-inch-long leaves that are white, woolly and wrinkled. Flowers are ¾ inch long and white, blue or purple. This is the herb used for seasoning. Zones 5-9. *S. splendens,* scarlet sage, grows from 3 to 8 feet tall. It is an annual in colder climates and a perennial in warmer areas. Leaves are ovate and 3½ inches long. Flowers are whorled, scarlet, white or rose, and held in rigidly upright racemes. Zones 8 and 9. 'St. John's Fire' grows 12 inches tall and has dark leaves with bright red flowers that bloom in spikes from July to frost.

Growing conditions. Grow salvia in full sun and moist but well-drained light soil. It will tolerate dry weather, but will produce fewer blooms. Garden sage can stand a richer soil. It flowers in its second year and needs pruning in spring. Propagate perennials from seeds, by division and from cuttings. Annuals can be propagated from seeds sown indoors in February or March. Transplant seedlings after danger of frost is past.

Uses. Salvia can be used fresh as a line flower in a centerpiece, or dried to use in a mixed fall arrangement or dried bouquet. The flower also retains good color when pressed. Mealy-cup sage turns blue when dried, and can be used for its color in a mixed dried arrangement. The dried leaves of garden sage can be added to kitchen wreaths or potpourris.

Harvesting and preparing. To use dried, pick mealy-cup sage when four-fifths of the spike is developed; air-dry plants by hanging upside down. Air-dry the leaves of garden sage.

Satin flower see *Clarkia*

Scabiosa (skab-ee-O-sa)

Genus of annuals and perennials having leaves that are opposite, entire or dissected, ovate or lance-shaped. Flowers are surrounded by two rows of small, leafy bracts in blue, purple, brownish black, reddish brown, pink, cream or white. Flower heads are terminal atop long stems and resemble small, round pincushions. Zones 2-9.

Selected species and varieties. *S. caucasica,* pincushion flower, is a hardy perennial that grows from 1½ to 2½ feet tall. Basal leaves are blue-green and lanceolate-linear; stem leaves are divided. Flowers are blue, 3 inches across and occur in flat heads with tufted round centers; they bloom in July and August. 'Miss Willmott' has creamy white blossoms. Zones 3-9. *S. stellata,* starflower, paper moon, is a 1½-foot-tall, hairy annual with pinnately cleft leaves. Flower heads are blue or rose-violet, 1¼ inches across and bloom in summer. They are followed by globular seed heads made up of papery spheres, called calyxes, and starlike pistils.

Growing conditions. Plant pincushion flower and starflower in full sun and moist soil. Pincushion flower likes neutral to alkaline soil, and can be propagated by division in early spring. Propagate starflower from seeds sown indoors or in a cold frame in early spring and transplanted outdoors after danger of frost is past. In mild climates, plant starflower seeds in late summer for a second crop. Space 1 foot apart.

Uses. Pincushion flowers make good focal flowers in fresh arrangements. Starflower seed heads can be used in dried wreaths or in other mixed arrangements, whether fresh or dried.

Harvesting and preparing. Pick the strong-stemmed seed heads of starflowers when the green stars begin to turn black; air-dry by standing them upright in an empty container.

Scarlet oak see *Quercus*
Scotch heather see *Calluna*
Sea holly see *Eryngium*

Sea lavender see *Limonium*
Sea myrtle see *Baccharis*
Sea pink see *Armeria*

Sedum (SEE-dum)
Stonecrop

Large genus of succulent perennials and small shrubs having mostly alternate and sessile leaves that are often small and overlapping. Flowers are usually terminal and usually occur in broad or flat-topped cymes of two or more. They grow alternately left and right and not in one direction. Colors range from white, yellow, pink and red to purple. Zones 3-9.

Selected species and varieties. *S.* × 'Autumn Joy' grows to 2 feet tall with leaves scattered along the stems. Flowers are ¼ to ¾ inch across and grow in platelike, 3- to 4-inch-wide clusters. Flowers are pink when they start to bloom in late summer, changing to salmon and rosy russet in late fall. *S. spectabile,* showy stonecrop, is a perennial that grows from 12 to 22 inches tall. Leaves are opposite or occurring in threes or fours, somewhat toothed, blue-green and 3 inches long by 2 inches wide. Flowers are pink, ½ inch wide and bloom in flat clusters 3 to 4 inches across in early fall. 'Album' has white flowers. 'Brilliant' grows to 18 inches tall with raspberry red flowers.

Growing conditions. Stonecrop can be grown in full sun or light shade in well-drained soil; it is drought-resistant. 'Autumn Joy' tolerates wet soil. Propagate from seeds, by division or from stem cuttings. Space plants 15 to 18 inches apart.

Uses. Fresh stonecrop flowers can be used to create focal points in fresh arrangements. 'Autumn Joy' lasts especially well in water. Both the flower clusters and the seed heads of stonecrop can be used dried in wreaths and other mixed dried arrangements.

Harvesting and preparing. To use the flowers dried, pick when the clusters are fully open and hang to air-dry. Allow the seed heads to remain on the plant to dry.

SCABIOSA CAUCASICA 'MISS WILLMOTT'

SEDUM × 'AUTUMN JOY'

SENECIO CINERARIA

SOLIDAGO CANADENSIS 'PETER PAN'

Senecio (se-NEE-see-o)

Large genus of annual, biennial, perennial vines and shrubs and small trees having alternate or basal leaves. Flower heads are generally yellow, but sometimes purple, red, blue or white, and may be solitary or clustered. They are usually composed of ray and disk flowers, but sometimes lack ray flowers.

Selected species and varieties. *S. cineraria,* dusty miller, silver groundsel, is a perennial grown as an annual that reaches 2½ feet tall. Leaves are white, woolly, deeply cut into blunt parts and 2 to 5½ inches long. Flowers are yellow to cream and bloom in ½-inch-wide terminal clusters from late spring to autumn.

Growing conditions. Grow dusty miller in full sun and well-drained soil. It is well suited to coastal areas. Propagate from seeds sown indoors in early spring and transplant seedlings two to three weeks before the last frost date. Space plants 1 foot apart.

Uses. Dusty miller leaves may be used fresh or dried to add texture and a silvery color to centerpieces, tall arrangements, bouquets and garlands. They are especially attractive when used with pink flowers in a small fresh arrangement.

Harvesting and preparing. To dry dusty miller, first poke tissue into the gaps along the stems to keep the plant from closing in on itself; then either hang it or stand it upright in an empty container.

—

Shasta daisy see *Chrysanthemum*

Shellflower see *Moluccella*

Shield fern see *Polystichum*

Siberian larkspur
see *Delphinium*

Sideoats gramma
see *Bouteloua*

Silk tree see *Albizia*

Silver dollar see *Lunaria*

Silver dollar gum see *Eucalyptus*

Silver groundsel see *Senecio*

Silver lace vine see *Polygonum*

Smokeweed see *Eupatorium*

Snapdragon see *Antirrhinum*

Solidago (so-li-DAY-go)

Large genus of erect, somewhat woody perennials having stems that are seldom branched, and simple, alternate leaves that are either toothed or entire. Ray and disk flowers are yellow, occasionally white and about ¼ inch wide. They are borne in a wide variety of frequently one-sided terminal clusters, and bloom in late summer and early fall. Zones 3-9.

Selected species and varieties. *S. canadensis,* Canada goldenrod, grows from 1 to 4 feet tall with lanceolate leaves up to 5 inches long. Flower heads are yellow and compactly arranged in branched, one-sided, terminal panicles. 'Peter Pan' is a compact plant reaching only 2½ feet tall and having canary yellow blossoms. *S. sempervirens,* seaside goldenrod, grows from 2 to 5 feet tall. Leaves are thick, narrowly lanceolate with slender tips, and closely alternating on the stem. Lower leaves are stem-clasping. Flower heads are borne on one-sided terminal or axillary panicles. Blooming occurs late summer to late fall. Zones 4-9.

Growing conditions. Grow goldenrod in sun or partial shade in well-drained soil. It will tolerate moist soil. If the soil is too rich, growth goes into the foliage. Propagate from seeds or by division. Goldenrod self-sows readily. Space plants 18 inches apart.

Uses. Goldenrod can be used in a fresh or dried arrangement as a filler flower. Small parts of the flower can be used in pressed designs.

Harvesting and preparing. To use goldenrod dried, pick when it begins to flower; it will continue to open and will hold its color. Hang to air-dry.

—

Sorghum (SOR-gum)

Genus of annual and perennial grasses that usually have long, flat leaf blades. Flowers occur in loose or compact panicles formed by many spikelike racemes. Spikelets occur in pairs: one stalkless and fertile, the other stalked and male, or barren.

Selected species and varieties. *S. bicolor* is a coarse annual with robust stems that grow up to 12 feet tall. Leaves are 2 feet long and 2 inches wide. Flowers occur in large panicles. *S. bicolor technicum,* broomcorn, has stiff branches that are 12 to 30 inches long with twisted fruit heads. The household broom is made from these branches.

Growing conditions. Grow sorghum in sun and in fertile soil that is neutral to slightly acid. Propagate by sowing seeds outdoors in the spring.

Uses. Sorghum flower panicles can be used fresh or dried; they make good filler in mixed grass arrangements. Dried branches of broomcorn can be used to establish line in vertical and Oriental arrangements.

Harvesting and preparing. Air-dry both the panicles and the branches of sorghum and broomcorn by hanging them upside down.

—

Southern magnolia
see *Magnolia*

Southernwood see *Artemisia*

Southern yew see *Podocarpus*

Speedwell see *Veronica*

Spindle tree see *Euonymus*

Spirea see *Astilbe*

Sprenger fern see *Asparagus*

Squirreltail grass see *Hordeum*

—

Stachys (STAK-is)
Woundwort

Large genus of annuals and perennials that are usually hairy and that have opposite and ovate or broadly lance-shaped leaves. Flowers are white, yellow, pink, red or purple, and bloom in whorls on terminal spikes. The tubular corolla opens into two lips. Zones 4-9.

Selected species and varieties. *S. byzantina,* lamb's-ears, is a perennial that grows 1 to 1½ feet tall and has soft, woolly, silver leaves shaped somewhat like lambs' ears. Flowers are pink to purple and 1 inch across, growing in densely flowered whorls on furry spikes; they bloom from July to frost.

Growing conditions. Grow lamb's-ears in full sun and in fertile, well-drained soil. It tolerates dry

soil. Divide and replant every third or fourth year only if the plant is not thriving. Propagate from seeds, by division in spring or early fall, and by rooting cuttings in a cold frame in summer. Flower spikes bloom the second year. Space plants 12 inches apart.

Uses. Used fresh, the delicate foliage and furry flower spikes lend contrast and background to fresh arrangements. The young foliage shoots and the flower spikes can be dried and used in mixed arrangements. The leaves can be dried for use in wreaths, or pressed for flat designs.

Harvesting and preparing. Air-dry the young foliage shoots in a horizontal position. To use the flower spikes dried, pick when the spike is two-thirds developed, and air-dry by hanging upside down or by laying the stalks flat on a screen. Press or air-dry the leaves.

—

Starflower see *Scabiosa*

Star of Persia see *Allium*

Statice see *Limonium*

Stock see *Matthiola*

Stonecrop see *Sedum*

Strawberry bush see *Euonymus*

Strawflower see *Helichrysum*

Sugar maple see *Acer*

Sultan's flower see *Centaurea*

Sumac see *Rhus*

Summer's darling see *Clarkia*

Sunflower see *Helianthus*

Sweet Annie see *Artemisia*

Sweetgum see *Liquidambar*

Sweet pea see *Lathyrus*

Sweet sultan see *Centaurea*

Sweet violet see *Viola*

Sweet William see *Dianthus*

Sword fern see *Nephrolepis*

Sword lily see *Gladiolus*

—

Syringa (sy-RING-ga)
Lilac

Genus of deciduous shrubs and small trees having opposite leaves. Flowers are small, fragrant, white,

SORGHUM BICOLOR TECHNICUM

STACHYS BYZANTINA

SYRINGA VULGARIS

TAGETES PATULA × ERECTA (NUGGETS SERIES)

TANACETUM VULGARE

lilac, pink, red or purple, and occur in showy clusters. They are tubular with four spreading lobes and two stamens. Zones 3-9.

Selected species and varieties. *S. vulgaris,* common lilac, grows to a height of 20 feet. Leaves are heart-shaped, smooth and 5 inches long. Flowers are pale purple, borne on 10-inch-long lateral panicles and bloom in May. Zones 4-8. 'Alba' has white flowers.

Growing conditions. Plant lilac in full sun with good air circulation. Soil should be fertile, moist, and neutral or slightly alkaline. Lilac transplants easily. Blooming occurs on the previous year's growth. Prune after flowering to remove suckers and older, crowded branches. Apply fertilizer and limestone every two years.

Uses. Lilacs make attractive filler in fresh arrangements, or they can be grouped alone in a vase. Starting in mid-January, the branches may be cut for forcing indoors.

Harvesting and preparing. Hammer the stem ends of lilac before conditioning normally.

—

Tabasco pepper see *Capsicum*

—

Tagetes (ta-JEE-teez)
Marigold

Genus of annuals and a few tender perennials that are erect and branching, having opposite leaves that are usually fernlike and strong-scented. Flower heads vary in size and may be single, semidouble or double.

Selected species and varieties. *T. erecta,* African marigold, is an 18- to 36-inch-tall half-hardy annual that is branched and bushy. Leaves are pinnately divided. Flower heads are yellow or orange, 2 to 6 inches wide with long rays and bloom from late summer to frost. *T. patula,* French marigold, is a 6- to 18-inch-tall half-hardy annual that is much branched with pinnate leaves. Numerous rays form a 2- to 3-inch-wide flower head that is yellow with red markings, orange or red-brown. Flowers bloom from summer to frost. *T. patula × erecta,* hybrid marigolds, are 10 to 16

inches high and sterile. Nuggets Series bear 2-inch double flowers that may be yellow, orange, red or bicolored; flowers blossom all summer.

Growing conditions. Marigold grows in full sun and in fertile, porous soil. It prefers warm weather. Afternoon shade will prolong bloom in the South and Southwest. African and French marigolds have low germination rates. Propagate marigolds from seeds sown indoors at 65° to 70° F about six to eight weeks before the last spring frost. Set outdoors once the soil is warm. Space African marigold 1 to 1½ feet apart; French marigold, 8 inches to 1 foot apart.

Uses. Fresh marigold lasts long and makes an excellent focal flower in a fresh arrangement. Dried marigold can be used as a filler flower in a mixed dried bouquet or a wreath. The fernlike leaves can be used in pressed designs.

Harvesting and preparing. To use dried, pick marigold blossoms when they are in midbloom to full bloom; dry in silica gel or in a microwave oven to retain the best shape and color. Press the foliage.

—

Tailflower see *Anthurium*

Tampala see *Amaranthus*

—

Tanacetum (tan-a-SEE-tum)

Genus of aromatic annuals, perennials and small shrubs having alternate, entire, lobed leaves. Flower heads are solitary and terminal or in clusters. Disk flowers are yellow and are sometimes surrounded by yellow ray flowers. Zones 3-9.

Selected species and varieties. *T. vulgare,* tansy, golden buttons, is a coarse, rhizomatous perennial that grows 3 to 4 feet tall and 4 feet wide. Leaves are pinnate and 4¾ inches long with toothed or incised leaflets. Flower heads are golden yellow, ¼ to ½ inch across and bloom in flat-topped clusters. Flowers bloom in summer.

Growing conditions. Plant tansy in sun or partial shade and in well-drained soil. It is highly invasive and needs to be divided in spring or fall to prevent it from spreading.

Propagate by dividing clumps and from seeds. Space plants 4 to 5 feet apart.

Uses. Tansy makes an excellent filler flower in a fresh arrangement; it retains good color when dried, and can be used in a mixed dried bouquet or a wreath. The leaves can be added to the base of a fresh arrangement or they can be used in pressed designs.

Harvesting and preparing. Air-dry flower heads by hanging them upside down; press the leaves.

—

Tansy see *Tanacetum*
Tassel flower see *Amaranthus*
Teasel see *Dipsacus*
Texan bluebell see *Eustoma*

—

Thalictrum (tha-LIK-trum)
Meadow rue

Large genus of graceful perennials having alternate, basal leaves that are twice- or thrice-compound. Small petal-less flowers have showy colored sepals and stamens and occur in large, often branching, panicles or racemes. Zones 2-9.

Selected species and varieties. *T. dioicum,* early meadow rue, is a 1- to 2½-foot-tall perennial having leaves separated from one another by branching petioles as long as or longer than the leaflets. Flowers are nodding, have greenish yellow stamens and bloom in 12-inch-long loose panicles in early summer. Zones 4-9. *T. polygamum,* tall meadow rue, is an 8-foot-tall perennial with many branches. Leaflets are rounded and three-lobed. Flowers have white stamens and sepals of about equal length on 1-foot-long panicles; they bloom in early summer. Zones 3-9.

Growing conditions. Meadow rue grows in sun or partial shade and in fertile, moist, well-drained soil. Divide every fourth or fifth year for good growth. Propagate by division in spring. Sow seeds of early meadow rue in summer. Space plants 12 to 15 inches apart.

Uses. The fresh flower sprays of meadow rue can be used to create focal points in fresh arrangements or used as filler. The dried flower sprays can be used in mixed dried arrangements. The delicate, soft foliage makes a good background in a fresh arrangement.

Harvesting and preparing. Air-dry the flower sprays by hanging them upside down.

—

Thistle see *Cirsium*
Thoroughwort see *Eupatorium*
Thrift see *Armeria*
Thyme see *Thymus*

—

Thymus (THY-mus)

Large genus of aromatic perennials and small shrubs, mostly evergreen, with stems that are generally prostrate or creeping and woody at the bases. Leaves are opposite, small and entire. Few to many flowers are crowded in terminal heads. Zones 3-8.

Selected species and varieties. *T. vulgaris,* thyme, is a 6- to 15-inch erect shrub with woody stems. Leaves are linear to elliptical and up to ½ inch long. Flowers are lilac-colored to purplish, ³⁄₁₆ inch long and bloom on upright spikes in late May. 'Argenteus', silver thyme, is a variety that has foliage variegated in silver. Zones 5-8.

Growing conditions. Grow thyme in full sun and in dry neutral soil. Prune plants halfway back when spring blooming starts; feed and water heavily at that time. Divide every three to five years. Propagate from cuttings, by division and from seeds.

Uses. Both the leaves and the flowers may be used to provide a warm aroma and delicate shape in small fresh arrangements. The dried leaves may be used in potpourris or herbal wreaths, and both leaves and flowers may be pressed.

Harvesting and preparing. Press the leaves, or air-dry them by hanging them upside down; press the flowers.

—

Tickseed see *Coreopsis*

THALICTRUM POLYGAMUM

THYMUS VULGARIS 'ARGENTEUS'

TITHONIA ROTUNDIFOLIA

TRACHYMENE COERULEA

TRITICUM HYBRID

Tithonia (ty-THO-nee-a)

Genus of annuals, perennials and shrubs having alternate, broadly ovate, deeply lobed or coarsely round-toothed leaves. On the lower stem, the leaves are sometimes opposite. Flower heads are usually solitary on long, hollow stems.

Selected species and varieties. *T. rotundifolia,* Mexican sunflower, is a 4- to 6-foot-tall tender annual that is woody and shrubby. Leaves are 6 inches long and have three lobes. Flower heads are bright orange or orange-scarlet, almost 3 inches in diameter and bloom on 1-foot-long stalks from midsummer until frost. 'Sun Dance' grows 3 to 4 feet high in a compact form and bears deep orange-colored blossoms.

Growing conditions. Mexican sunflower prefers warm weather. Grow it in full sun and average soil, giving each plant abundant space. Water during dry spells. Staking may be useful. Propagate from seed sown indoors in peat pots six to eight weeks before the last spring frost date. Plant outdoors after danger of frost is past. Seeds may be sown outdoors in a seedbed or where plants are to grow. Space plants 2½ to 3½ feet apart.

Uses. Mexican sunflower can be used fresh or dried. Used fresh, it is long-lasting and makes a good mass flower; when dried, it retains good color and can be used to create a focal point in a wreath or other dried arrangement.

Harvesting and preparing. Dry Mexican sunflower in silica gel or in a microwave oven.

—

Toad's mouth see *Antirrhinum*

—

Trachymene (tra-KIM-e-nee)

Small genus of annuals and perennials having erect, weak stems and twice- or thrice-compound leaves whose end segments are narrow and three-lobed. Flowers are white or blue, tiny and numerous, and borne in flat umbels with lanceolate bracts beneath.

Selected species and varieties. *T. coerulea,* blue lace flower, is a hardy annual that grows to 2 feet

tall. Flowers are light blue to lavender and bloom on 3-inch umbels in summer.

Growing conditions. Grow blue lace flower in full sun and in well-drained, average soil. Plant densely. Propagate from seeds sown in spring or in a cold frame in winter for spring bloom. Space plants 4 to 8 inches apart.

Uses. Used fresh, blue lace flower is long-lasting, and can be used as a delicate mass flower in a fresh arrangement. It can be used dried in a bouquet or a wreath.

Harvesting and preparing. Dry blue lace flower in silica gel or in a microwave oven.

—

Transvaal daisy see *Gerbera*

—

Triticum (TRIT-i-kum)

Genus of annual and biennial grasses having leaf blades that are flat. Flowers are two to five in crowded spikelets that form a solitary, thick spike. Fruit and seed are one and grooved.

Selected species and varieties. *T. aestivum,* wheat, is a 4-foot-tall annual grass with leaves up to 16 inches long and ½ inch wide. Fruit spikes are bearded and 4 inches long. Flowering occurs in summer. There are numerous varieties and many hybrids of both spring and winter wheat. Spring wheat is planted in spring and harvested in summer or fall. Winter wheat is planted in fall in areas where winters are moderate, and is harvested the following summer.

Growing conditions. Wheat grows well in full sun and ordinary soil that is slightly acid or neutral. It prefers warm weather. Propagate from seeds sown outdoors in the spring. Where winters are warm, plant wheat in the fall.

Uses. Wheat may be used to add form and line to a wreath or other dried arrangement.

Harvesting and preparing. To obtain different shades of wheat, pick at different stages before the seeds drop. Air-dry the stalks by hanging in bundles or by standing them upright in an empty container.

Trumpet flower see *Campsis*

Trumpet vine see *Campsis*

Tulip see *Tulipa*

—

Tulipa (TOO-lip-a)
Tulipa

Large genus of hardy, spring-blooming, deciduous perennials having bulbs that are usually pointed and covered with a thin, brown skin. Basal or stem leaves are lance-shaped, strap-shaped or linear, slightly fleshy and usually blue-green. Some leaves are mottled, streaked or marked with red-brown or chocolate brown. Flowers are cup-shaped, saucer-shaped or urn-shaped, and are usually solitary, but some species have two to five blossoms. When they open their petals widely in full sun, some form a starlike shape. Tulips come in all colors except for blue. Fruit is a many-seeded three-valved cap. Zones 4-8.

Selected species and varieties. There are thousands of *T.* hybrids providing a seemingly endless variety of shapes and color combinations. The flowers may have the standard shape of the species, or they may be frilled, fringed or double. Cultivars are available in a wide range of single colors and bicolors.

Growing conditions. Plant tulips in fall in full sun and in well-drained, sandy-textured soil. Renew plantings, since tulips last only one or two years. Use a bulb fertilizer or balanced slow-release fertilizer at planting time and once each year. Bulbs should be stored below 70° F. Propagate from bulbs ready to bloom or from offsets, the small bulbs that form on the existing plant. It takes two years before the new, small bulbs are large enough to bloom. Space bulbs 8 to 9 inches apart.

Uses. Freshly cut tulips can be grouped loosely in vases by themselves or placed in mixed spring arrangements. When dried, the flowers retain their color and can be used in mixed arrangements. The seedpods, too, are appropriate in dried arrangements.

Harvesting and preparing. When using tulips fresh, leave space in the arrangement for the flowers to grow as much as 2 inches more after they have been cut. Preserve the flowers in silica gel or in a microwave oven, and keep them away from moisture once dried. To obtain seedpods, leave a few blossoms on the plant; when pods develop, harvest and hang them to air-dry.

—

Typha (TY-fa)

Erect, aquatic perennial having a creeping rootstock. Leaves are mostly basal, linear or sword-shaped with their lower parts sheathed. Tiny flowers are usually crowded in dense, erect terminal spikes. The male flowers appear on the upper portion and the female flowers are mixed with sterile flowers on the lower portion of the spike. Fruit is a tiny nutlet containing mealy seeds. Zones 2-10.

Selected species and varieties. *T. angustifolia,* narrowleaf cattail, lesser reedmace, grows to 4 feet tall with ½-inch-wide leaves. Flower spikes are ⅝ to 1¼ inches in diameter. Flowers bloom in summer. *T. latifolia,* common cattail, bulrush, greater reedmace, grows from 4 to 6 feet tall with sword-shaped leaves up to 1 inch wide. Flowers occur in a brown, clublike spike without a definite space between male and female portions.

Growing conditions. Plant cattail in rich, loamy soil in an open, wet area. It spreads aggressively, but will not invade dry ground. Cattail can be confined to tubs. Propagate by dividing creeping rootstalks in spring or summer and from seeds sown in pots sunk in water almost to their rims.

Uses. Cattail can be used in a fresh or dried arrangement for its unusual form. Narrowleaf cattail has a dainty look; common cattail is larger and heavier.

Harvesting and preparing. Harvest cattails when the upper portion of the stems (the part above the club) is still in flower; if harvested much later, the clubs will shatter. To prevent shattering, spray the clubs with acrylic sealer after picking. Air-dry cattails by standing them upright in an empty container.

TULIPA 'DUTCH FAIR'

TYPHA ANGUSTIFOLIA

VENIDIUM FASTUOSUM

VERBASCUM PHOENICEUM

VERONICA SPICATA

Venidium (ve-NID-ee-um)

Genus of annuals and perennials having alternate leaves that are lobed or lobeless, toothed or toothless, and usually woolly. Flower heads are solitary and bisexual, and have tubular disk flowers surrounded by a single row of female, petal-like ray florets.

Selected species and varieties. *V. fastuosum,* cape daisy, is a gray, hairy, hollow-stemmed annual that grows from 2 to 3 feet tall and has leaves that are lanceolate to oblanceolate, irregularly lobed and 5 to 6 inches long. Flower heads are 4 to 6 inches long and have brownish purple or black disk flowers and numerous bright orange rays with purple-brown bases. Flowers bloom in midsummer.

Growing conditions. Plant cape daisy in full sun and in well-drained, sandy soil. It tolerates dry periods and grows better on the West Coast than the East Coast. Flowers tend to face the sun. Propagate from seeds sown indoors six to eight weeks before the last frost.

Uses. Cape daisies make good focal flowers in fresh arrangements and in dried arrangements, such as dried flower wreaths.

Harvesting and preparing. Even when cut, the fresh flowers close at night and open in the morning. To use dried, preserve the flowers in silica gel or dry them in a microwave oven.

Verbascum (ver-BAS-kum)

Large genus of biennials, perennials and small shrubs that are tall and erect. Leaves are alternate, undivided and sometimes lobed; basal leaves are larger than stem leaves. Flowers are yellow, tawny, red, purple or white, and occur on terminal spikes or racemes. Zones 3-9.

Selected species and varieties. *V. blattaria,* mullein, moth mullein, is a biennial that is unbranched and grows from 3 to 4 feet tall. Leaves are stalkless, hairless, lanceolate with serrate margins, and are 2½ inches long or more. Flowers are 1 inch wide and are yellow or pink in bud, opening to white in loose racemes. Flowers bloom from June to September. Zones 6-9. *V. phoeniceum,* purple mullein, is a 5-foot-tall

perennial. It resembles moth mullein, but the leaves are sparsely hairy on the undersides and the slender flower spikes are white, salmon, pink, rose, red or lavender. Flowers bloom in early summer. *V. thapsus,* common mullein, flannel mullein, is biennial, grows from 4 to 7 feet tall and is woolly-textured. Rosettes of basal leaves are 12 to 14 inches long, narrowing toward the base, with a strong central rib. The flower stalk is unbranched and has alternate, clasping leaves. Flowers are ½ to 1¼ inches wide, yellow, cuplike and spaced along the spike.

Growing conditions. Plant mullein in full sun and in well-drained, light, sandy, alkaline soil. Purple mullein prefers some shade. Mullein tolerates dry periods. Propagate from seeds sown outdoors or in a cold frame in May or June and from root cuttings taken at the same time or earlier. Transplant in early fall or spring. Seedlings spring up near the previous year's growth. Space plants 6 inches apart.

Uses. Mulleins can be used in fresh or dried arrangements for their line and varied colors. When dried, common mullein flowers add a silver color to mixed arrangements. The soft, gray-silver leaves of mullein can be used in fresh or dried arrangements or in pressed designs.

Harvesting and preparing. Hang common mullein to air-dry. Dry moth mullein and purple mullein in a drying agent. Press the leaves.

Veronica (ver-RON-i-ka)

Large genus of annuals and perennials that range from prostrate to erect. Lower leaves are sometimes alternate, rarely whorled. Upper leaves are simple, entire or toothed. Flowers are small, white, rose-purple or blue in terminal or axillary spikes or racemes. Zones 3-9.

Selected species and varieties. *V. incana,* speedwell, is a 2-foot-tall perennial with woolly stems. Leaves are oblong to lanceolate and 3 inches long. Flowers are blue, borne on one or several terminal spikes that are 6 inches long and bloom from mid-June to late July. *V. latifolia,* Hungarian speedwell, is a

2-foot-tall erect perennial having ½- to ¾-inch-long linear leaves. Flowers are ½ inch across, blue, rose or white, and occur in loose racemes; they bloom in May and June. Zones 4-9. *V. longifolia* is a 2½-foot-tall perennial. Leaves are 4 inches long and sometimes occur in threes. Flowers are small, lilac-blue, borne on pyramidal spikes and bloom in summer. Zones 4-9. *V. spicata*, spike speedwell, is a 1½-foot-tall perennial with leaves that are lance-shaped and 2 inches long. Flowers are blue or pink and are borne in dense racemes from late June to early August. Zones 4-9.

Growing conditions. Speedwell grows in full sun or light shade in fertile, well-drained soil. Spike speedwell tolerates heat and dry spells. It will repeat bloom in September if deadheaded. Propagate by dividing plants in spring or fall, from cuttings in summer and from seeds sown in late spring. Space plants 1 foot apart.

Uses. Speedwell makes a good line or filler flower in a fresh or dried arrangement. The dried seed head can be used in a mixed dried bouquet or in a wreath.

Harvesting and preparing. To use the flower spikes dry, pick them at the peak of their flowering stage and hang in bundles. Air-dry the brown seed heads by hanging them upside down.

Viola (VY-o-la)
Viola, violet

A large genus of hardy, low-growing, tufted annuals and perennials having basal leaves that are simple, heart-shaped or ovate, and slightly wrinkled, and stem leaves that are simple, alternate and ovate with round-toothed margins. Flowers are solitary, stalked and nodding, and are violet, blue, reddish purple, yellow or white. Pods are three-celled and many-seeded. Zones 5-8.

Selected species and varieties. *V. odorata*, sweet violet, is a source of perfume. It grows from 4 to 6 inches tall and has long stolons. Leaves are heart-shaped, ovate to kidney-shaped and toothed. Flowers are ¾ inch across and have a short spur. They range from deep violet or white to rose, are fragrant and bloom from mid-April through May and again in the fall. *V. tricolor*, Johnny-jump-up, is a perennial grown as a hardy annual and grows to 12 inches high. Flowers are ¾ inch long with a roundish corolla and overlapping petals; they are tricolored (purple, white and yellow) and bloom in May and June. *V. × wittrockiana*, pansy, heartsease, grows 9 inches high or more. It is a perennial treated as a hardy annual. Flowers are 2 to 5 inches long and are flat with facelike markings. Colors range from purple, blue, maroon and red to yellow, orange and white. Flowers are sometimes tricolored and bloom in the spring.

Growing conditions. Grow viola in sun and in fertile, sandy, well-drained soil. It prefers cool weather. In warm climates, blooming can be prolonged by providing afternoon shade. Propagate by dividing clumps, or the stolons of sweet violets, and from seeds sown 10 to 12 weeks before the last frost for bloom in late spring. Space Johnny-jump-up about 6 inches apart; allow 12 to 18 inches between sweet violet plants.

Uses. Viola makes a good focal flower in a fresh or dried arrangement. Sweet violet adds scent to a fresh bouquet. When dried, the flower retains good color, making it useful in flower wreaths. When the flower is pressed, its color and form make it a striking addition to flat designs.

Harvesting and preparing. Preserve the flower in silica gel, dry in a microwave oven or press.

Violet see *Viola*

Vitex (VY-teks)

Large genus of trees and shrubs having compound, opposite, long-stalked leaves, and three to seven often grayish green, hairy leaflets that are arranged palmately and are sometimes stalked. Flowers are white, yellow, red, blue or purple, and bloom in dense, showy, terminal or axillary panicles. Fruit is plumlike and has four seeds. Zones 6-10.

VIOLA TRICOLOR

VITEX AGNUS-CASTUS

WISTERIA SINENSIS

XERANTHEMUM ANNUUM

Selected species and varieties. *V. agnus-castus,* chaste tree, monk's pepper tree, is an aromatic shrub or small tree that grows from 6 to 25 feet tall. Leaves are 4 inches long and are lanceolate or elliptical. Flowers are ⅓ inch long. Flowers are fragrant, lilac- to lavender-colored and bloom in 5- to 12-inch-long panicles. Flowers bloom from July to September. Zones 7-10.

Growing conditions. Chaste tree grows in full sun and in almost any well-drained soil. Blooming occurs on the current year's growth. Where winters are cold, chaste tree dies to the ground. Where winters are warm, prune to keep low before new growth starts.

Uses. Chaste tree flowers provide line in fresh or dried arrangements. Branches with many panicles can be used as filler in fresh arrangements. The seed heads may be used in mixed dried bouquets of seed heads and grasses.

Harvesting and preparing. Preserve the individual panicles in silica gel or dry them in a microwave oven. Air-dry the seed heads.

—

Wahoo see *Euonymus*

Wandflower see *Galax*

Water lily see *Nelumbo*

Wattle see *Acacia*

Wax myrtle see *Myrica*

Waxwork see *Celastrus*

Western sage see *Artemisia*

Wheat see *Triticum*

Wild bergamot see *Monarda*

Wild carrot see *Daucus*

Wild indigo see *Baptisia*

Willow see *Salix*

Windflower see *Anemone*

Winged everlasting see *Ammobium*

—

Wisteria (wis-TEER-ee-a)

Genus of woody vines with twining stems having leaves that are alternate and compound, and leaflets that are alternate and pinnate with an odd one at the end. Pealike flowers bloom profusely in pendulous racemes that are usually terminal. Flower petals are blue to purplish, pink or white. Fruit is a thick, flat, knobby, velvety pod. Zones 4-9.

Selected species and varieties. *W. floribunda,* Japanese wisteria, grows 35 feet or more. Leaflets, 13 to 19 in number, are ovate-elliptical and 3 inches long. Flowers are ¾ inch long, fragrant, and violet-blue, pink or white. They bloom in clusters from 8 to 18 inches long in spring after the leaves have opened. *W. sinensis,* Chinese wisteria, grows 40 feet high and usually has 11 leaflets similar in size and shape to those of Japanese wisteria. Flowers are nonfragrant and bloom on 1-foot-long racemes in early spring, before the leaves appear, and again in August with a smaller display. Zones 5-9.

Growing conditions. Wisteria grows well in full sun and in fertile, moist but well-drained soil. It is drought-resistant. Wisteria does not transplant readily. Feed with a superphosphate fertilizer; nitrogenous fertilizer will lessen flowering and increase vegetative growth. Prune the roots and vigorous young shoots to control the plant's spread. Propagate from seeds, by division and from hardwood cuttings.

Uses. Wisteria can be used as a filler flower in a fresh arrangement; its drooping flower heads make it especially useful for draping over the rim of a container to soften a hard edge, or to unite container and arrangement. The younger vining stem can be used to make a vine wreath. The seedpods are also useful in dried arrangements.

Harvesting and preparing. Sear the freshly cut stems of wisteria before conditioning normally. Shape the fresh, twining stems into wreath form and allow them to dry in place. Air-dry the pods at different stages of ripeness for an assortment of colors and sizes.

—

Woad see *Isatis*

Wolfsbane see *Aconitum*

Wormwood see *Artemisia*

Woundwort see *Stachys*

Xeranthemum
(ze-RAN-the-mum)

Small genus of annuals having erect, branching stems with alternate, entire leaves. Flower heads are solitary, appear on long stalks and consist of tubular disk flowers surrounded by small, chaffy, petal-like bracts. The disk flowers and bracts are lilac-colored, rose, purple or white.

Selected species and varieties. *X. annuum*, immortelle, grows to 2 feet tall and has white, downy leaves that are oblong to lanceolate and 1 to 2 inches long. Flower heads are 1½ inches across and bloom from August to early frost.

Growing conditions. Grow immortelle in full sun and in well-drained ordinary soil. It prefers cool weather. Rich soil produces vigorous foliage at the expense of flowers. Staking may be necessary. In areas where the growing season is short, propagate from seeds sown indoors six to eight weeks before the last frost date. In areas where the growing season is long, sow seeds outdoors after all danger of frost is past. Space plants 6 inches apart.

Uses. Immortelle flowers can be used in fresh or dried arrangements. Their shape and size make them good filler flowers; they can also be grouped to form focal points. The dried flowers can be used in mixed dried bouquets, nosegays and wreaths, or to decorate the top of a bowl of potpourri.

Harvesting and preparing. To use dried, pick the flowers in mid-bloom to full bloom and air-dry. Flowers will dry naturally on the plant, but will fade more.

Yarrow see *Achillea*
Youth-and-old-age see *Zinnia*

Yucca (YUK-a)

Semidesert perennial that may be stemless or have an erect, woody trunk with tough, leathery, sword-shaped leaves occurring in a basal rosette. Flowers are nodding, waxy, white, rarely purple-tinged, and borne in showy, erect, terminal panicles. Flowers are usually fragrant at night. Some species bloom only at night. Zones 4-10.

Selected species and varieties. *Y. filamentosa*, Adam's needle, needle palm, grows from 3 to 15 feet tall. Leaves are 2½ feet long and about 1 inch wide, stiffly upright and evergreen. Pendulous flowers are 2 to 3 inches across, occur in 1- to 3-foot spikes and bloom in mid-July.

Growing conditions. Yucca tolerates dry spells, open exposure and seaside conditions. Plant it in full sun and in sandy, gravelly, well-drained, slightly alkaline soil. Propagate by separating the well-rooted basal offshoots, by cuttings from roots, from rhizomes and from seeds. Leave plenty of space for each plant.

Uses. The tall stalks of striking flowers can be used by themselves or with other flowers in tall fresh arrangements. Individual flowers, dried seed heads and leaves can be preserved for use in dried arrangements.

Harvesting and preparing. To use the fresh stalks of flowers, cut and sear the stem ends before conditioning normally. Preserve individual flowers in silica gel or dry them in a microwave oven, but keep them dry afterwards, so that the flowers won't reabsorb moisture. Air-dry the leaves by laying them on a screen; air-dry the seed heads by hanging stalks with the seed heads upside down.

YUCCA FILAMENTOSA

ZANTEDESCHIA AETHIOPICA

Zantedeschia
(zan-te-DES-kee-a)

Genus of stemless tropical perennials having short, thick rhizomes and long-stalked basal leaves that are ovate to heart-shaped, arrow-shaped or lanceolate. Showy, solitary flowers consist of a dense spike containing tiny, unisexual, true flowers and a large, conspicuous corolla-like bract (spathe) that forms a white, yellow or pink trumpet around the spadix. Fruit is a berry. Zones 8-10.

Selected species and varieties. *Z. aethiopica*, calla lily, arum lily, grows to 3 feet or more with arrow-shaped leaf blades that are 18 inches long and 10 inches wide. The

151

ZINNIA ANGUSTIFOLIA

spathe is velvety white or cream-white, 4 to 6 inches across and has a yellow spadix. Calla lily is fragrant and blooms in June and July. *Z. rehmannii,* pink calla, red calla, grows to 2 feet and has narrow leaves that are sometimes spotted with white. Showy spathes are 3 to 4 inches long and rosy purple to white with pink margins.

Growing conditions. Plant calla lily in sun or partial shade and in deep, moist, fertile, alkaline soil. It likes boggy sites. Propagate by division, by separating offsets and from seeds. From Zone 7 north, lift rhizomes and store them over the winter. Space plants 12 to 18 inches apart.

Uses. Used fresh, calla lilies make graceful form flowers. They can be grouped in a vase or used in mixed arrangements for line or as focal points. Calla lilies can also be preserved for use in mixed dried arrangements.

Harvesting and preparing. Dry calla lilies by placing them face up in sand.

—

Zinnia (ZIN-ee-a)

Genus of annuals, perennials and low shrubs with stiff, erect stems that are hairy with short bristles. Leaves are opposite, ovate or lance-shaped, and usually stem-clasping. Flower heads are showy, solitary, flattish or cone-shaped, with ray flowers of many colors and yellow or purplish brown disk flowers.

Selected species and varieties. *Z. angustifolia,* formerly called *Z. linearis,* has single golden orange flower heads with yellow stripes. Plants grow from 8 to 12 inches high and have very narrow leaves. *Z. elegans,* common zinnia, youth-and-old-age, grows 3 feet tall. Flower heads are 4 inches wide. There are numerous varieties; some have double flowers, some are 6 inches across and some have quilled petals. Flowers bloom in summer and fall.

Growing conditions. Zinnia prefers warm weather. Plant it in fertile soil where it will receive full sun. Keep it moist until it is established. Water in hot, dry weather. Afternoon shade helps in very hot areas. Where the growing season is short, propagate from seeds sown indoors six weeks before the last frost. Where the growing season is long, sow seeds outdoors in early spring.

Uses. Zinnias will provide both color and mass to fresh or dried arrangements.

Harvesting and preparing. To use fresh, remove the foliage from the stems before conditioning normally. Preserve the flowers in a drying agent to maintain their size; the flowers retain their color when they are air-dried, but they will shrink in the process.

FURTHER READING

Ascher, Amalie Adler, *The Complete Flower Arranger.* New York: Simon and Schuster, 1974.

Black, Penny, *The Book of Pressed Flowers.* New York: Simon and Schuster, 1988.

Conder, Susan, *A Complete Guide to Making and Arranging Dried Flowers.* New York: Gallery Books, 1988.

Cowles, Fleur, *Flower Decorations.* New York: Gallery Books, 1989.

Derbyshire, Jane, *The Flower Arranger's Year.* London: Collins, 1981.

Donald, Elsie Burch, ed., *Flower Arranging.* New York: Gallery Books, 1985.

Forsell, Mary, *The Book of Flower Arranging.* Philadelphia: Courage Books, 1988.

Harper, Janice, *Flower Arranging.* New York: Gallery Books, 1988.

Hillier, Malcolm, *The Book of Fresh Flowers.* New York: Simon and Schuster, 1988.

Hillier, Malcolm, *Decorating with Dried Flowers.* New York: Crown Publishers, 1987.

Hillier, Malcolm, and Colin Hilton, *The Book of Dried Flowers.* New York: Simon and Schuster, 1986.

Horton, Alvin, *Arranging Cut Flowers.* San Francisco: Ortho Books/ Chevron Chemical Company, 1985.

Ingham, Vicki L., *Elegance in Flowers.* Birmingham, Alabama: Oxmoor House, 1985.

Jacobs, Betty E. M., *Flowers That Last Forever.* Pownal, Vermont: Garden Way Publishing, 1988.

Joosten, Titia, *Flower Drying with a Microwave.* New York: Sterling Publishing, 1989.

Nehrling, Arno, and Irene Nehrling, *Gardening for Flower Arrangement.* New York: Dover Publications, 1976.

Piercy, Harold, *The Constance Spry Book of Flower Arranging.* New York: Exeter Books, 1984.

Piercy, Harold, *Dried and Artificial Flower Arranging.* New York: Gallery Books, 1987.

Silber, Mark, and Terry Silber, *The Complete Book of Everlastings.* New York: Alfred A. Knopf, 1988.

Thorpe, Patricia, *Everlastings: The Complete Book of Dried Flowers.* Boston: Houghton Mifflin, 1985.

Tozer, Zibby, *The Art of Flower Arranging.* New York: Warner Books, 1981.

Vaughan, Mary Jane, *The Complete Book of Cut Flower Care.* Portland, Oregon: Timber Press, 1988.

Westland, Pamela, *Flower Arranging for Special Occasions.* London: Columbus Books, 1985.

PICTURE CREDITS

The sources for the illustrations in this book are listed below. Cover photograph by Saxon Holt. Watercolor paintings by Nicholas Fasciano and Yin Yi except pages 80, 81, 82, 83: Lorraine Moseley Epstein. 84, 85: Catherine Dolcini. Maps on pages 74, 75, 77, 79 digitized by Richard Furno, inked by John Drummond.

Frontispiece paintings listed by page number: 6: *White Callas,* 1925-1927 by Arthur B. Carles. Courtesy The Pennsylvania Academy of the Fine Arts, Gift of Harry G. Sundheim, Jr. 16: *Quince Blossoms,* 1878 by Charles Caryl Coleman. Courtesy Jordan-Volpe Gallery, New York. 24: *Vase of Flowers with Watch and Key,* by Simon Pietersz. Verelst(1644-1721). Private Collection. 46: *Wreath of Flowers,* 1866 by John LaFarge. Courtesy National Museum of American Art, Smithsonian Institution, Gift of John Gellatly.

Photographs in Chapters 1 through 4 from the following sources, listed by page number: 8: © 1990 Walter Chandoha. 10: Saxon Holt. 12: Wanda LaRock/Envision. 14: Horticultural Photography, Corvallis, OR. 18: Ann Kelley/Garden Picture Library. 20: Bob Grant. 22, 26: Saxon Holt. 28: Elvin McDonald. 32: Bob Grant. 34: Elvin McDonald. 38: Bob Grant. 40: Wayne Ambler. 42, 44: Bob Grant. 48: Harry Smith Horticultural Photographic Collection. 52: Barry Runk/Grant Heilman Photography. 56: Renée Comet. 58: Wayne Ambler. 62, 66: Saxon Holt. 70: Bob Grant.

Photographs in the Dictionary of Plants from the following sources, listed by page and numbered from top to bottom. Page 88, 1: Elvin McDonald; 2: Thomas Eltzroth; 3: © 1990 Walter Chandoha. 89, 1, 2: Pamela Harper. 90, 1: Pamela Harper; 2: Thomas Eltzroth; 3: Horticultural Photography, Corvallis, OR. 91, 1: Pamela Harper; 2: Grant Heilman/Grant Heilman Photography; 3: Saxon Holt. 92, 1: Larry Lefever/Grant Heilman Photography; 2: Pamela Harper. 93, 1: Saxon Holt; 2: Ann Reilly; 3: Maggie Oster. 94, 1, 2: Pamela Harper; 3: Joanne Pavia. 95, 1, 2: Pamela Harper; 3: Elvin McDonald. 96, 1: Derek Fell; 2: Saxon Holt; 3: Pamela Harper. 97, 1, 2: Pamela Harper. 98, 1: Robert E. Lyons/Color Advantage; 2, 3: Pamela Harper. 99, 1: Pamela Harper; 2: Derek Fell. 100, 1: Derek Fell; 2: Joanne Pavia; 3: Ann Reilly. 101, 1, 2: Derek Fell; 3: Steven Still. 102, 1: Ann Reilly; 2: Thomas Eltzroth. 103, 1: Derek Fell; 2: Saxon Holt; 3: Joanne Pavia. 104, 1: Thomas Eltzroth; 2: Barry Runk/Grant Heilman Photography. 105, 1: Robert E. Lyons/Color Advantage; 2: Saxon Holt. 106, 1: Pamela Harper; 2: © John Smith/Photo-Nats; 3: Robert E. Lyons/Color Advantage. 107, 1: Joy Spurr; 2, 3: Pamela Harper. 108, 1: Grant Heilman/Grant Heilman Photography; 2: Saxon Holt. 109, 1: © 1990 Walter Chandoha; 2, 3: Horticultural Photography, Corvallis, OR. 110, 1, 2: Pamela Harper; 3: © 1990 Walter Chandoha. 111, 1, 2: Pamela Harper. 112, 1: Derek Fell; 2: Thomas Eltzroth. 113, 1: Grant Heilman/Grant Heilman Photography; 2: Lefever/Grushow/Grant Heilman Photography. 114, 1: William D. Adams; 2: Derek Fell; 3: Pamela Harper. 115, 1: Derek Fell; 2: Pamela Harper. 116, 1: Jane Grushow/Grant Heilman Photography; 2: Pamela Harper; 3: Thomas Eltzroth. 117, 1: Saxon Holt; 2: Steven Still. 118, 1: Pamela Harper; 2: Elvin McDonald; 3: Pamela Harper. 119, 1: Jane Grushow/ Grant Heilman Photography; 2: Pamela Harper. 120, 1: Tyler Gearhart/Envision; 2: Steve Rannels/Grant Heilman Photography; 3: Pamela Harper. 121, 1: Pamela Harper; 2: Saxon Holt. 122, 1: Pamela Harper; 2: Elvin McDonald. 123, 1: Grant Heilman/Grant Heilman Photography; 2: Derek Fell. 124, 1: Pamela Harper; 2: Fry's Herb Farm, photo by Lefever/Grushow/Grant Heilman Photography; 3: Pamela Harper. 125, 1: Robert E. Lyons/Color Advantage; 2: Thomas Eltzroth. 126, 1: Thomas Eltzroth; 2: Pamela Harper. 127, 1: Thomas Eltzroth; 2: Derek Fell; 3: Steven Still. 128, 1: Pamela Harper; 2: © Virginia Twinam-Smith/Photo-Nats; 3: Grant Heilman/Grant Heilman Photography. 129, 1: Thomas Eltzroth; 2: Saxon Holt. 130, 1, 2: Pamela Harper. 131, 1, 2: Pamela Harper; 3: Elvin McDonald. 132, 1: Horticultural Photography, Corvallis, OR; 2, 3: Pamela Harper. 133, 1: Derek Fell; 2: Thomas Eltzroth. 134, 1: Steven Still; 2: Pamela Harper. 135, 1: Saxon Holt; 2: Thomas Eltzroth. 136, 1: Robert E. Lyons/Color Advantage; 2: Steve Rannels/Grant Heilman Photography; 3: Pamela Harper. 137, 1: Grant Heilman/Grant Heilman Photography; 2: Horticultural Photography, Corvallis, OR. 138, 1: © Tyler Gearhart/ Envision; 2: Bob Grant. 139, 1, 2: Pamela Harper. 140, 1: Pamela Harper; 2: Derek Fell. 141, 1, 2: Pamela Harper. 142, 1: Thomas Eltzroth; 2: Steven Still. 143, 1: © 1990 Walter Chandoha; 2: Pamela Harper. 144, 1: Horticultural Photography, Corvallis, OR; 2: Gary Mottau; 3: Saxon Holt. 145, 1: Pamela Harper; 2: Susan A. Roth. 146, 1, 2: Pamela Harper; 3: Elvin McDonald. 147, 1: © John Smith/Photo-Nats; 2: Wanda LaRock/Envision. 148, 1: Thomas Eltzroth; 2: Jane Grushow/Grant Heilman Photography; 3: Pamela Harper. 149, 1: Pamela Harper; 2: Jane Grushow/Grant Heilman Photography. 150, 1: Pamela Harper; 2: Ann Reilly. 151, 1: Derek Fell; 2: Thomas Eltzroth. 152, 1: Pamela Harper.

ACKNOWLEDGMENTS

The index for this book was prepared by Lee McKee.
The editors also wish to thank: Kenneth E. Hancock, Annandale, Virginia; Thanh Huu Nguyen, Alexandria, Virginia; Jayne E. Rohrich, Alexandria, Virginia.

INDEX

REDEFINITION

Senior Editors	Anne Horan, Robert G. Mason
Design Director	Robert Barkin
Designer	Edwina Smith
Illustration	Nicholas Fasciano
Assistant Designers	Sue Pratt, Monique Strawderman
Picture Editor	Deborah Thornton
Production Editor	Anthony K. Pordes
Editorial Research	Mary Yee (volume coordinator), Gail Prensky, Barbara B. Smith, Elizabeth D. McLean
Picture Research	Caroline N. Tell
Text Editor	Carol Gardner
Writers	Gerald Jonas, Joan E. Prior, Ann Reilly, David S. Thomson
Administration	Margaret M. Higgins, June M. Nolan
Finance Director	Vaughn A. Meglan
PRESIDENT	Edward Brash

Time-Life Books Inc.
is a wholly owned subsidiary of

THE TIME INC. BOOK COMPANY

President and Chief Executive Officer	Kelso F. Sutton
President, Time Inc. Books Direct	Christopher T. Linen

TIME-LIFE BOOKS INC.

EDITOR	George Constable
Executive Editor	Ellen Phillips
Director of Design	Louis Klein
Director of Editorial Resources	Phyllis K. Wise
Director of Photography and Research	John Conrad Weiser
PRESIDENT	John M. Fahey Jr.
Senior Vice Presidents	Robert M. DeSena, Paul R. Stewart, Curtis G. Viebranz, Joseph J. Ward
Vice Presidents	Stephen L. Bair, Bonita L. Boezeman, Mary P. Donohoe, Stephen L. Goldstein, Juanita T. James, Andrew P. Kaplan, Trevor Lunn, Susan J. Maruyama, Robert H. Smith
New Product Development:	Yuri Okuda, Donia Ann Steele
Supervisor of Quality Control	James King
PUBLISHER	Joseph J. Ward

Editorial Operations

Copy Chief	Diane Ullius
Production	Celia Beattie
Library	Louise D. Forstall
Computer Composition	Gordon E. Buck (Manager), Deborah G. Tait, Monika D. Thayer, Janet Barnes Syring, Lillian Daniels
Correspondents	Elisabeth Kraemer-Singh (Bonn), Christina Lieberman (New York), Maria Vincenza Aloisi (Paris), Ann Natanson (Rome)

THE CONSULTANTS

C. Colston Burrell is the series consultant for The Time-Life Gardener's Guide. He is Curator of Plant Collections at the Minnesota Landscape Arboretum, part of the University of Minnesota. He was formerly Curator of Native Plant Collections at the National Arboretum in Washington, D.C., and is the author of publications about ferns and wildflowers.

Robert E. Lyons, co-consultant for the series, is an associate professor of horticulture at Virginia Polytechnic Institute and State University in Blacksburg, Virginia, where he teaches courses in herbaceous plant materials. He has written numerous articles on flowering plants.

Wayne Ambler, consultant for *Flowers for Cutting and Drying,* is a teacher of horticulture. He is a member of the adjunct faculty at J. Sargeant Reynolds Community College and at Patrick Henry High School in Ashland, Virginia.

Library of Congress Cataloging-in-Publication Data
Flowers for cutting and drying
    p. cm.—(The Time-Life gardener's guide)
    Includes bibliographical references.
    ISBN 0-8094-6656-2.—ISBN 0-8094-6657-0 (lib. bdg.)
    1. Flower gardening.   2. Flower arrangement.
I. Time-Life Books.   II. Series.
SB404.9.F56   1990   635.9'66—dc20   89-20666 CIP

Time-Life Books Inc. offers a wide range of fine recordings, including a *Rock 'n' Roll Era* series. For subscription information, call 1-800-621-7026, or write Time-Life Music, P.O. Box C-32068, Richmond, Virginia 23261-2068.